SOCIOPOLITICAL ASPECTS OF
CANAL IRRIGATION IN THE VALLEY OF OAXACA

Plate 1. Frontispiece. The main village *tanque*, or reservoir, above San Agustín Etla.

MEMOIRS OF THE MUSEUM OF ANTHROPOLOGY
UNIVERSITY OF MICHIGAN
NUMBER 6

PREHISTORY AND HUMAN ECOLOGY
OF THE VALLEY OF OAXACA

Kent V. Flannery, General Editor

Volume 2

SOCIOPOLITICAL ASPECTS OF
CANAL IRRIGATION IN THE VALLEY OF OAXACA

BY

SUSAN H. LEES

ANN ARBOR
1973

© 1973 by the Regents of the University of Michigan
The Museum of Anthropology
All rights reserved

ISBN (print): 978-1-949098-45-7
ISBN (ebook): 978-1-951538-18-7

Browse all of our books at sites.lsa.umich.edu/archaeology-books.

Order our books from the University of Michigan Press at www.press.umich.edu.

For permissions, questions, or manuscript queries, contact Museum publications by email at umma-pubs@umich.edu or visit the Museum website at lsa.umich.edu/ummaa.

AN INTRODUCTION TO VOLUME 2 OF THE SERIES

By Kent V. Flannery

This *Memoir* is the second step in our series of final reports on The University of Michigan Museum of Anthropology project, "Prehistoric Human Ecology of the Valley of Oaxaca." It builds directly on the foundation laid by Ann Kirkby in Volume 1, *The Use of Land and Water Resources in the Past and Present Valley of Oaxaca, Mexico,* and in turn it provides a theoretical base for several projected future publications on the rise of the Zapotec state. As in the case of Volume 1, the research herein reported was supported by National Science Foundation Grants GS1616 and GS2121, and the publication itself was financed by NSF Grant GN35572.

Dr. Susan Lees joined the Oaxaca Project in 1967, and during four field seasons (through 1970) she slogged through the mud and dust of backwoods Oaxaca collecting data on the social and political aspects of the land-use systems which Anne Kirkby reported in Volume 1. Often, in fact, Lees and the Kirkbys worked hand-in-hand—interviewing amiable farmers, recalcitrant village officials, garrulous drunks, and tight-lipped social climbers whose words concealed more than they communicated about their accumulated wealth and prestige. By jeep, truck, Volkswagon, and sometimes on foot, Lees reached 22 villages with canal irrigation systems and pried out data on the use, distribution, and regulation of water. She waded through fertilizer, fell in at least one river, and once—in Matatlan—found herself ankle-deep in mezcal tailings. In the course of this ethnographic seasoning, she found time to participate extensively in our archaeological excavations at San Jose Mogote, Abasolo, Tierras Largas, and Hierve el Agua; finally, she directed her own excavation, with Henry T. Wright, at Santo Domingo Tomaltepec. Seeing the traces of pre-Columbian canal irrigation come to light in our excavations, Lees was constantly reminded that one day she would have to address herself to the role of irrigation in the rise of the state. Her conclusions are spelled out in the final chapters of this *Memoir*.

Lees found the regulation of water in the Valley of Oaxaca as varied as the communities she studies: the solutions found by each community came from within its pre-existing sociopolitical institutions. No new polity arose to deal with water, no despotism separated upstream and downstream villages. But canal irrigation, more than any other local form of water control, made the village vulnerable to the intervention of the state. Where communities appealed for Federal dams, the price of development was loss of autonomy: the dams came under Federal jurisdiction, the regulation of water changed, and new rules were imposed on village governments which had changed but little in the previous three or four centuries. Canal irrigation in Oaxaca thus provides a setting in which state organization has a selective advantage, and the development of local canal resources becomes an important vehicle for change. Irrigation does not create the state, as some have argued; but the state can use canal irrigation to increase its centralization in ways that it cannot manipulate other land-use systems in Oaxaca.

Since she completed this manuscript, Dr. Lees has carried her work to a still higher level of abstraction. At the December 1972 meeting of the American Anthropological Association, Lees presented a major new hypothesis on the difference between (1) the state's organizational response to clear, short-term degradation of its environment or water resources, and (2) its organizational response to long-term, almost imperceptible degradation.[1] We are pleased to think that her continuing theoretical contribution—work still in progress, with much promise for the field of anthropology—grew out of those days spent wading through canals in the Oaxaca hills.

Ann Arbor, Michigan
June 1, 1973

---

[1] Susan H. Lees, *Irrigation, Organization and Stability in Complex Societies.* Paper presented at American Anthropological Society meetings, New York, New York, December 1, 1972.

CONTENTS

Tables	ix
Maps	ix
Figures	x
Plates	x
Acknowledgments	xi
Introduction	1
Area of Investigation	3
Method of Investigation	5

I. Community Organization

Introduction	9
The Village	9
Historical Background	9
The Civil-Religious Hierarchy and the *Cargo* System	10
Economic Organization: Land and Wealth	11
Economic Organization: Exchange and Cooperation	13
Economic Organization: Community Cooperation	15
The Village and the State	16
Political Units	16
Village Government	18
The Village and the State	20

II. Problems of Water Control and Their Solutions

Introduction: Problems	23
Construction	23
Maintenance	29
Allocation	30
Conflict over Water	40
Change	43

III. Political Control and Access to Water

Introduction	45
Tlalixtac de Cabrera	45
San Juan del Estado	69
San Agustín Etla	73
Summary and Conclusions	79

IV. The Roles of the Village and the State in Water Control

Introduction	83
Intra-Village and Inter-Village Water Control	83
The Village and the State	84
Change in Water Control Organization and the State	85
Summary and Conclusions	87

V. The Role of Water Control in Oaxaca's History

Introduction	89
Origins	89
Post-Classic History	96
Colonial Period	97
Post-Colonial, Pre-Revolutionary History	100
Since the Revolution	102
Summary and Conclusions	104

VI. Oaxacan Irrigation Compared with Other Regions
    Introduction 107
    Social Change 109
    Variation According to Resource Type 110
    Cooperative Labor 110
    Water Distribution 112
    Disputes 116
    Village-State Relations and Water Control 118
    Summary and Conclusions 119

VII. General Conclusions   123
    Oaxaca as a Case Study 124
        Environment 124
        Technology 124
        Allocation 124
        Social Change, the State, and Water Control 125
    Mass Labor and Allocation in Oaxaca 126
        Mass Labor 126
        Allocation 127
    Environment, Technology, Adaptation, and Evolution 129
        Variation in Response and the Nature of the Resource 129
        Environment and Technology 131
    The Origins of Statehood 132

Resumen en Español 135

References 139

TABLES

1.	Distritos of the Valley of Oaxaca	18
2.	Location of irrigating villages	24
3.	Irrigating villages: size, type, source and control	39
4.	Political careers: Tlalixtac de Cabrera sample	50
5.	Public offices held: Tlalixtac de Cabrera sample	51
6.	Service in ceremonial offices: Tlalixtac de Cabrera sample	51
7.	Age group and political career: Tlalixtac de Cabrera sample	53
8.	Residential distribution: Tlalixtac de Cabrera sample	55
9.	Political office and residence by sector: Tlalixtac de Cabrera sample	55
10.	Political office and residence by barrio: Tlalixtac de Cabrera sample	56
11.	Canal use and population by barrio: Tlalixtac de Cabrera sample	57
12.	Political career and canal use by barrio: Tlalixtac de Cabrera sample	58
13.	Political career and canal use by sector: Tlalixtac de Cabrera sample	59
14.	Residence and canal use: Tlalixtac de Cabrera sample	59
15.	Land tenure and political career: Tlalixtac de Cabrera sample	60
16.	Multiple plots of irrigated land: Tlalixtac de Cabrera sample	61
17.	Parcel size of irrigated land: Tlalixtac de Cabrera sample	61
18.	Size of irrigated plots by canal used: Tlalixtac de Cabrera sample	63
19.	Political career and amount of irrigated land owned: Tlalixtac de Cabrera sample	63
20.	Political status by age group: Tlalixtac de Cabrera sample	65
21.	Residence by age group: Tlalixtac de Cabrera sample	65
22.	Location of canal use by age group: Tlalixtac de Cabrera sample	66
23.	Land tenure by age group: Tlalixtac de Cabrera sample	66
24.	Multiple parcel-holding by age group: Tlalixtac de Cabrera sample	67
25.	Size of landholding and political status by age group: Tlalixtac de Cabrera sample	67
26.	Size of plot amount of irrigated land and location of canal use: San Juan sample	69
27.	Political status and amount of land owned: San Juan sample	71
28.	Political office and location of canal use: San Juan sample	72
29.	Political office and ownership of irrigable land: San Juan sample	73
30.	Political office and irrigable land held: San Juan sample	73
31.	Size of irrigated parcels and location of canal use: San Agustín sample	76
32.	Political status and amount of irrigated land: San Agustín sample	76
33.	Location of canal use and political status: San Agustín sample	77
34.	Age and political status, irrigable land holders: San Agustín sample	77
35.	Political office held and age: San Agustín sample	78
36.	Political office and irrigable land held: San Agustín sample	78

MAPS

1.	District centers in the Valley of Oaxaca	17
2.	The northern arm of the Valley of Oaxaca	25
3.	The eastern arm of the Valley of Oaxaca	26
4.	The Mixtepec River	27
5.	Tlalixtac de Cabrera	47
6.	San Juan del Estado	68
7.	San Agustín Etla	75
8.	Monte Albán I period sites in the Valley of Oaxaca as of 1969	91
9.	Early Monte Albán I: Santa Domingo Tomaltepec	92
10.	Sites on a piedmont tributary stream	93

FIGURES

1. a & b. Age breakdown by political career 54
2. Size of irrigated plots in Tlalixtac de Cabrera 62
3. Amount of land and political career in San Juan del Estado 72
4. Amount of irrigated land and political status in San Agustín Etla 79
5. Bar graph of officeholders by age group.. 80

PLATES

(following page 141)

1. Frontispiece. The main village *tanque*, or reservoir, above San Agustín Etla.
2. Canal-irrigating villages in the Valley of Oaxaca.
3. Irrigation facilities at Tlalixtac de Cabrera.
4. Irrigation facilities at San Juan del Estado.
5. Irrigation facilities at San Agustín Etla.
6. Irrigation in other parts of the valley.
7. Ancient and modern irrigation sites at Santo Domingo Tomaltepec.
8. Archaeological sites in canal-irrigation settings.

ACKNOWLEDGMENTS

I wish to thank all the members of the Oaxaca Project for their help and advice in the field. A special debt of gratitude is owed to Ernesto Martínez, who was my guide and Zapotec interpreter, to Marcus Winter, who loaned me his automobile for use in the field, and to my dissertation chairman Dr. Kent Flannery, without whose support and guidance this report would not have been possible. I also wish to thank Drs. Eric Wolf, Roy Rappaport, John Kolars, Marshall Sahlins, and Aram Yengoyan for reading the manuscript and offering advice and criticism.

Financial support for my work in the field was provided by National Science Foundation Grant GS-2121, by the National Institute of Mental Health, and by a Ford Foundation travel grant.

Finally, I thank Mrs. Wanita Rasey who patiently typed the manuscript.

INTRODUCTION

The subject of water control is a matter of concern not only to farmers, but to engineers and statesmen, archaeologists and ecologists, anthropologists, geographers, historians, and social theorists of all kinds. For many farmers, and for most engineers and ecologists interested in water control, it is a technical subject involving constructions and devices and their effects on plant populations and soil fertility. For statesmen, as well as anthropologists and other social scientists, it is more than a technical problem; it is a political one having to do with the organization and use of public resources, and the wielding of power, and with conflicts of interest among men.

It is the political aspect of water control that is the focus of this study. The scene of the study is the Valley of Oaxaca, Mexico. Here the hydraulic situation is quite complex, not because the hydraulic facilities are large or technically elaborate, but rather because there are several varieties of water resources and water control techniques. Canal irrigation, the subject of this study, is only one of several techniques used in the valley today. But canal irrigation itself has particular interest for anthropologists for a number of reasons.

First, it is an ancient and culturally widespread technique. Second, recent controversies in social anthropology and archaeology have centered upon the sociopolitical implications of its use (Adams, 1966; Millon et al., 1962; Palerm, 1955; Sanders, 1968; Wittfogel, 1957). And third, canal irrigation has particular importance in the Valley of Oaxaca because it appears to have first been used in this area during the early stages of the growth and development of statehood.

The widespread use of canal irrigation suggests a number of questions. Given the fact that the political institutions of societies using canal irrigation vary tremendously, perhaps far more than the techniques applied to water control themselves, we might conclude that there must be a variety of ways to manage the use of water. If this is so, we might ask:

1. Do the technology of or problems posed by irrigation limit or affect the selection of alternative control institutions? If so, how?

2. Are some alternatives more effective than others for the management of water use?

3. What guides or influences the selection of one alternative over another in any particular society?

These are not new questions. They have been posed repeatedly in what has become a classic anthropological controversy over the role of water control in the history of cultural development. It was precisely this problem of interpreting the historical influence of canal irrigation in the Valley of Oaxaca that led me to investigate the political organization of water control in contemporary Oaxacan villages.[1] Because we have archaeological and historical documentation

---

[1] This study was closely associated with the long-term multidisciplinary project, "The Prehistoric Cultural Ecology of the Valley of Oaxaca," directed by Professor Kent Flannery and funded by the National Science Foundation (see Flannery, et al., 1967). I worked in conjunction with the project, receiving help and advice from its members and offering them assistance in my own field of specialization. The general aims of the project have to do with understanding the sequence of cultural development in the valley and its relationship to the natural environment and to processes of production. Although its focus has been upon the Early and Middle Formative periods of the archaeological sequence, research has also been directed toward contemporary plant and animal resources, both wild and domestic, as

the existence of both canals and political change over a span of more than 2,000 years in this area (Flannery, et al., 1967; Neely, 1967), we may consider the questions listed above as applied to a single society in a single geographical setting.

In approaching these questions three main points will be made. First, this study will try to show that the form of water-use management emerges from the social structure of the society in which it is found. On the one hand, the form of the water-control devices themselves—the canals, the dams, the aqueducts—depends not only upon the available natural resources and geographical configurations but also upon the needs and the capabilities of the society which builds them. On the other hand, while the construction, maintenance, and use of these devices requires some sort of organization, the precise form of that organization is determined by the principles upon which social interaction in general is structured in the society. Finally, if we must understand the principles underlying social interaction in a society in order to understand the organization associated with water control, then we must carefully delineate what sort of society, or what segment of the society, is involved in the control of water and how. Although it is clear that many societies using canal irrigation are tribal, the main controversy over

well as climate, mineral resources, soils, drainage, topography, and land and water use. Most pertinent to my own study was the research of Anne Kirkby on the subject of land and water use (Vol. 1, this series). I hoped to complement her descriptions of the technical aspects of agricultural production with an analysis of the sociological aspects of one important factor in this production—water control.

Other research which had bearing on our work was carried out in the valley at more or less the same time, and we were fortunate to have access to the results of several of these studies. They are likely to be published at about the same time as our work. Dr. Joseph Whitecotton has made an ethnohistorical study of Zapotec social organization at the time of the Conquest, and Dr. William Taylor has made a historical study of land holding during the Colonial period. A number of students from Stanford University spent time in villages in the Valley doing ethnographic research; other studies are in progress. A study of market systems in Oaxaca, directed by Professor Ralph Beals, coincided in time with our work, and other independent studies by ethnographers were being made during the same period. Since most of these will be published within the next few years, the Valley of Oaxaca should soon become a relatively well-known, well-described area.

the implications of canal irrigation for political structure has to do with the relationship of irrigation to the emerging state. But states are complex, and the relationship of canal irrigation to the state is likely to be similarly complex.

The second point to be made in this study is that there is at least one intermediate control step between the canals and the superstructure of the state: the peasant community. The principles of organization at the peasant community level are often different and apart from those at the more remote level of the state. It is the peasant community which directly controls the individual irrigators, use of water from the small, localized canals typical of the region examined in this study. This is not to say that the existence of the state is irrelevant to the construction or the use of canals; rather, the relationship of the state to the canals is often indirect, mediated by the peasant community, which has its own distinctive form of organization.

If organization at the level of the peasant community is different from that at the state level and if the community itself directly controls the use of water by individual irrigators, then even societies which are similar in organization at the upper levels may differ widely in their organization of water control. Still, they do share common features, not necessarily in the organization of water control, but in the manner in which water control is related to the interaction between community and state. This shared characteristic is especially relevant to archaeological interpretations of the origins and development of statehood, because it applies only in reference to social change and—for lack of a better term—progress.

The search for similarities in social response to the problem of water control brings up some important and difficult questions concerning cultural adaptation in general. Water, as an agricultural resource, has certain distinctive characteristics regardless of social setting. It has been suggested by some authors, particularly by Wittfogel (1957), that the peculiarities of water, as opposed to other agricultural resources, determine to some extent the social response to its use, while other aspects of the environment

INTRODUCTION

determine the relative importance of this response in structuring the society. As I have indicated above, this study will show how cultural, rather than environmental, factors determine the form of response in a society. But it will also suggest that neither the peculiarities of water as a resource in canal irrigation nor other factors in the environment are entirely irrelevant. The question is, how are they relevant, if social response is rooted in the more general structure of the society?

The third point made in this study is that both the environmental factors and the distinctive characteristics of the resource itself play a significant role in particular contexts of cultural change, specifically in the relationship between the local community and the state. This study will attempt to explain the ways and contexts in which the characteristics of water as a resource, and canal irrigation as an exploitative technique, become significant in cultural adaptation. Such an explanation will be facilitated by our first understanding the contexts in which these environmental characteristics do *not* play a significant part and why. This understanding will help to account for the diversity of social response among societies which use canal irrigation and to evaluate the role of such environmental factors in cultural evolution.

Like Gray's study of the Sonjo (1963), this paper, in order to relate canal irrigation to social organization, presents ethnographic data collected in the field with a view toward providing more material for analysis and comparison. The chapters which follow will present a brief, general description of the social setting of canal irrigation in the Valley of Oaxaca, the organization of its management in contemporary villages, and its history from the earliest evidence of its use in this area. Chapter I will attempt to show how the general principles of social interaction in this society are brought to bear upon canal irrigation; Chapters II and III will discuss whether or not the physical properties of a canal irrigation system affect the organization of its management or the political organization in the community in general. While these two chapters concentrate mainly upon organization at the village level, Chapter IV will focus upon the role of the state in canal irrigation.

Chapters V and VI attempt to place irrigation in contemporary Oaxaca into both historical and cross-cultural perspective. From these perspectives, we are better equipped to evaluate the meaning of variation in response and the significance of particular responses in the context of long-range cultural evolution. Although ethnographic descriptions of contemporary societies do not necessarily provide a good basis for archaeological reconstruction, certain generalizations, discovered through analysis of contemporary societies, can be useful for archaeological interpretation. In my conclusions, I will attempt to make generalizations which will be useful in this way.

Before proceeding any further, however, I will briefly introduce the area in which the study was made, and describe the manner in which it was carried out.

AREA OF INVESTIGATION[2]

The Valley of Oaxaca is located in the southern highlands of Mexico at an average altitude of 1550 meters above sea level. Immediately north of the valley is the Mixteca Alta; to the south lie the valleys of Miahuatlán and Nexapa. Following a mountain route to the south, one reaches the coast of Tehuantepec; by way of a deep canyon pass to the northwest, one may reach the Valley of Tehuacán, Puebla. Although the mountains encircling the Valley of Oaxaca give it clear definition, they have not prevented intensive contact and communication with these and other neighboring areas throughout the history of human occupation of the valley.

The valley is drained by the upper Río Atoyac and its main tributary, the Río Salado or Tlacolula, which flows from east to west to join

---

[2]This short outline is meant merely to place the area of study more concretely for the reader. An extensive geographical description of the area appears in volume 1 of this series by Dr. Anne Kirkby. Dr. Kirkby's monograph presents a detailed analysis of methods of agriculture and irrigation in the Valley of Oaxaca, and in order to avoid repetition, I refer the reader to her report.

the Atoyac near the center of the valley. This drainage pattern gives the valley the shape of a "Y," with three major arms, one to the north (Etla), one to the south (Zaachila-Zimatlán-Ocotlán), and one to the east (Tlacolula). From the northern end of the valley, where the Río Atoyac enters from the Mixteca Alta, to the southern limit, at the Ayoquesco gorge where the Atoyac drains down toward the Pacific Ocean, the distance is about 90 kilometers. The distance across the valley does not exceed 15 kilometers in any of the arms of the valley; in the northern arm, which is the narrowest, it rarely exceeds 5 kilometers.

The environment is complex, including a number of subzones and many different microenvironments, but it can be generally divided into three main physiographic zones: the flat, humid alluvium of the valley floor; the dry, hilly piedmont; and the steep, forested mountains. Despite its proximity to the equator, the Valley of Oaxaca has a cool climate due to its high elevation. Unlike the valleys of Mexico or Cholula-Puebla, however, Oaxaca suffers little from seasonal frost. Precipitation is sometimes a major environmental problem for Oaxaca, for the climate is generally dry; there are few permanent streams, and the humid alluvial land is quite limited. The mean annual rainfall varies locally from about 490 to about 740 mm, while the evaporation rate is about three to five times that of precipitation.[3] Rainfall is confined mainly to the months of late May or June through September, and it is variable from place to place, month to month, and year to year. Variability is at least as important a characteristic of the rainfall as its seasonality and general scarcity.

Among the many languages spoken in the state of Oaxaca, Zapotec and Mixtec are the most important in terms of numbers of speakers and geographical spread. Zapotec is the main Indian language of the Valley of Oaxaca and has been so for as long as historical documents and human memory can record, although colonial documents also report a large number of Mixtec speakers in the valley (Paddock, 1966). Valley Zapotec is a regional dialect, differing considerably from those spoken in the Isthmus of Tehuantepec, on the Pacific coast, and in the mountains. Even in the valley itself, there are subdialects which the speakers sometimes claim are mutually unintelligible, though this may be exaggerated.

Thus, with the exception of some small immigrant groups of Mixtecs, Mixes, and Spaniards, most inhabitants of the valley today can be classified as Zapotec, a term which denotes not only their language but also their shared customs, traditions, and history. This history may date back some 10,000 years or more, for the valley has been continuously occupied since the time of the early hunters and gatherers (Flannery, 1968a). Positive evidence for cultural continuity is available in the archaeological record from at least 1200 B.C. through the Spanish Conquest (Flannery, et al., 1967).

Its location and environmental characteristics place the Valley of Oaxaca in the "culture area" of the southern Mexican highlands. Thus, it falls into the same cultural-environmental pattern as other major valleys previously reported in this area and on the Central Plateau, such as the valleys of Tehuacán, Mexico, Cholula-Puebla, and the Mixteca Alta. All of these areas share similar agricultural methods and characteristics of social organization; furthermore, contact between them has led to a mutual participation in one another's cultural development (Palerm and Wolf, 1957).

With the conquest and later with the revolution came many changes in the way of life of the valley Zapotecs. Although these changes were not as drastic or as rapid as those experienced elsewhere in Mexico, they eventually eliminated many earlier Zapotec cultural traditions. The Zapotec language has disappeared in nearly all the villages of the northern arm of the valley, and although it is still widely spoken in the eastern and southern regions, Spanish is gradually replacing it there as well. Social structure, religion, and agriculture were all radically altered through Spanish influence. The result was a new set of traits showing these influences, as well as others which are distinctly those of the post-Hispanic Mesoamerican rural peasantry, or more

---

[3]This varies by zone. See Flannery, et al., 1967.

specifically, of the Mesoamerican southern highlands peasantry.

Unlike the populations of northern parts of Mesoamerica, the people of Oaxaca managed to retain a large proportion of their land after the conquest (Taylor, 1969). Thus, on the whole, they were only indirectly affected by the rise of the hacienda system. They continued to live in nucleated villages, depending upon subsistence agriculture managed on a household basis and supplementing their incomes by specialization in cash crops and craft production and participation in weekly regional markets. The revolution, by eliminating what haciendas there were in the valley and by redistributing their lands to villagers in small parcels, served mainly to protect and perpetuate this way of life. The Valley of Oaxaca seems to lag behind much of the rest of the nation in industrialization, urbanization, modernization of agricultural technology, and political integration of the villages into the larger sphere of the Mexican nation. Clearly, the valley is making progress in these directions, particularly in certain villages (Iszaevich Fajerstein, 1969), but it is equally evident that this progress is slow and recent.

Unlike many of the more backward mountain areas, the Valley of Oaxaca is not poor in resources. According to some anthropologists (Palerm and Wolf, 1957; Flannery, et al., 1967), the high fertility of its alluvial plain, the diversity of environmental subzones, and the variety of techniques which could be used to exploit them have, in the past, continually placed the Valley of Oaxaca in the forefront of cultural development in Mesoamerica. Thus, the Valley of Oaxaca was one of the few areas of Mesoamerica that remained nuclear throughout its pre-Hispanic history.

Irrigation resources certainly played an important role in Oaxaca's cultural leadership. They also account to a considerable extent for the great interest displayed by the Spanish colonists in certain areas of the valley, particularly the northern region. But the main concern of this report is with the present, with the role of one type of irrigation, canal irrigation, in the social and political organization of the rural villages in the valley today.

METHOD OF INVESTIGATION

Before I began work on canal irrigation, I had spent two seasons in the valley, six months in 1967 and three in 1968, acquainting myself with the ethnographic situation and the archaeological sequence. For seven months in 1969 I devoted almost all of my time to studying canal irrigation, although my research was considerably curtailed in the last month by bad weather and the lack of a vehicle for transportation. During that season I did ethnographic research in villages, consulted with government officials in Oaxaca de Juárez, did archaeological surveys of early canal-using sites, and made a limited test of one of these sites.

For reasons I shall discuss below, I decided to make a survey of canal-irrigating villages rather than an intensive study of water control in a single village. Early in my study, I designed a questionnaire for use in each of the villages I visited. I believed it would be more efficient and rewarding to have these questionnaires answered by one or more officials in each village than to seek out peasants in their homes and fields, since the officials were likely to be more familiar with the rules and problems involved in water control. Soon, however, I had to discard my questionnaire. I suspected that holding a printed form before them made my informants uncomfortable and reticent, and furthermore I found that the wording appropriate for one village was meaningless or distorting in another.

Therefore, I modified my approach by simply memorizing a list of topics I wished to discuss and improvising questions as I went along. In each case I would ask how many people lived in the towns, how many were irrigating and how much land was irrigated, whether or not there was an *ejido*, who was in charge of water control, how water was distributed, when and how often people irrigated, what crops they grew, what they did for canal maintenance, and so forth. In many cases I asked about other municipal offices, how they were filled, and what the duties were of various officials. I often tried, in an indirect way, to find out whether there were disputes over water or problems of delinquency associated with water control and, if so, how they were solved. After asking these questions, I would ask to see the canals.

I had originally selected three areas, one in each arm of the valley, on which to concentrate. Later, however, I found that some of the villages in these areas no longer used canal irrigation and others, some discovered by accident, were more interesting because they illustrated variation. Therefore, I decided to survey a larger number of villages in a greater number of areas. The time I needed to gather information varied from village to village, depending on the cooperation of the informants and the amount of detail they offered. I knew I could not plan my timing very precisely, and that I could never cover all the canal-irrigating villages in the valley. As I visited more villages, I also found that they varied so greatly that I could not predict beforehand, on the basis of their location or size, what sort of water-control arrangements I would find. Under these circumstances, it seemed impossible to devise a set sampling procedure; I simply had to decide as I went along which villages to visit, and let the available time determine how many I would cover. I did try to get information from each of the three arms of the valley, but the sample was too small for me to predict on a statistical basis how close I came to finding the full range of variability. In short, my decision to survey a number of villages led me into some difficulties.

Why, then, did I continue to survey? First, my initial reason—that I wanted to find out about the interconnections between villages using the same source—still held. Second, as I continued my study, I realized that a survey might be useful to underline the range of ways water control could be handled in a single society. I found, moreover, that a similar diversity extends to other aspects of local organization. Thus, I had a way of tracing a characteristic of the larger society which might not be observed at the community level. Furthermore, the very existence of diversity told me something about the relationship between water control and political organization—a matter which I will discuss in detail below. My third reason for making the survey was that I believed it should be possible to determine which variables affect the form of water control in each case and how.

I have suggested some of the limitations and advantages of my survey method, but neglected to mention one further disadvantage which is a matter likely to concern many ethnographers. That is, one cannot, from a survey of many villages, gain the depth of understanding of the interconnections between institutions and activities; of the relationships among individuals, families, and larger groups; of what they do and how and why, that one can gain from an intensive study of a single community. Nor can one in a brief visit gain the confidence of the informants, the judgment needed to interpret what they say, or establish the rapport with the community as one often can through long-term "participant observation."

No doubt this is an important consideration. But just how important it is depends on the questions one asks and the kind of answers one wants to get. To illustrate the advantages of the survey method in this case, let me give an example. My aim was to gain an understanding of the relationship of water control to political structure in Oaxaca's peasant society. If I had made a community study of the village of Tlalixtac, I would have discovered that the municipal *presidente,* the highest ranking and most powerful village official, has complete control of the distribution of water. I might have concluded that, because irrigation water was very important in this community, it was only natural that the highest-ranking official would control it. Since control of water in itself would be a source of power, placing control in the hands of the presidente would enhance his position so that he could more effectively execute his other duties. If I had, instead, made a community study of San Juan del Estado, I would have found something rather different. There water is distributed by five relatively low-ranking officials, one for each main canal, who are apparently not very powerful at all. I might have concluded that the knowledge necessary to distribute water from so many canals to so many people requires a division of labor so that several people could supervise this distribution separately and independently. This supervision would be time consuming and tedious, and thus would be assigned to lower-level officials who were not engaged in important decision-making. I might further have assumed that the administrative tasks of these officials give them no special power, that they are merely public servants.

These two communities are more or less similiar in size, water resources, and technology, and in the relative importance of irrigation. Thus, my interpretation of the relationship between water control and political structure in either one would not only have been wrong for the other but wrong for both. If I had studied both of them, and no others, I would have been hard put to make a generalization, and I might have devised some sort of complicated explanation about why they are different. If I had instead compared about 10 or 15 villages, I would have learned that water distribution is never so complex as to require that five men supervise it at once; and I would have learned that water control is only very rarely a task of the presidente and that its relative importance has nothing to do with who controls it. By the time I had conducted interviews in 20 villages I might have been ready to generalize and say that although the form of water control varies from village to village, it is always present where people use canal irrigation because someone is needed to see that they take turns and do not fight; without it they could not irrigate at all. In fact, it was not until after I had actually surveyed 20 villages that I came across two which had no official organization of control. Only by sacrificing the admitted advantages of an intensive community study–rapport and participant observation—could I have gained the perspective I needed to understand the nature of social response to canal irrigation in the larger society. This understanding is crucial, I believe, to the interpretation of what goes on at the community level.

Having made this point about the potential distortions in viewpoint which may arise from limiting research to a single village, I should take warning myself about the distortions to which a study of only one *kind* of water control is subject. A number of generalizations will be made about the role of water control on the basis of this one-sided view; these can be presented only with the qualification that they might convey this distortion. To balance the views presented here, similar studies should also be made of villages which do not use canal irrigation, in order to test the degree to which similarities among those which do use it might have been overlooked. Limitations of time, money, and manpower prevented me from extending my study in this way; therefore, I offer my conclusions as tentative, subject to change on the basis of more extensive study, particularly villages using other types of irrigation.

I

COMMUNITY ORGANIZATION

INTRODUCTION

Since the organization of water use is only one part of a larger organization, it is important first to understand the structure and operation of that larger organization, the rural community of Oaxaca. The organization of the community involves the political offices, the processes of selection of officials, the rights of village members, and the responsibilities of both officials and other members. It also involves economic interaction and exchange, which are central to the internal integration of the community. The rules which guide behavior in both the political and the economic spheres are based upon certain underlying principles which apply to the actual situations encountered by community members in their everyday lives. Thus, our description of the larger organization will include a description of the principles upon which particular rules for particular circumstances—such as the allotment of water—are based.

Similarly, the problems and conflicts involved in water control are reflected in the larger organization. They arise from such contradictions as the ideal of equality among community members in the face of actual differences in wealth, prestige, and power, and the ideal of shared community interests in the face of actual private, sometimes opposed, interests. In the first part of the chapter, several institutions are described in detail to show how some of these conflicts may be resolved. Although certain of these institutions are not directly related to canal irrigation, they demonstrate the fact that the principles that guide the resolution of conflicts through these institutions are the same principles functional in institutions related to canal irrigation.

The second part of the chapter is devoted to a discussion of an organization of a different kind which applies to the external relations of the community and its place in the regional, state, and national political network. Although these organizations are in many ways independent of one another, they meet from time to time. When they do meet—and such situations are occurring with increasing frequency—certain changes take place, particularly at the community level. Later on, I will describe the relationship of such changes to water control. The second part of this chapter describes the general circumstances under which confrontations and changes in village-state relations occur.

THE VILLAGE

Historical Background

To understand the organization of the rural community in Oaxaca, we should turn back four and one-half centuries to the historical events most responsible for its present-day form.[1] The pre-Hispanic Zapotec state consisted of an integrated hierarchy of social classes, with a broad base of primary producers (commoner-peasants) and a smaller, specialized group of professional governors (noblemen and *caciques*) who main-

---

[1]This brief analysis of the relationship between community organization and Spanish colonial policies agrees closely with, and owes a great deal to, the suggestions made by Eric Wolf in a number of his writings on the subject of the closed-corporate community in Mesoamerica. See, for example, Wolf, 1955.

tained order within, and controlled relations between, the communities in which they lived and served.2 Although the impact of Spanish Colonialism upon the Zapotec nobility was less harsh and rapid than elsewhere in Mexico, its eventual result was a thorough decapitation of the Indian state:3 the class which had once served to maintain order and regulate intercommunity relations was effectively eliminated by absorption into either the Spanish colonial elite or the Indian rural peasantry.

While the Spanish colonial government easily replaced the Indian nobility as an intermediary among communities, it did not replace it within the communities. The Spanish restricted the power of the communities to sell land freely, made them pay tribute, and granted them internal self-government (Taylor, 1969).

Faced with a vacuum in their organization—once filled by the specialized class whose business it was to govern—communities were forced to devise new systems for maintaining internal order on the one hand and fulfilling responsibilities to the colonial state on the other. The result was a reworking of pre-Columbian institutions into a new system, containing a number of institutions which not only lacked a social class hierarchy but effectively prevented such a hierarchy from forming. By institutionalizing a method of selecting individuals from the community to serve in administrative positions, the new system prevented such individuals from specializing in administration. Finally, the new system organized relations only within communities, not among them. Intercommunity relations were almost entirely the responsibility of the colonial government.

When Mexico broke away from Spain, the new national government merely replaced the colonial government without really altering the community systems. Nor did the revolution bring radical change at the community level. In certain ways, it even protected and perpetuated existing arrangements. Only in the past two or three decades has the traditional community system in the Valley of Oaxaca begun to weaken, but its collapse is far from complete.

The Civil-Religious Hierarchy and the *Cargo* System

I have refrained from calling Oaxacan communities "closed corporate communities," a term initially proposed by Wolf (1955) for a certain type of Mesoamerican community, because, although they share many of the characteristics of the villages which seem to fall into this category, they diverge from the ideal type Wolf described in important ways. Unlike some of the villages in the mountain areas of this region, which seem to fit the "ideal type" more closely, the valley villages are not situated entirely upon "marginal land," and in most the bulk of the agricultural land is privately owned, not communally controlled. The combined features of a limited amount of highly productive arable land and a strong emphasis upon private ownership of property have presented Oaxacan communities with special problems perhaps not shared by "ideal" Mesoamerican "closed corporate communities."

In most other respects, however, Oaxacan communities traditionally conform to the general patterns outlined by Wolf. Central to their organization is a set of institutions referred to in the literature as the "civil-religious hierarchy" and the *cargo* system. A cargo is a public service position, a public office; in the cargo system every able-bodied male member of the community takes his turn at filling various offices in the civil-religious hierarchy: judge, policeman, church warden, and others. The "civil-religious hierarchy" refers to the ranking of these offices, or cargos, and the steps one must take to fill them. Traditionally, at some point as a man proceeds up the hierarchy, he is expected to sponsor with his own private means a public celebration of a religious occasion.4 These cele-

---

2For a detailed description of the various pre-Hispanic social classes in Oaxaca, see Whitecotton, 1968.

3For a discussion of the reasons for the less severe impact of the Colonial government upon the Oaxacan nobility, see Taylor, 1969.

4This is not a universal requirement; in fact, it has been outlawed in a number of the more progressive communities.

brations are called *mayordomías* and their sponsors, *mayordomos*. Participation in government, then, entails expenditure of private surpluses on the community.

All male community members are ideally expected to seek to approach the top of the hierarchy, serving in successively higher offices and sponsoring successively more costly and more important mayordomías until they can go no further. This system operates on a principle of equal and successive participation in the internal community government by every male member of the community. Traditionally, it was nearly impossible for members of the community to avoid participation, though lately this has changed.

If the civil-religious hierarchy and the cargo system are classified as political institutions, they imply a certain type of economic and social organization as well. They imply, for example, social and economic equality, at least in terms of resources, power, rights, and opportunities. Though this equality may not in fact exist, in certain contexts people, as well as the system, act as if it did. The institutions imply the existence of private economic resources and the social pressure to meet responsibilities to the public by using these resources. Finally, they imply a sharing of responsibility, resources, and benefits by all the members of the community, but never all at once. Everyone takes turns at giving and receiving, and eventually everyone is supposed to give and receive as much as everyone else.

Economic Organization: Land and Wealth

Turning now to economic institutions, we find a variety of patterns of organization, some of which create basic contradictions in the larger social structure in terms of coexistence of equality and inequality, public and private realms of ownership and access, independence and interdependence, and individual reciprocal exchange and collective cooperation.

I will begin with the question of property and land tenure. Almost every village in the valley has, within its municipal boundaries, two or more different types of land: barren, forested, or otherwise not agriculturally productive land, and fertile, well-situated land. Some, if not most, of the poor land is owned collectively by the community. If it is not cultivated, anyone may use it for pasture or collecting firewood, or may request permission from a community official to clear and cultivate it. Once it is cultivated, the cultivator generally has indefinite and exclusive rights of usufruct as long as he continues to cultivate it, or expresses his intention to do so, and periodically pays a small fee for this right. It may be passed on to his heirs, but it may not be sold—by an individual, or (generally speaking) by the whole community.

Some, though by no means all, villages have *ejidos,* organizations which collectively own land. These organizations allow members usufructory rights similar to those applied to communal village land with the further stipulation that the cultivator be not only a member of the community but also of the ejido.[5] Generally, there is more land of the communal type available than there are people who want to cultivate it. Ejido lands by contrast may vary in quality, but are generally scarce and in demand, with none to spare for newcomers.

The more fertile, humid land is better situated in relation to the village and is privately owned. Almost all villages have a private sector, and unless the ejido is large, the private sector constitutes the bulk of the more productive land.[6] This land may be bought and sold by individuals to other members of the community or to outsiders at any time. Individuals may or may not own land privately, depending on what they have inherited, bought, or sold up to any particular point in time. Prime land is generally

---

[5]Ejido lands are generally redistributed lands from pre-Revolution haciendas, though not all such redistributed land became cooperatively controlled by ejido organizations. There is only one ejido to a village; many villages have none. Nonresidents may not become ejido members. Membership may be obtained, if there is extra land available, by placing an application with the ejido and paying a membership fee.

[6]There are exceptions. San Bernardo Mixtepec and San Miguel del Valle, for example, have only communal land—no private or ejido property. San Sebastián Etla and Santiaguito Etla, on the other hand, have almost nothing but ejido land, and virtually every member of these two communities is an ejido member as well.

quite scarce in relation to the number of people who want to cultivate it. Privately-owned plots tend to be small and irregular in size and shape. They may be divided up for sale and inheritance and thus tend to become fragmented into smaller and smaller pieces. Although some land redistributed as private property after the revolution was allotted to villagers in equal portions, different rates of inheritance and buying and selling have resulted in differences in the sizes of plots on these lands as well. Therefore, in any one community some individuals will own much more land than others, and some will own none at all. The proportions vary from village to village. Landless individuals are often younger men who have not yet received an inheritance or had enough time to accumulate sufficient funds to buy land, but in many villages a large proportion of even middle-aged and older men have no land of their own.

Good land is scarce and expensive; wages are low, and money is hard to come by. Most villagers live at a subsistence level, producing just enough to get by on in an ordinary year. In a bad year—if there is a drought or a flood or sickness in the family—individuals must often resort to selling their land, if they have any, in order to survive. But an individual who by chance manages to transcend the subsistence level and acquire more land than survival requires becomes less and less vulnerable to such emergencies.

Even though there is almost always some land to which everyone has equal access, the best land, often the only productive land available, is generally privately owned and not accessible to many or most of the population. Those who own more land than they themselves can cultivate have three alternatives: they may rent some or all of it out; they may hire laborers to work it; or they may sharecrop it with a landless person.[7] The first alternative is rarely taken because those who would need land are not likely to have money to rent it. But the second two alternatives are frequently used. If someone in the village owns more land than he can cultivate, there must be someone who owns less, who must resort to working the land of others in order to survive. Thus the private landowner with more land than he needs for minimum subsistence tends to become a landlord or an employer or both. The hiring of labor or sharecropping of the land implies a social relationship, a "patron-client" relationship, albeit on a very small scale, at the community level.

All this takes place without the emergence of a stratified class structure at the village level (although in some villages there seems to be a slight trend in this direction), several factors counteract its development. First, the villagers live by an ideal of equality: value is placed on hard work and a modest life style. Poverty is a virtue of sorts; wealthier citizens are reluctant to display their unequal status, hoping to avoid social disapproval as well as requests for charity from friends and relatives. What is not displayed can be ignored, and without social recognition of differences of status no class structure can arise.

Another restraint on the development of class structure has to do with the actual existence of an economic class structure in the larger society. Although members of the upper class rarely live in rural communities, they can be observed by members of the lower classes from a distance, and differences between the styles of life of the former and the latter are recognized by both. Until recently, Mexico had had only two classes—nothing in between. Since even wealthier villagers cannot really approach the life style of the upper class, they are grouped with the lower; while such villagers may get ahead of their neighbors, the chasm between upper and lower class is nearly impossible to cross. Should the almost incredible occur, that a wealthy villager rise so high as to approach the upper class style of life, it is even more inconceivable that he would remain in the village. Either way, community members do not become divided into distinct upper and lower classes at the local level. (The situation is beginning to change now, with the growth of a new middle class in Mexico.)

---

[7]Sharecropper arrangements vary, but a common arrangement is one in which the landowner supplies the land and seed, the sharecropper supplies the labor, plow and oxen, and each gets half the harvest.

A third restraint is that the Federal government tries to limit individual accumulations of wealth by placing a ceiling on the amount of land that any one person may own. Although not always effective, this legislation probably arrests a widening division between rich and poor. And finally, accumulations or concentrations of land rarely last more than two or three generations, for successions of heirs divide the property into smaller and smaller holdings.

It has been suggested by Wolf and others[8] that the civil-religious hierarchy, particularly the institution of the mayordomía, tends to level differences of wealth by establishing a limited range of differences or by preventing them from becoming permanent. Theoretically, sponsorship of a mayordomía would immediately absorb any surplus wealth an individual might have accumulated. This might be so if surplus wealth could only be acquired through personal labor. But the truly significant surpluses here are not based upon personal labor; they are based upon private ownership of highly productive agricultural land.

Cancian (1967) and others have proposed alternative interpretations of the effects of the mayordomía and the cargo system upon social differentiation based upon wealth. They argue that these institutions enhance, rather than impede, such differentiation. For example, wealthier individuals who are landlords and employers are likely to be more influential than others in the village and thus tend to be selected more frequently to serve in higher public offices. In addition, wealthier individuals may more easily afford to sponsor mayordomías (which makes them eligible for high office) and sponsor more expensive ones, more frequently. Poor individuals either cannot afford sponsorship at all, or become completely impoverished or indebted for years afterward. Furthermore, wealthier individuals can afford to hire laborers to work for them, leaving them time to devote to public affairs. Poor men have to devote all their time to earning a living, and thus are less likely to seek office and tend to be less effective in office in the unlikely event that they are elected.[9]

Both of these interpretations probably hold true to some extent in most traditional villages, but there are many other complications as well. I have mentioned these interpretations in order to point out that the egalitarian ideal often disguises a nonegalitarian reality, and that this contradiction with the ideal, which partly arises from the existence of private property in productive land, may have important consequences for other institutions in the social organization.

Economic Organization:
Exchange and Cooperation

In addition to the buying and selling of agricultural land and labor, other economic exchanges take place between private individuals. Money has become an increasingly important medium of exchange. Most villages specialize in the production of one or another of the cash crops or craft goods which villagers exchange for money in the local markets in order to purchase goods in either the market or the stores in the village and city. Further, most villages have within them a variety of local specialists: barbers, butchers, bakers, masons, carpenters, tailors, curers, and others, who perform their services for cash payments. As many anthropologists have pointed out, markets play an important role in the peasant economy.[10] Since they are not central with respect to the topic of this study, I will not discuss market institutions in detail but mention them only in contrast to another form of exchange.

Guelaguetza, another traditional institution of economic exchange, has been described in Oaxacan villages several times. The term is apparently a Hispanicized version of a Zapotec term, suggesting that the origins of the institution in this region are ancient. Although it is frequently described as ceremonial in context and nature, guelaguetza actually has a more

[8]See Cancian, 1967.

[9]See Lewis (1964) for a discussion of the trials of a poor man holding high public office in a Mexican village.

[10]For a discussion of the Oaxaca market system, see Malinowski (1957). More recent studies have been made by Beals (1967) and Cook (1969).

general meaning, referring to delayed exchanges of equivalent goods or services in equivalent contexts. The parties to the exchange are either friends or relatives, but not members of the same household. One of the parties to the exchange, in need of help for a specific project (almost always either for sponsorship of a religious ceremony or for an agricultural task—planting or harvesting), asks one or more of his friends and kinsmen to help him. Both parties keep careful accounts of what help was given, and at a later time, when the individual who gave help needs assistance in a similar enterprise, he may expect it from those whom he assisted in an amount exactly equivalent to that which he previously gave. It is considered morally reprehensible for a party to receive guelaguetza assistance if he knows he will be unable or unwilling to repay it when called upon.[11] Guelaguetza creates debts which must be repaid in full and in equivalent items. Although it strengthens social bonds, its primary purpose is economic. If one knows he will not need or want repayment in kind, one does not offer or agree to give help through guelaguetza.

As I have already observed, one of the two main contexts in which guelaguetza takes place is in planting or harvesting. Generally, a group of men decide they will cooperate on the job. They all work together, first in one man's field, then in another's, until all the men's fields are done. Because there is no monetary payment involved, this cooperation is considered to be guelaguetza: it is neither an obligation nor a favor done by one man for another, but an exchange of assistance.

The other context in which guelaguetza occurs is in sponsorship of religious mayordomías or wedding, baptismal, or funeral ceremonies. Friends and kinsmen contribute what they can—perhaps a few pesos, some chocolate, some bread or coffee. Those who have received similar contributions in the past from the sponsor bring an amount equivalent to what they received, although it need not be precisely the same goods.

For example, if a donor gives two pesos worth of chocolate, one peso worth of candles, and one peso worth of bread, he may receive three pesos in cash and one peso worth of coffee or four pesos worth of beer when he himself later sponsors a ceremony. He cannot, so far as I know, receive or ask repayment for this donation in labor at harvest time, since neither the type of assistance nor the context would be equivalent.

Guelaguetza, as a form of mutual aid, is an important means of overcoming some of the contradictions which have been mentioned. First, though individuals own and work land privately, they sometimes need help from others for executing certain tasks. Since no man has a particular interest in what others produce on their own lands or any obligation to help them, and since he must rely upon his own private resources and personal effort, he must be offered recompense for his labor on the land of another. Most men are too poor to offer money or even goods, such as a share of the harvest, in order to get the help of others. This is a system in which almost every man has what every other has, only each has it separately—they do not customarily share their resources. Guelaguetza is a device for allowing them not only to have the same things separately, but also to share them as members of a group by letting the members take turns at having access to their pooled resources. This sort of resource would not be available to most men other than as members of a guelaguetza group.

In this society men are expected to take turns at sponsoring religious ceremonies; yet the accumulation of sufficient wealth to do so is extremely difficult for most individuals. Although most people are more or less equally poor at any given time, one of them is supposed to be wealthy. While the system impedes the private accumulation of wealth, it also rewards such accumulation with prestige and social favor—if such accumulation is dispersed through immediate expenditures upon the behalf of the whole community. In fact, since private sponsorship of public festivities is a moral obligation on the part of all community members, such accumulations seem to be required if the system is to operate. The sponsorship of these religious

---

[11]Sometimes, individuals carefully avoid or refuse guelaguetza exchange, because delayed debts in kind may turn out to be more costly in the long run than immediate cash payment (see Cook, 1965).

ceremonies provides the second context in which guelaguetza is important; it provides the means by which everyone can take turns at being wealthy, while just about everyone remains equally poor.

There are further implications. Guelaguetza is limited to certain specific contexts, and these contexts are mutually exclusive. Once a person has engaged in a guelaguetza transaction, then he must at a later time engage in the same type of project, though in a different role. Thus, for example, if he gave help to a religious sponsor, then he must later become a religious sponsor, so that he can receive repayment. In the ceremonial context, the project is one in which private funds are used for public enjoyment. A person cannot help another to sponsor such a ceremony and then use the debt to add to his personal wealth; he can only use the debt to sponsor another public ceremony. Guelaguetza, then, is an equalizer in that all who engage in the transaction must eventually carry out the same sorts of projects, each one taking his turn.

In some ways, my description of guelaguetza has been exaggerated and oversimplified. Everyone is not, in fact, equally poor, and the wealthy sometimes prefer not to engage in guelaguetza; furthermore, part of the sponsorship funds are accumulated by individuals without guelaguetza help. But I have chosen to emphasize two basic characteristics of guelaguetza—the equality of the participants and the process of sharing by taking turns—and the attendant conflict between private interests and cooperative efforts. The joint characteristics of equality and turn-taking, in conjunction with this conflict, constitute a basic theme of this society which is reflected in other institutions and in other contexts of social interaction. I have already noted its appearance in political organization.

Economic Organization: Community Cooperation

Though agricultural and craft production and sponsorship of certain religious celebrations are private household responsibilities, other aspects of economic organization lie in the public realm.

Water for domestic and agricultural use, electricity, roads, public buildings, and such services as school and church are managed by public institutions and paid for, at least in part, by the whole community in several ways.

Community taxes pay for such public services as the initial installation of electricity, the building of a new school, some religious celebrations, etc. Sometimes a set sum of money is collected from each member of the community; sometimes people are asked to pay different amounts according to their known incomes; sometimes people are asked to contribute voluntarily according to their desire or ability. While the first alternative stresses the equality of community members in participation and contribution, the second and third recognize real differences among them. Communities may use any one of the three on different occasions.[12]

Sometimes schools and churches are paid for in another way. They may have attached to them a plot of good agricultural land. In some cases, this land is rented or sharecropped by private individuals, whose payments go into school or church funds. In other instances, community members work the land collectively, the proceeds going to the school or church.[13]

This sort of communal labor, along with other kinds directed toward building or maintenance such as construction and repair of roads and irrigation canals is managed through an institution called *tequio*. Every able-bodied adult male in the community, with the exception of certain public officials, is required to give a certain number of work days each year to the community for such projects. Usually so many projects are underway that an individual can choose which days he will work. Thus, if every individual must contribute five work days each year and community projects take up eight work days, an individual may refuse to work three times during the year. Generally, careful accounts are kept by

---

[12]Payment for services which are used differentially by different households, such as water and electricity, may be made according to the amount used by the household.

[13]In at least one case, communal land was worked by means of tequio for community emergency funds (Cook, 1965).

the public officials of who has worked, when, and how much. If an individual is seriously inconvenienced by the requirement to work on a particular day, he may hire a replacement for himself, if he can afford it, and notify the officials. But individuals who continually refuse to contribute labor when they are called may be severely punished by fines, incarceration, and negative public opinion.

Projects are organized by public officials, who decide what must be done, where, and when. Some time in advance they make known the day or days on which a tequio labor project is scheduled. That day a public official announces the project and calls laborers to the village center by blowing a conch shell trumpet which can be heard everywhere in the community. Together the villagers walk out to wherever the work is to be done, led by the official(s) in charge. Tequio is a very ancient institution of pre-Hispanic origin.[14] Although once used in the service of the Indian nobility and later the Spanish colonial government and church, it does not require the authority of an outside or socially remote force. It is an internal arrangement by which the community exerts its own authority over individual members.

In the institution of tequio evidences of the themes of equality and inequality, the conflict of private and public interests, and the process of taking turns appear again, only in a different arrangement. Equality is expressed in the fact that everyone is required to do the same work; inequality, in the fact that work is and must be directed by an official who stands in a position of superordination in relation to others. Inasmuch as men take turns in occupying offices, superordination itself is shared successively by all. Thus, he who works as a laborer on a public project one year may be administrator the next, and he who directs any project will find himself being directed in the same sort of work at another time. Accommodation is made for the conflict of public and private interests through the possibilities of arranging alternative work days or hiring substitutes on the one hand, but also through the possibility of exercising sanctions to assert the dominance of public over private interests, on the other.

The existence of a public sphere of the economy for communal labor, property, and redistribution of goods and services, along with a set of public officials who organize and direct activities in this sphere, is perhaps a major distinguishing characteristic of peasant, as opposed to tribal, societies. Though tribal peoples may work and own property collectively, they do so through the organization provided by a kinship structure. Kinship in the peasant society belongs in the private sphere; the public organization has an entirely different and separate structure. This structure may or may not be linked directly to the larger structure of the society of which peasants are a part; in the case of Oaxaca, as we shall see, there are certain elements or characteristics of public management at the community level which separate it from that of the state.

THE VILLAGE AND THE STATE

Political Units

The structure of the community has remained more or less constant since the conquest, but the details of its political organization have varied through time. The basic political unit at the time of the conquest was the "lordship," which usually comprised a number of villages, one of which was its political center or *cabecera* (Whitecotton, 1968). The lord or *cacique* generally resided in the cabecera and directed political affairs from there. As time went on, the lords disappeared, but the political unit of cabeceras and dependent villages or *sujetos* remained. In the Valley of Oaxaca, these units had a tendency to fragment, becoming smaller and more numerous; many of them now contain only a single village, though others still contain several.

Today the state constitution recognizes this unit as the basic unit of the political structure (Pérez Jiménez, 1968). It is called the *municipio libre*; its dependencies are called *agencias*.

[14]Carved conch shell trumpets of the type used for tequio are known archaeologically in Oaxaca since at least 900 B.C. (Flannery, private communication). (See Whitecotton, 1968.)

Though the constitution states that a *municipio* must have a population of 5,000 or more, most Valley of Oaxaca municipios are much smaller, ranging between 500 and 5,000 inhabitants. Cabeceras themselves generally range between 400 and 4,000 inhabitants. Agencias fall into two categories: according to the constitution, communities with populations of 500 to 5,000 are *agencias municipales;* those with less than 500 are *agencias de policia.* For most practical purposes, agencias are independent and separate communities, the larger ones more so than the smaller. For certain administrative purposes, municipios are grouped into larger units called *distritos,* which also have administrative centers, or cabeceras. The cabeceras of the distritos are large towns which give the distrito its name and provide the locus for the regional market. In the Valley of Oaxaca there are six distritos (See map 1, Table 1).

The head village of a municipio is a more or less independent unit, with its own body of political administrators. Most agencias also have a separate set of political offices and frequently take affairs needing decisions by higher authorities directly to the district or state officials, bypassing the municipio cabecera entirely. As an important official of one large agencia said of its municipio cabecera, "We don't bother them, and they don't bother us." Agencias

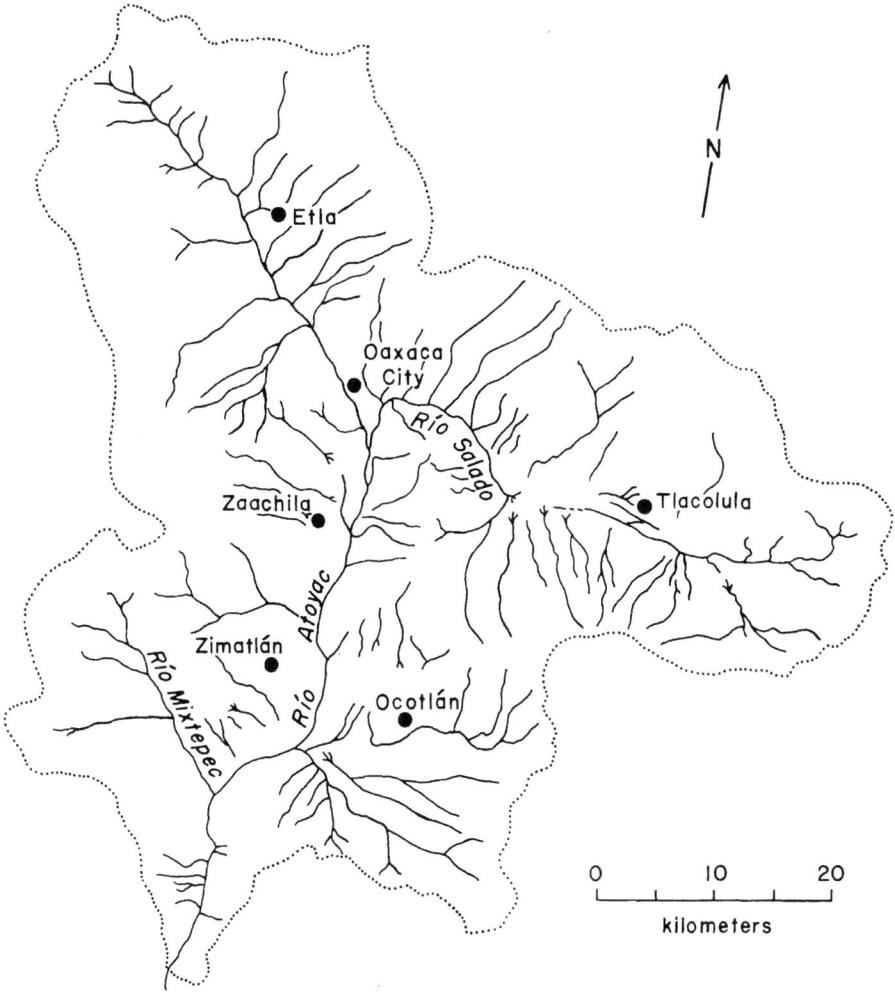

Map 1. District centers in the Valley of Oaxaca.

TABLE 1
DISTRITOS OF THE VALLEY OF OAXACA

Distrito	Municipios	Agencias Municipales	Agencias de Policía	Market
Tlacolula	25	15	10	Sunday
Etla	23	27	30	Wednesday
Zimatlán	13	15	7	Wednesday
Zaachila	6	3	10	Thursday
Ocotlán	32	11	16	Friday
Centro	21	12	37	Saturday
Total	120	83	110	

generally have their own schools, churches, and various types of officials to run their community affairs. The main administrative difference between municipio cabeceras and agencias is that the chief administrator of the former is a presidente and of the latter, an agente. Though agencias tend to be smaller, some agencias are larger than some municipio cabeceras.

Village Government

The principal governing body of the municipio is the *ayuntamiento,* whose core is a council of five men. These men are elected by the population at large for a term of three years and cannot be reelected to the same office for two consecutive terms. From their number, the group selects one man to be presidente and another, his second-in-command, as *síndico.* The remaining three are called *regidores* (or *consejales*). The latter three officials are frequently assigned different responsibilities, though the division of labor varies from village to village. For example, in one village there may be one regidor in charge of the school, another in charge of public works, and a third in charge of water control; in another, they may all three be responsible for different aspects of public works—one for finances, one for labor, one for materials—while school and water administration are assigned to different public officers.

In the council there are also five alternates, or *suplentes,* one for each principal member, who serve in the absence of one or another member and may have additional tasks as well. In addition, the ayuntamiento may have a *secretaria* and/or a *tesorero,* either of whom may be elected by the population at large or appointed by the ayuntamiento. Sometimes the secretaria and tesorero are paid a small allowance for their services; other members of the ayuntamiento are never paid. The ayuntamiento has a public office in the center of the village where it meets to make decisions and execute its administrative tasks. Attached to this office are a number of lesser officials who serve as messengers, police, guards, and custodians. In some villages, the ayuntamiento office is kept open all day, with one or more officials available for duty and a messenger waiting to fetch others if necessary. In others, generally the smaller ones, the office is opened for only a few hours each day. Council members take turns at sitting in the office during the slow hours so that all need not be there at once.

Outside the ayuntamiento proper, but also a part of the core governing body, is the office of the *alcalde*—the justice department—which hears cases which do not involve the state government, such as petty crimes and local disputes, but not major crimes such as homicide. There are generally two alcaldes, who may take turns or serve together. These also generally have suplentes and sometimes a secretaria and tesorero as well, in addition to messengers and other servants. Rules for election of these officials are the same as those for the ayuntamiento.

Another office, apart from the ayuntamiento, is the *Comisariado de Bienes Comunales,* which is mainly responsible for the administration of communal lands, though it may also have other tasks. It may consist of a committee, with a presidente, secretaria, tesorero and so forth, or may have only one official, the *comisariado*.

Agencias, as I have already noted, have no ayuntamientos proper but rather an *agente,* who is elected annually in agencias de policía and every three years in agencias municipales. The agente always has a suplente and sometimes a secretaria and/or tesorero and a set of messengers and other functionaries. Agencias municipales also have alcaldes and comisariados.

Certain public facilities are managed by special committees. There is generally one assigned to the church and another to the school; these are frequently large enough to have presidents, secretaries, treasurers, messengers, servants, and other officials. There are also committees for electricity, sometimes for fire-fighting, occasionally for water control, and so on, which vary from village to village. Agencias, like municipios, may have few or many of these committees, depending on their needs and interests.

Many villages have no ejidos, and many others have very small ones, which have little influence in community affairs. A few villages, however, are composed almost entirely of a single ejido. In these cases, ejido affairs are really identical to public affairs, and the ejido plays a major role in their management. Ejidos also have presidents, secretaries, treasurers, committees, and so forth. They do not replace the ayuntamiento or agente but govern along side of them and often share administrative tasks with them.

Most villages, even the smaller ones, have a large number of public offices and require a large number of people to fill them. At the base of the structure is the office of *topil* (sometimes called night policeman or messenger or servant). Each village generally has a large number of topiles, sometimes 20 or more. Individuals more or less automatically begin to serve in these positions as they reach a certain age or as they marry. Though they do not serve continually, they serve repeatedly at lower levels until they reach higher levels of the organization. For example, they may be required to serve one year out of every three or one out of every six as a public official of this sort for a certain period of time in their lives. Everyone starts at this level, and everyone serves. Generally there are so many young men serving in these offices at any one time that groups of them can take turns by weeks or days or months. For example, if 10 men must serve as night policemen every night, and if there are 30 men in the police force altogether, they might divide into three groups, each serving for a week at a time with two weeks off.

As men get older, they may volunteer or be appointed or elected to serve on various committees. Again, these committees generally have more members than are needed to serve at any one time, so they alternate, one working one week, another the next. Officials become fewer near the top of the hierarchy, but even in the ayuntamiento members divide up the work and take turns at performing the more time-consuming duties.

Because these offices do take up time and are nonremunerative, most individuals are reluctant to serve. But refusal to serve if one is elected or appointed is generally considered a crime, punishable not only by public disapproval but sometimes by fine, incarceration, or even banishment from the community. If people are not allowed to refuse public service, they also rarely volunteer. Political ambition at the village level, though not unheard of, is generally not strong.

Some villages are divided into factions: the rich against the poor, the progressives against the conservatives, or some other opposition. In one village, where half the community were ejido members and half were not, ejido membership was the basis of the factional split. Factions sometimes compete for control of the political offices. In the case of the community split between ejido and nonejido members, a compromise was reached whereby half the offices were filled by members of one faction and half by members of the other (Reichmann, 1964).

By now most villagers know about the Mexican national party system, for they vote in the national and state elections and are exposed to vigorous compaigns at regular intervals. There are three major parties: the Partido de Acción Nacional (PAN), the Partido Popular Socialista (PPS), and the Partido Revolucionario Institucional (PRI). Party politics have not really penetrated the village level, although the PRI has representatives in many villages and wins nearly all the state and national elections.

Despite the occasional existence of factions, villages tend to present a united front to the outside world, whether other villages or federal and state governments. One village, severely factionalized, found that it could only achieve internal peace and accord through its perpetual feud with another village (Reichmann, 1964). It was my impression that within most villages, officials and others were reluctant to argue, take stands, or make decisions with which they knew others would disagree; they sought consensus before taking action. Not that arguments did not occur; they did. Outbreaks of violence, both within and between villages, are rare because villagers seem to prefer litigation through government channels. Oaxacan communities were outstanding for their recourse to such litigation even in the early colonial period (Taylor, 1969). Disputes between villages almost invariably concern land and municipal boundaries.

The Village and the State

While the political structure of the state includes that of the village, the reverse is not true. Although the state, like the village, is in principle egalitarian and democratic and villagers do vote in national elections, the villagers usually do not participate directly in government at the state level except by voting. Democracy at the village level means not only that villagers select their own officials, but that they rotate the offices among themselves. Democracy at the state level is a representative democracy, in which the people elect representatives to make decisions for them. These representatives, unlike village officials, are full-time specialists. Their jobs are not rotated among members of the population at large, nor even among the specialists themselves. All these specialists are remote from the villagers, both physically and socially. Most of them live and work in the cities and have attitudes and interests far removed from those of the villagers.

But although the state may seem remote in some ways, its actions and policies do affect the everyday lives of the villagers. In addition to voting in its elections, supporting it by paying taxes, and obeying its laws in addition to their own, the villagers also apply for financial and technical assistance from state agencies and benefit from its health, education, transportation, communication, agricultural, hydraulic, and environmental development programs. Villagers use government-installed electricity; travel on government-built roads, often in government-controlled transportation powered by government-owned gasoline; they send their children to school to meet government educational standards with the help of government-trained teachers; they drink water brought from government-built wells by government-built pumps; they receive advice about the use of fertilizers from government agronomists, and assistance in building new hydraulic constructions from government engineers; they borrow money from government banks; they send letters with government stamps. If the government affected the daily lives of villagers little in the past, it will certainly have a much greater effect in the future.

The fact that the government is now increasing its impact on village life will force some changes in the relationship between the two. Villages have developed their own ways of managing their public affairs which do not always concur with that of state agencies. For example, sponsorship of religious celebrations is traditionally prerequisite to eligibility for higher offices in the village. This procedure provides the village with not only administrative service from the individual, but also a share of his surplus wealth. The state provides no support or sanction for the sponsorship requirement. But it does require that all office holders, even at the village level, be literate. Many of the older men in the community, generally the more religious-minded and the more well-to-do, have already sponsored mayordomías but are illiterate. The younger men, more frequently literate, are not as likely to have sponsored mayordomías. The government law—which the villagers must obey—makes ineligible people who by traditional standards would be eligible to serve, and those who would be ineligible by traditional standards are now eligible. The village standards, of course, must change, as in fact they have in the past few years. Now few villages hold to the old mayordomía requirement, and all have accepted the new literacy requirement. As the mayordomía has become detached from the village political structure, it has been set aside as a purely religious matter, a personal responsibility which one may or may not decide to fill. Eventually, private sponsorship of public celebrations will disappear, as it already has in many villages and a number of other, related institutions will lose their purpose. Guelaguetza, for example, will lose one of its major functions. Indeed, it is reported that in one very modern village, guelaguetza has disappeared within the lifetime of the current generation.

Some of these changes are welcomed by villagers; others are not, for reasons discussed in a later chapter. In any case, through developmental programs, the state can alter community structure more than has any historical event, law, or decree in the past 450 years. By making the community look outside itself for solutions to internal problems, these programs begin to eliminate the functions of the traditional organization, and thus undermine its effectiveness.

II

PROBLEMS OF WATER CONTROL AND THEIR SOLUTIONS

Introduction: Problems

The problems of water control referred to in this chapter are concerned not with the technical devices themselves,[1] but rather with their use. These problems are solved by systems of organization generally embodying rules of behavior and some sort of formal administration. The responsibilities of these organizations fall into three basic categories: construction, maintenance, and allocation. Construction involves the acquisition of building materials and equipment, labor, and sometimes special technical expertise. Maintenance includes surveillance and the application of labor at more or less regular intervals. Allocation refers to a set of rules pertaining to rights, a method of dividing the resource into segments which are to be allocated, and an administrative organization. Each task, particularly the last, involves dealing with conflict, potential or realized. Conflict over water use is solved in various contexts: some aspects of water control are restricted to internal village organization while others involve relationships among communities or, sometimes, between communities and the state government.

Data relating to these problems were collected for 24 villages (see Table 2 and Maps 2, 3, and 4), two of which did not rely upon canal irrigation: one depended primarily upon well irrigation in the alluvial zone, and the other upon dry farming in the piedmont. Even these villages had water control problems, and thus illustrate situations and solutions encountered in the two other types of agricultural communities. Other communities will be referred to for which information was obtained indirectly, through village informants, government records, or other anthropologists.

Construction

The task of building major dams or canals today is almost entirely relegated to the state branches of the federal hydraulic agencies. Although traditional small canals and irrigation wells are widespread, major canals are rarely built because water resources are diminishing; in fact, many of the devices already available have been abandoned for lack of water. Facilities of the traditional variety built in recent times include brush-dams on tributaries (and on the main Atoyac River until 40 years ago) and small floodwater terraces using rainfall which are located in the eastern arm of the valley (Kirkby 1973). These were built through the private arrangement of individuals and small groups of individuals and were not the concern of the community at large.

Formerly, *hacendados* and other private entrepreneurs also constructed dams and canals on permanent streams, paying for the materials and labor with private funds. But few such facilities have been built by private individuals since the revolution. No information exists to date concerning the construction of radically new irrigation devices by villages or caciques during the colonial or pre-Hispanic eras. In modern times, so far as we have evidence, none were constructed under state or federal government auspices in the valley until the past few decades. At present, the evidence indicates a shift in the control and

[1] See Volume 1 in this series (Kirkby, 1973) for a description of canal irrigation technology.

TABLE 2
LOCATION OF IRRIGATING VILLAGES

Village	Arm of Valley	Water Source	Zone
San Sebastián Abasolo	Tlacolula	High Water Table	HA
San Pablo Mitla	"	Primarily Rainfall	UP–LP
Teotitlán del Valle	"	Stream	UP
Santo Domingo Tomaltepec	"	"	UP
Tlalixtac de Cabrera	"	"	UP–LP
San Bernardo Mixtepec	Zimatlán	Mixtepec River	UP
Santa Cruz Mixtepec	"	"	UP
Rincón de Tlapacoyan	"	"	UP
Emiliano Zapata	"	"	UP–LP
Santa Ana Tlapacoyan	"	"	HA
San Juan del Estado	Etla	Stream	UP
Magdalena Apasco	"	"	LP
San Juan Bautista Guelache	"	"	UP
Santos Degollados Etla	"	"	LP
San Gabriel Etla	"	"	UP
San Miguel Etla	"	"	LP
San Agustín Etla	"	"	UP
San Sebastián Etla	"	"	LP
Santo Domingo Barrio Alto	"	"	LP
San José Mogote	"	"	LP–HA
Santiaguito Etla	"	"	LP–HA
Guadalupe Etla	"	Atoyac River	HA
San Andrés Zautla	"	Stream	UP–LP
Santa Tomás Mazaltepec	"	"	UP

Zone: HA = High Alluvium UP = Upper Piedmont LP = Lower Piedmont

direction of any large irrigation-device construction from the native caciques (in late pre-Hispanic times) to both the egalitarian colonial communities and private entrepreneurs in the pre-revolutionary period, to state and federal government agencies in recent times.

The current government policy for this area rests on a project to construct a large number of state-supported irrigation devices, which, for the most part, are not total innovations, but rather improvements of older irrigation systems. In a few cases—that is, when a relatively large dam is built—the transformation is radical, as in Teotitlán del Valle and Santo Domingo Tomaltepec, for example. Smaller, bit-by-bit improvements are more common, however. In Zautla, for example, a small diversion dam, two *galerías* (underground conduits) and a siphon were added over the past 10 years, and more additions are expected in the future.

When a community—an ordinary village or an ejido—decides it needs a major new water-control device, it generally applies in writing to the Secretaria de Recursos Hidráulicos (SRH), the specific governmental agency in charge of this operation. For the relatively small-scale type of federal installation built nowadays in the Valley of Oaxaca, the SRH generally turns to a section of the Secretaria de Agricultura y Ganadería (SAG), which has its own staff of hydraulic engineers. The SRH mainly restricts itself, in actual construction, to major projects such as those found today in the area of Jalapa del Marquez, near Tehuantepec.[2] Thus, an SAG representative (engineer) is usually sent to the village to review the situation, find an appropriate location for the new construction, estimate expenses, and advise the community on the feasibility of the project and on how to proceed. Often requests will be denied by the agency if the water supply is insufficient, or the device can not be constructed or not enough

[2] See Secretaría de Agricultura y Ganadería publications (1968-69), for a description of this agency's role in construction and development of hydraulic works and its general policies.

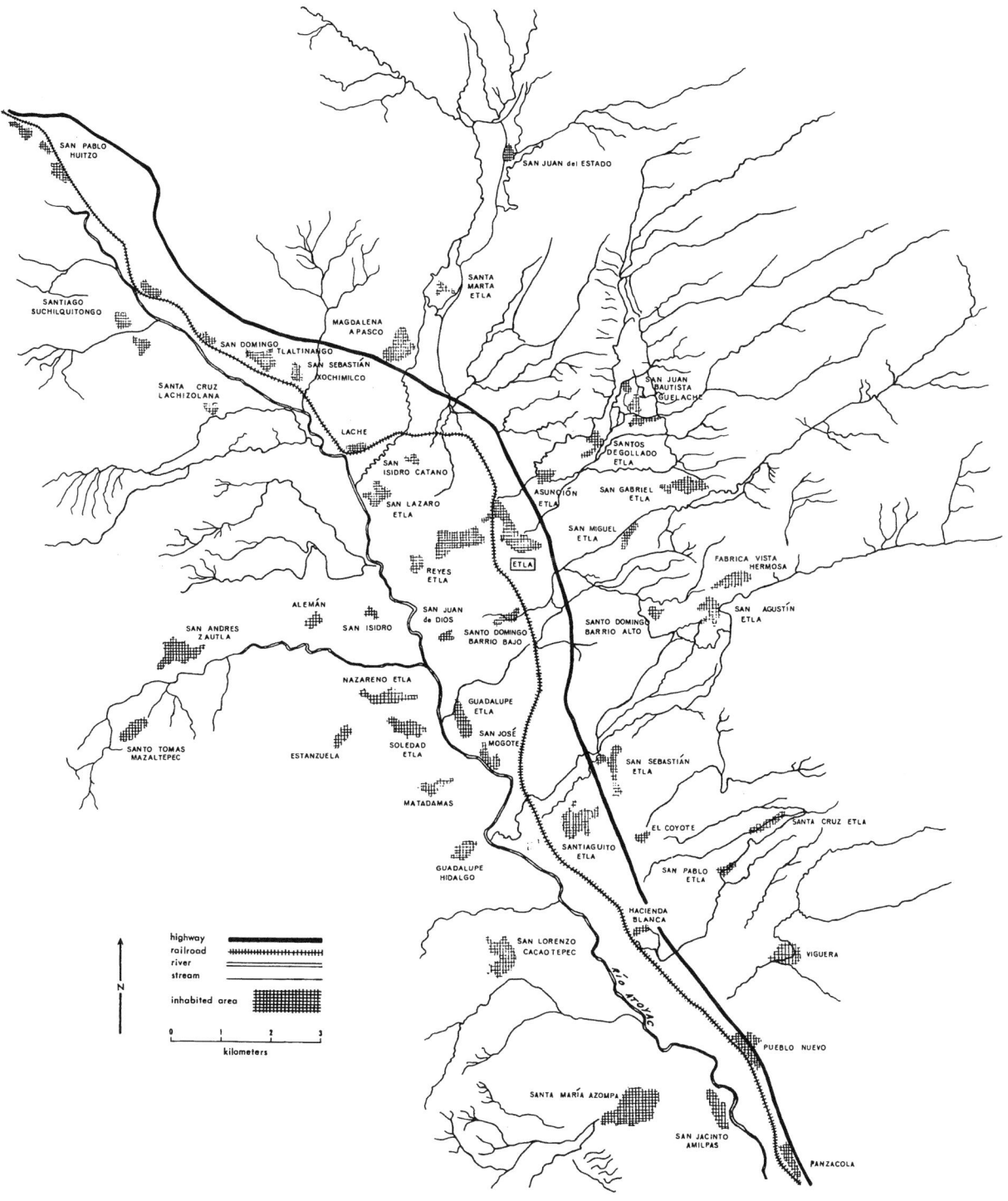

Map 2. The northern arm of the Valley of Oaxaca.

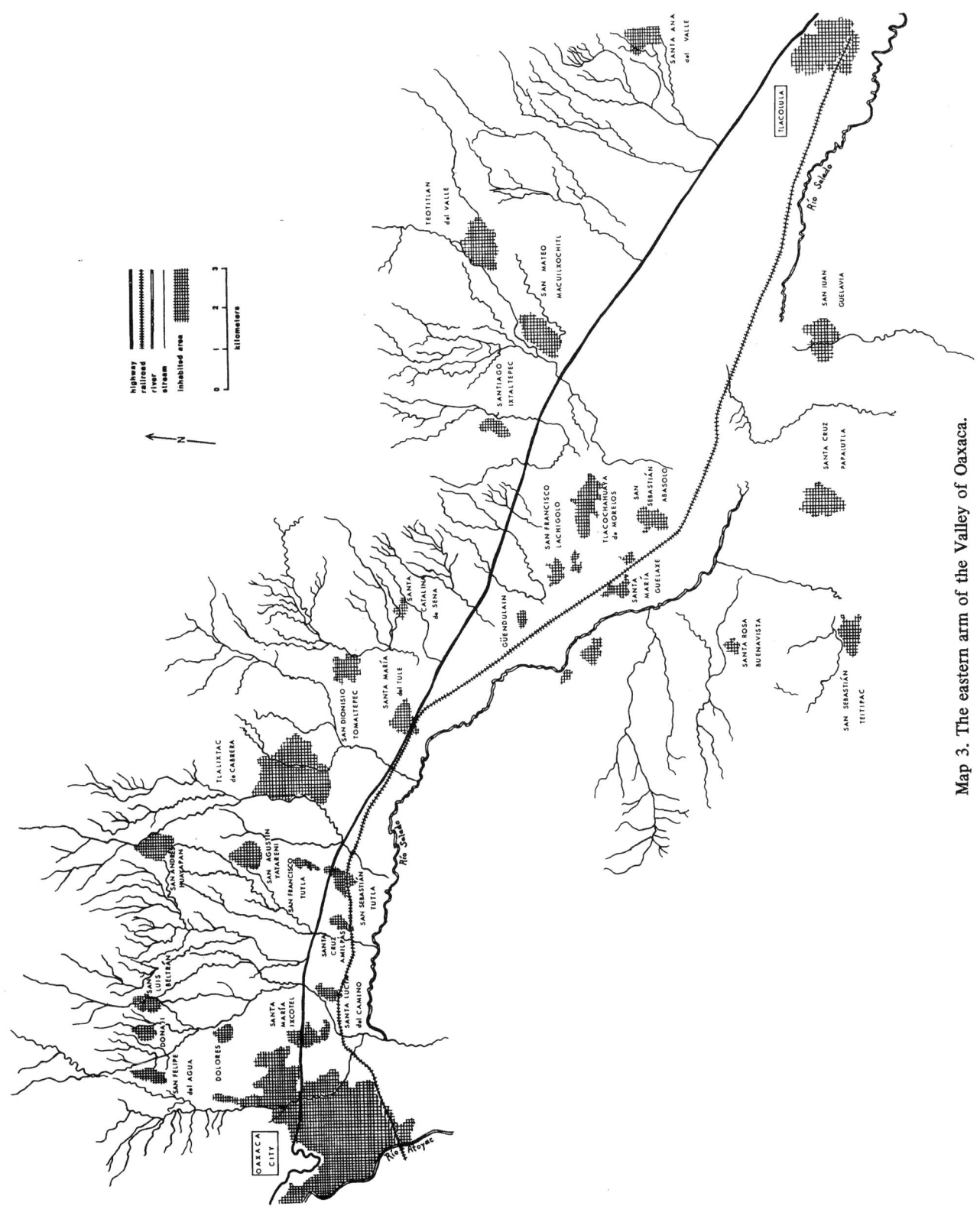

Map 3. The eastern arm of the Valley of Oaxaca.

PROBLEMS OF WATER CONTROL AND THEIR SOLUTIONS

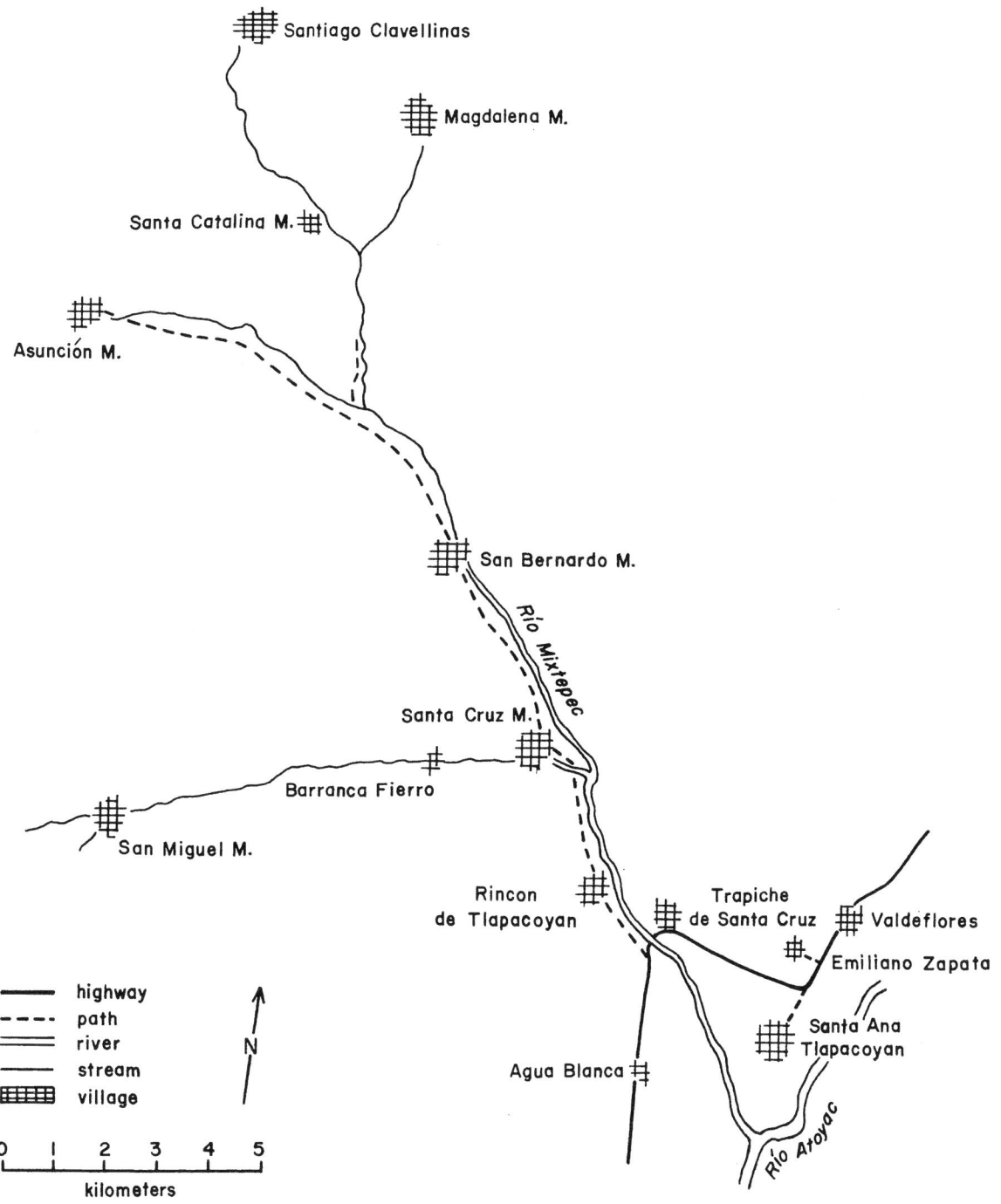

Map 4. The Mixtepec River.

money exists for the project. If the project is approved, the costs and labor of construction are shared by the government and the community. The government agency informs the community of how much money it must provide and how and when labor will be required, and the community is then left to its own devices to provide its share. There are a variety of ways of raising the money—immediate taxation or loans from banks or other government agencies and long-term fund raising to repay the loans are two alternatives popularly used. But once the community has applied for aid and the government agency has agreed to give it, the expenditure of funds and labor is ultimately in the hands of the agency officials. As we will see, this relationship of the government agency with the village does not necessarily end with the completion of the new works—it may apply to the use of the works as well.

It is still possible, though exceptional, for a village to initiate and carry out the construction of new, modern devices independent of the government. For example, San Juan del Estado raised its own funds to build a large and costly village water-storage tank and a diversion dam because villagers felt that it would take too long to go through government channels. The design clearly required advanced technical know-how, and lacking knowledge to the contrary, it is likely that engineering assistance actually was provided for through a government agency. In fact, the need for government expertise in this respect may explain why villages do tend to wait for assistance, rather than to take the initiative.

As construction becomes more complicated and costly, the villagers become more and more dependent upon government aid. The problem of technical know-how is obvious—only specialists are capable of designing large water-control works. The financial problem is also not difficult to understand. Villages generally do not have the resources or power to accumulate large amounts of money over short periods of time; only an organization as large and powerful as the state government is capable of raising adequate funds for a project of this sort. But it is only in recent times, with the introduction of new engineering techniques and such materials as cement, that the expense of construction has grown beyond the ordinary capacity of the village. The more traditional devices could be built easily with local community resources—mainly labor. In fact, given the nature of the resources and of traditional water-control techniques, higher level aid or intervention simply for purposes of construction would have been pointless. The tasks would still have had to be executed by the villagers, who have their own ways of organizing collective labor, and there would be no particular function for the government to perform.

The reasons for the initiation of new construction at any one place are not always clear. Villagers generally believe that they can improve their lot by the use of devices they know are modern—cement and steel are quite impressive—and through the aid of engineers. In practice, villagers have sometimes been disappointed. New dams sometimes silt up; water sources seem to diminish despite all efforts at conservation and efficient use. The government agents also seem to have great faith in their ability to improve the processes of production by the introduction of modern engineering devices. However, they rarely check afterward to see if their new installations have increased productivity or the effectiveness of land and water use. There is a certain mystique involved in the modernization process. Engineers are regarded by villagers as a combination of sage and magician, while the engineers often seem to regard the villagers as children: dependent, without judgment or understanding. Modernization often becomes an end in itself.

The effectiveness of the government's development program in the valley is limited, not only by diminishing water resources, but also by the extent to which it is dependent upon the cooperation of the communities as partners in the program. And new constructions are not always welcomed unanimously by the community. Long debates and arguments frequently precede the completion of a new project; many villagers are reluctant to contribute the sums of money involved. In at least one village, and probably others, construction had to be interrupted due to a lack of cooperation by community members in fund raising. This may be another reason why so few villages try to build new projects on their own—without some outside authority, the debates might go on forever.

The construction of waterworks is at present such an important part of the government development program that a large full-time staff of hydraulic engineers and bureaucrats is a permanent part of the central government structure. Water control is directed by SRH, which works in conjunction with other agencies on special construction programs. For a large proportion of villages, contact with the central government is made primarily through this particular agency. The importance of the agencies involved in hydraulic construction at present is closely related to the fact that Mexico is now in a state of accelerated development. It is too early to judge what role the construction of hydraulic works will assume in the government if and when the water-control development reaches a state of equilibrium. But if Mexico is to continue to develop with any speed, hydraulic construction must continue to be important. The bulk of Mexico's population is concentrated in arid areas, and the productive potential of these areas depends upon the control of water. As population continues to grow and water resources at best remain the same, it is only through the addition of more devices to control the water for productive purposes that the people can expect to continue supporting themselves and the urban populations on their land.

Maintenance

While the construction of new works is a continuing process for government agencies, it is only a fleeting problem for the villages. Maintenance is their persistent concern. Maintenance problems associated with new types of devices are often specialized, requiring knowledge and equipment not yet available to villagers. Such problems must be dealt with by government engineers, but so far the devices are so new and so scarce in the valley that the villagers have hardly begun to worry about maintaining them.

For the more widespread traditional devices—brush dams and small gravity-flow canals—the tasks involved are few and simple. Brush dams do not pose a major silting problem, nor is silting generally a serious problem in the canals. Vegetation, however, may become troublesome, obstructing the waterflow in the canals. In addition, the earthen canals and small aqueducts may require occasional patching and cleaning. Basically, then, maintenance involves clearing away weeds and trash that collect in and around the canals, and seeing to it that the canals and aqueducts remain straight, clean, and unbroken. The tools required for maintenance are simply machetes and shovels. Cleaning takes place once a year (or at most, twice), generally during the dry season—November through March. It rarely requires more than a few days of collective work.

The actual organization of maintenance tasks varies little from village to village. In every case, responsibility for the maintenance of the smallest canals, those which lead water into individual fields, belongs to the cultivator of the fields to which they run. Since it is in the cultivator's interest that they be maintained, no sanctions are necessary for enforcing cooperation. And since this task is small, the individual cultivator performs it himself whenever he feels it is necessary. Work on the larger canals must be done cooperatively and must be more or less standardized so that downstream irrigators do not suffer from neglect of canals at upstream locations; maintaining larger canals requires the work of a large number of individuals. Responsibility for organizing or supervising this task falls to one of the village officials—which one depends on the village. In almost all cases, no matter which official is in charge, the work is carried out by villagers through tequio (see Chapter I). In cases where not everyone uses canal water, only canal users are expected to participate; in others, everyone participates. Where different canals benefit different individuals, individuals may either be expected to work on the canals they themselves use, or all may work together on all the canals. The procedure for calling out tequio labor is more or less standard everywhere. In one case, Guadalupe Etla, cleaning was not a public communal task (tequio) but a private one. Every individual was expected to maintain the segment of canal that bordered his own land. The official in charge periodically inspected the canals, and if he found that an individual was not maintaining his section of the canal, the delinquent would be jailed and fined.

Two of the villages under study—Abasolo and Mitla—do not use canal-irrigation. Yet they, too, have water-control maintenance problems. Abasolo has large drainage ditches in the fields which must be cleaned periodically. This is done privately for the small ditches and by tequio for the larger ones. Mitla has a tank and canals for domestic water. In this case, maintenance is the responsibility of the four topiles (one of the lowest-level public offices) who are in charge of domestic water. This is the only case where actual cleaning is done by the official in charge.

Waterwork maintenance is almost invariably an intravillage problem. Except in the case of its own constructions, the government never intervenes. Nor does any village direct the maintenance of canals in another or contribute to maintenance in another. The one exception is the case of San Gabriel and San Miguel Etla. Here, since the two communities jointly own the source and the main canal, they cooperate in its maintenance with a large, annual joint tequio in which villagers from both communities work together. Except for the fact that the two communities work together, maintenance proceeds just like a one-village operation, with the same tasks and sanctions. Neither village has more responsibility or more authority than the other, nor was there any special official for this occasion.

Inspection and judgments, as well as organization of labor on the canals, are the constant responsibility of the village official in charge of water control, even between major maintenance operations. As they make their rounds, such officials often rearrange stones in a dam, move aside brush in a canal, and carry out similar minute repairs.

The structure and organization required for maintenance of water-control devices are not specific to water control itself; they are only one application of a more generalized institution. Canal maintenance is neither a major problem nor a special one; it is carried out through a generalized communal labor institution, with its own generalized sanctions, and it is directed by an official who has other, more pressing and important tasks.

Allocation

Water allocation poses greater problems to the Valley of Oaxaca communities than do construction and maintenance of water-control devices, and these problems, in contrast, are specific to the resources and the communities which use it. In fact, water is the only economic resource in the society which is continually redistributed by means of political institutions. Although communal and ejidal lands, in theory, might be redistributed from time to time, they tend to be treated as though they were private property even though they cannot be sold. All other goods are redistributed privately by means of various dyadic arrangements.[3] But water which flows through canals is never owned or redistributed privately. This was not true for certain historical periods, as we shall see in a later chapter.

In the following sections, we will consider three aspects of contemporary water allocations: who has jurisdiction over the resource, how the allotments are made up, and who is in charge of redistribution.

JURISDICTION

The major sources of water for canal irrigation lie in the high mountains above the valley; some small springs in the piedmont and on the valley floor provide minor secondary sources. Whether or not the source lies on private, communal, or municipal land, ultimate jurisdiction over the water lies with the state and federal government and not the municipality or private individual. This rule is incorporated into constitutional law; there are no exceptions. However, the state does not always exercise its jurisdiction and almost never does so directly at the community level.

---

[3] Cook (1965) noted an exception, Teitipac, which had a community welfare fund.

State jurisdiction intervenes only in the distribution of water between villages.

When the state does not intervene, jurisdiction over water lies with the community on whose land the initial diversion point of the canal from the source, the *toma de agua,* is situated, the upstream village. If the source is big enough, as is the case with the Atoyac and Mixtepec rivers, there may be a number of tomas in a number of different municipalities. If one of these tomas is used by several communities, jurisdiction lies with the community on whose land the toma is located, even though the source passes through the lands of other upstream and downstream communities. Once the water leaves the upstream segment of the canal, two alternatives may be followed: the upstream community may retain jurisdiction and allocate the water to individual downstream community members; or the downstream community may assume jurisdiction over all the water allocated to it by the upstream communities once the water enters its land.

1. *Mixtepec River* The Mixtepec River is large enough so that a number of different upstream communities may use their tomas for a number of different canals at once without affecting one another. Near the valley floor, the government has installed a dam from which canals flow to three different villages, one of which is Emiliano Zapata. Although the government has not intervened in the allocation of water from upstream towns, it does control allocation from the toma which feeds this dam. By government ruling, each of the villages which use the water from the dam is allocated a specific number of days per week to irrigate; on the remaining days, the water is permitted to flow to the other communities.

2. *San Agustín River* San Agustín Etla once controlled all of the water which flowed from a large stream originating far beyond it in the mountains. Before the revolution, it sold water in large quantities to haciendas on the valley floor. But since then, the state and federal governments have assumed control of the resource. The federal government uses the stream to provide power for two electric plants: one 20 km upstream in the mountains, the other just above the town. After the water leaves the second plant, it enters a small enclosed structure which is always kept under lock and key by a state agent who resides in the town. It is there divided into two unequal parts. One-fourth of the water is channeled into a small canal which, when it leaves the structure, comes under the total jurisdiction of the community of San Agustín. The rest passes on to be used as a power source by a large textile factory below. After this use, it is again divided into two parts. One part goes into a tube in which it is conveyed to Oaxaca City; the rest goes into a canal which is used by two communities yet farther downstream, San Sebastián and Santiaguito Etla.

San Agustín now controls only the water in the canal allotted to the village by the government and receives no recompense for the use of the rest of the water from the government or the users themselves. Naturally, the villagers of San Agustín are somewhat bitter about the loss of control over a resource they had considered to be their own. Nevertheless, until recently San Agustín has still had enough water left from the fraction it was apportioned to sell shares to outsiders living in Santo Domingo Barrio Alto. At one time, as many as 400 individuals per year requested and paid for the use of the lower part of San Agustín's canal to irrigate their fields. But the number dwindled, and now San Agustín claims that it does not have enough water even for itself, much less to sell to outsiders.

The two downstream villages, San Sebastián and Santiaguito Etla, share the water from the southern canal allotted to them by the government in equal parts. San Sebastián, the upstream of the two, gets water for 12 hours during the day; Santiaguito Etla gets it for 12 hours during the night. If there is enough water, either village might sell shares to individuals from San José Mogote. In one or two cases, farmers from San José Mogote claimed that, though they purchased water from the upper San Sebastián canal and paid San Sebastián for the water, they were required to pay an additional fee to Santiaguito because the water passed over Santiaguito land before it reached their fields. Others had lands directly bordering San Sebastián and only had to pay once. Some Santiaguito people had fields upstream with access only to those upper sections of the canal which belong to San Sebastián. In these cases, the inhabitants of San Sebastián would sell shares to Santiaguito people for water they did not need themselves. When there was a scarcity of water, the upstream individuals from Santiaguito had to go without, even though their village had rights to the water.

According to government allocation San Agustín, San Sebastián, and Santiaguito all "owned" shares of the San Agustín River. Once the water entered their own canals, each village had complete jurisdiction. Santo Domingo Barrio Alto and San José Mogote were not allotted shares; they had no jurisdiction. These latter villages could not contract to buy water as villages; their members could only purchase water as individuals, and then only at the discretion of the other villages.

3. *Guelache River* Santos Degollados, San Gabriel, and San Miguel Etla are three agencias of the municipio of San Juan Bautista Guelache. Santos Degollados, which shares the use of a stream with Guelache, recalls that it was formerly a *barrio* of Guelache and gives this as a reason why it is entitled to a share in the water from the canal that originates in Guelache. San Gabriel and San Miguel share another stream and formerly considered themselves as two parts of a single community. In these two cases, the government has not intervened in the allocation of water between the communities; rather, such allocation is dictated by a traditional arrangement which, at least in the latter case, the people claim has existed since pre-Hispanic times. Within each community, the community itself has jurisdiction over the water, but between the communities, the upstream and downstream villages are considered to have joint jurisdiction.

The government did intervene, however, when San Miguel requested a share in the stream used by Guelache. San Miguel applied for government aid to construct a small diversion dam to channel off some of the water which had formerly been under the jurisdiction of Guelache. Guelache, which had enough water left over after its own lands were irrigated to sell the remainder to the local cabecera of Etla, protested this proposed encroachment to the government agency. The government apparently supported Guelache's claim, for San Miguel's request was denied. This case illustrates the manner in which the jurisdiction over water resources is shared on two different levels by the state and the community. The state may intervene between communities, and its word is final. But it may also delegate authority to the community, even over water used by another community. In this case Guelache was permitted to retain control over water which was used by the cabecera of Etla, but which might have otherwise been used by San Miguel, had Guelache not objected.

Natural properties of water flow obviously favor the upstream communities in the question of control. When there was enough water so that a large number of downstream communities could share water with upstream communities, it was general practice for the latter to sell water to the former, either to members of the downstream communities as individuals, or by contract to whole communities for a stipulated annual fee. In one case, an upstream community even attempted to exchange access to water for a portion of land owned by a downstream community. Selling water often constituted a source of considerable income for the community—or, in times when individuals could control water—for private entrepreneurs. The intervention of the state has tended, though not without exception, to deny this sort of control to the upstream communities. In the case of San Agustín, the state went so far as to place the division of the canal into the upstream and downstream segments under lock and key, guarded by its own salaried officials.

Within the community, it is up to the community to decide who gets how much water and when. However, when the government has constructed a major water-control device in the community—specifically, when the SAG constructs a retaining dam—it dictates to the community the rules for use of water and the form of the administrative body for water control, and authorizes the individuals who serve as administrators by its signature. Such authorization and conformity with government specifications of administrative structure are not required in cases where the government has contributed only a minor facility, or none at all. But there is clearly a trend now, as part of the development program, to standardize the administration of water control at the village level and place it under strict government supervision. Such changes in village structures only come about through the contribution of the state to village welfare— namely through its construction of major new irrigation facilities. The legal basis for such changes is written into national law. In a sense, the state purchases the right to intervene in the internal affairs of a village and to bring about change in village organization by installing irrigation devices for the villagers, who would otherwise not be obliged to pay any attention to the national law.

In fact, one informant expressed exactly that sentiment. The government had installed a diversion dam in his village and was under the impression that the village had conformed to the specified administrative organization of water control in government installations. But the dam had silted up within the first year after its installation, and the village still used its traditional form of water-control administration. When I asked the informant why his village had not changed its water-control administration, he told me, "If the government pays, it may tell a village how to behave. If not, the people decide themselves." As far as his village was concerned, the government had not fulfilled its promise— therefore, the people were under no obligation to change their ways according to its specifications.

TYPES OF ALLOTMENT

Because there is a limited amount of water in a canal at any one time and users at different points upstream and downstream of one another, two basic problems are involved in the allocation of water among users. First, it must be decided how much water may be used by an individual; second, if there is not enough for all to use the canal at once, there must be a way to determine both the order and the timing of use among canal users so that people downstream will know when they will have access to the water and for how long. The problem of determining the amount that any one user may take at a time may be exaggerated by scarcity. If not enough water exists to enable every user to take as much as he needs or wants, there must be a way of determining either limits on individual use or priority of users. Similarly, the problem of order will be exaggerated if the canal is small or the water is scarce, for then a single irrigator must take all the water in the canal at once in order to irrigate his field.

1. *Intervillage allotments* In some intervillage sharing systems, the main canal is divided into large segments, containing specific fractions of water flow, which are kept open for passage of the water to the different villages at all times. This is the case, for example, with Guelache and Santos Degollados Etla and is generally so with San Agustín and downstream communities, although the government may cut off San Agustín's supply at night.

Alternatively, subcanals to different villages may be opened and closed at the division point at certain hours of the day. This is the case, for example, with San Sebastián and Santiaguito, each of which uses all of the water in the canal they share for half of a 24-hour period. Or villages may have full use of the water in the canal they share for a certain number of days in the week, as is the case with the lower Mixtepec villages using the government dam, or for a certain number of days each month, as is the case of San Miguel and San Gabriel Etla, which alternate use of the canal every six days.

When an upstream village "owns" or controls the canal and may open or close the subcanal leading to a downstream village at will, it may charge a fee for the use of the share carried by the canal. When San Juan del Estado had enough water to share with Magdalena Apasco, for example, it made a contract with Magdalena for the sale of water in exchange for a yearly fee of about 500 pesos. Guelache has a similar arrangement for payment by Etla for its water. And, of course, San Agustín and San Sebastián sell water, when they permit individuals from Santo Domingo Barrio Alto and San José Mogote to take water; but in these cases, the sale is for a certain number of hours or days, not full use of a large subcanal for a whole year at a time.

2. *Intravillage allotments* Of the 24 villages in my sample, two were not canal-irrigating villages (Abasolo and Mitla), two had no internal control over water allotments but did have external control (Santo Domingo Barrio Alto and San José Mogote), and two had no internal control over allotments at all (El Rincón de Tlapacoyan and Santa Cruz Mixtepec). Of the remaining 18, all had, or at least formerly had, a system of controlling the order in which individuals were permitted to use the canals. In each case, the order was determined not by geographical location on the canal, but by arrangements made by the official in charge of water allocation.[4] In no case was the succession of turns at the use of canal water so fixed and regular that it could operate without supervision; this supervision was the main and most important task of the official in charge of water control.

In at least half of the 18 villages, a list was made, some time in advance, of everyone who wanted to use the canal. A person was added to the list either in order of either his position on the canal, or in the order in which his request to irrigate was received. As each person took his turn, his name was checked off the list. In Tlalixtac, a new list was made every month; those who had not had a chance to irrigate the previous month were placed at the top of the list, and new requests were added at the bottom. In all cases, individuals would be informed by the official who kept the list that they might have a turn if they so requested, so long as someone had not made a prior request to irrigate at the same time. When they had completed their turns, they would have to wait an interval before a request for another turn was granted, so that requests by other irrigators could be granted. In the other half of the 18 cases, although a list was not kept, every canal user was required to check with the official in charge to see if anyone else had planned to use the canal at the time he wanted. If so, the canal user would be told to wait until a later time, and if not, he would be granted formal (official) permission to use the water for a specified length of time. Whether the water was scarce, as in Tlalixtac, or plentiful, as in Guadalupe Etla, penalties for taking water out of turn or without permission were severe, ranging from public reprimand to heavy fines and imprisonment. In almost every case, permission to irrigate was granted strictly on a first-come, first-served basis. In San Bernardo Mixtepec, irrigators were issued numbered tickets; each individual was permitted to irrigate when his number came up.

Though almost all the villages had a controlled system of taking turns, not all specified the exact nature of an allotment or turn. In many cases, irrigators could take whatever quantity of water they needed or wanted, as long as they asked permission and told the official when they would be finished. More frequently, however, and particularly where water was scarce, water was divided into timed allotments, often called *tareas*. I found no case where all the irrigators were given equal allotments; rather, the share varied according to both the needs of the individual and the amount of water available at the time. The needs of individuals in a village were never identical.

Individuals judge how long they will need to use a canal by the size of their fields, the needs of the plants, and the amount of water available in the canals, which might vary in the course of a year. Allotments vary in size—sometimes up to a 12- or 24-hour day or more, and sometimes as little as two or four hours, depending on the village. One might be permitted to take more than one allotment at a time or be forced to take a fraction of the normal allotment, if one's field were small or water abnormally scarce. But tareas are not necessarily standard even in one village—they may be longer or shorter than the length of time formally specified. Although the division of turns into timed allotments may be useful for determining in advance who may ir-

---

[4]There were exceptions to this, such as San Miguel del Valle and Díaz Ordaz, but they were not in my sample.

rigate when, it does not standarize or equalize use by individuals; rather, it has another, more important function in many cases.

In nine of the 22 villages in my sample which used canal irrigation, individual canal users were not required to pay in any way for the water they used. In another nine villages, individuals were required to make direct payments, by allotments, in terms of time or amount of land irrigated. In Mazaltepec, for example, the charge for water was one peso per *almud* (one-fourth *hectare*) of land irrigated. In Tlalixtac, the charge was six pesos per day. In Santiaguito, the charge was five pesos per almud. In Emiliano Zapata, it was 50 *centavos* (one-half peso) per day. When Magdalena Apasco bought water from San Juan del Estado, it charged canal users in the community for water, to repay the sum owed San Juan. In Tomaltepec and Teotitlán del Valle, where there are new government dams, canal users pay a *cuota* (tariff) for each irrigation. And of course villages without water sources of their own, such as Santo Domingo Barrio Alto and San José Mogote, must pay relatively higher rates for use of canal water than others.

Direct charges are not always made, however. A form of indirect payment is found in at least four villages in the sample: San Juan Bautista Guelache, San Miguel Etla, San Gabriel Etla, and Santos Degollados Etla. Here, the amount of water to which a villager is entitled when his turn comes up varies with the amount of "help" he has given to the village in monetary terms. These villages sponsor community projects by making periodic collections from the population at large. In Guelache, for example, such major projects as the construction of a new school are paid for with large "donations" by villagers. A villager who gave 100 pesos, for example, would then be entitled to one whole day of irrigation from the canal every time his turn came up until the next collection was made; while one who gave 300 pesos would be entitled to three days of irrigation, and one who gave only five pesos might be entitled to only one-half day of irrigation. It is not a matter of absolute amount of contribution, but proportions. In the other three villages, collections are made on a smaller scale and more frequently, five pesos here, 10 pesos there. In San Miguel, there are two categories of water allotments (two hours and four hours, respectively), while in Santos Degollados, there are three (two hours, four hours, and six hours, respectively). In each case, the size of the allotment varied with the proportional help, i.e., financial contribution, given by an individual to the village.

Although the connection between help given and amount of water needed is indirect, it is not arbitrary. One needs water according to the amount of land one has; the more land, the more water needed. But the more land one has, the wealthier one is likely to be. The wealthier one is, the more capable one is of helping the village finances. We will return to this point below.

Less formally, the same principle applies in many other villages. Contributions are always expected according to the wealth of the individual, but it is also judged fair that individuals who have contributed more to the village funds are entitled to a greater share of its water. In one village where there was no charge for the water (San Agustín), careful accounts of "voluntary contributions" were kept right on the irrigation list itself, suggesting that although water was free, the amount one got really did vary in accordance with one's voluntary contributions. Furthermore, discrete allowances are sometimes made for truly generous contributors in other situations concerning water. It is suggested in Tlalixtac, for example, that when a person who has given much to the community breaks a rule—takes more than his fair share of water, let us say—the officials are likely to look the other way, while a "less generous" or poor person attempting to do the same is jailed or fined. But such cases are either sublegal or illegal in contrast to the four mentioned above, where the relationship is formally a part of their system. On the other hand, when villages share water with outsiders as individuals, they may refer to the fee they get in return as "help" and insist at the same time that they do not sell the water but only receive help from outsiders in the form of financial contributions.

3. *Methods of Allotment* Allocation of water

within the village is more or less standard for all but two villages, which claimed to have no formal control in the handling of succession or rotation of use. Since the needs of irrigators are different in terms of timing—they may plant different crops at different times, and need irrigation at different times—there must be some flexibility in successive use among them. Their use of water is not determined among themselves or by the seasons or by the crops they plant. Rather, it is coordinated through a central clearinghouse for information: the official in charge of the canals. By requiring that every individual first check with the official, irrigators avoid confusion or conflicts among themselves over the use of water. In fact, the system seems to work very well. It was explained to me repeatedly, when I asked about conflict within the community over water, that such conflicts are nonexistent because it is the job of the water official to see that there is no occasion for them to arise. Underlying the cooperation among the canal users is a principle already mentioned: participation in the public sphere of village life—which automatically includes water—entails taking turns.

On the other hand, the existence of public officials to coordinate canal use permits the individuals to continue to operate privately. One individual has no personal control over another, nor does the group control any individual by forcing him to plant or irrigate at any particular time. Thus, an individual may continue to operate independently with regard to his agricultural activities, while an official sees to it that his activities do not conflict with another's and deals with each person separately in the matter of irrigation. As in the cargo system, different individuals are ready to participate (in this case, take water) at different times. Each one's readiness is determined privately, as in the cargo system; they also all take turns, even though many of them may be ready at once.

Egalitarianism is also essential to the allocation process. No individual has the right to take a turn before another on the basis of personal, acquired, or inherited characteristics; turn-taking is determined on a first-come, first-served basis. Differences in wealth do not affect (except illegally, in some isolated cases) the sequence of turns, nor do differences of age or status or political position. This system makes no allowances for such differentiation; if it exists, it is ignored; were it recognized, the system would not work as it does.

Differences in wealth, particularly those based on landholding, do sometimes affect allocation, though not the aspect of turntaking. The reason is simple—those who have more land need more water. Where water is relatively plentiful, or differences in landholding are not pronounced, amounts are more or less disregarded. But in the other cases, differences in amounts of water needed by individuals may be capitalized upon by the system. This is perhaps particularly true of the systems in which water is paid for indirectly, given to individuals in the proportions to which they have given unspecified quantities of financial help to the community. In these systems, the disproportionate needs of the wealthier for water are directly linked to their disproportionate ability to contribute to community welfare. The fact that land is privately owned leads to such inequalities of need and of capacity to pay. For the community at large, water is free—communities today generally do not have to pay anyone for water. By making community members pay privately for water by contributions to the community funds, the community links private welfare to public welfare in much the same way as public religious ceremonies are paid for by private individuals. But the difference between the two lies in the fact that the "need" of an individual to sponsor public ceremonies derives from public pressure, while the "need" to contribute funds in proportion to the water he takes, derives directly from the source of his wealth—land. The cases in which the sums contributed are unspecified are more flexible and far-reaching than the cases in which water is paid for directly with a specified fee. In the second instance, the income from water sale is constant, but low and unchanging; in the first, it is irregular, but can be altered to particular ends.

Indirect sale of water (in exchange for help)

permits a community to act as though contributions were voluntary—which, indeed, they are. The community needs no special institution to force people to contribute according to their means. Thus, the community may maintain a sort of public fiction about the equality of its members. No one is required to give any more than anyone else; officially everyone is equal. At the same time, it can give differential rewards for differential contributions, hence motivating contributions according to means without using direct force or giving direct recognition to differences in means. Requiring direct payments for water disregards differences in means and places water use more in the private sphere: individuals purchase water, rather than receive water from the community, as a result of generous contributions. Stress upon generosity and dependence upon the community as a whole for survival are perhaps two of the most basic elements of the traditional, egalitarian, closed corporate community ideology with its undercurrent of inequalities based on private property. They have diminished in force and importance in recent times, as greater participation in the market and less reliance upon subsistence agriculture have become possible.

ADMINISTRATION

The greatest variation among communities occurs in the selection of water-control officials. In fact, actual variation was so complex that it is difficult to summarize on a chart, at least without some detailed explanation. In two of the canal-irrigating communities in the sample, there was no official supervision (Santa Cruz Mixtepec, Rincón de Tlapacoyan). In the two villages with no canals of their own (Santa Domingo Barrio Alto and San José Mogote), supervision came from another community. In the remaining 20 villages (two of which did not canal irrigate), each had one or more official supervisors whose relative rank, title, manner of selection, and character of office varied from community to community.

In two of the villages, the municipal presidente himself is in complete charge of water allocation. In Tlalixtac, the presidente keeps a list of canal users in the ayuntamiento offices, and canal users come to him to make requests and payments for each turn they take. In San Bernardo Mixtepec, where formerly no one was in charge of canal use, a recent deficiency of water has caused the presidente to institute a system of control. Now, he issues numbered tickets to all irrigators and sees to it that they take turns in an orderly fashion. San Bernardo was the only village studied in which all village land was communal—there was no private or ejido land.

In two communities, the comisariado de bienes comunales (the same official who supervises the use of communal land) is responsible for water control. In Mazaltepec, the comisariado himself supervises and collects the fee. In Zautla, the comisariado appoints five *repartidores,* one for each of the community's five main canals, who supervise allotments of water. Comisariados, like ayuntamiento officials, are generally elected every three years. San Miguel del Valle, a community not in my sample, was a village like San Bernardo with only communal land but in which water control was directed by the comisariado (Klug, 1965).

Three of the villages in the sample were all-ejido communities. The ejido structure contains two basic parts: a *comisariado ejidal* and a *consejo de vigilancia.* Each has at least a presidente, secretaria, and tesorero, and a suplente for each, all of whom are generally elected every three years. These officials, and others who may be elected or appointed, may perform a variety of administrative tasks. When the ejido includes the entire village, ejido officials may perform most of the tasks usually performed by municipal and agencia offices, even though these offices actually exist within the community as well. All three of the ejido communities in my sample were agencias. In one of them, Emiliano Zapata, water control was the responsibility of the consejo de vigilancia itself. In another, San Sebastián Etla, the ejido members elected two ejidal *jueces de agua* (water judges) in addition to their regular ejido officers, one to supervise each of the two main canals of the village. In the third, Santiaguito Etla, the ejidal authorities, as a body, appointed two jueces de agua to supervise the canals. Thus, in the three ejidos water control was always a responsibility of ejidal officials; but in one case it was part of a general office, and in the other two a specialized office (elected in one and appointed in the other).

In five of the villages in the sample, one of the municipal regidores was specifically assigned the task of water control. In a sense, this is a specialized office although regidores also serve on the municipal council which consults and decides upon more general matters. In two of the communities, Santa Ana Tlapacoyan and Magdalena Apasco, the job has been dropped from the roster of duties for regidores in recent years because there is no longer enough water to make it necessary. In Guadalupe Etla, one of the three regidores still retains the title regidor de aguas. In San Agustín, the responsibility for water control rotates among the three regidores, each serving one of his three years in office at this job. Sometimes, however, the community elects a special *repartidor*, apart from the regidores. In Abasolo, which does not canal irrigate but does use trenches for drainage of the fields, there is also a regidor de aguas who is in charge of maintenance of the trenches.

In one village, San Juan del Estado, water control is in the hands of the five suplentes to the five principal members of the ayuntamiento, one for each of the five main canals. Like the office of regidor, the suplente has other, more generalized responsibilities, but the suplente tends to be a less highly ranked official than the regidor. Suplentes are also elected by the community at large every three years.

In one village, the agencia of San Gabriel Etla, the suplente of the agente serves as juez de agua, one of the more highly ranked officials in the community, along with the agente and the alcaldes. Like the agente, he is elected every three years.

In San Juan Bautista Guelache, canal use is supervised by two repartidores who are appointed by the municipal ayuntamiento for indefinite periods of time and generally serve for about a year.

In Santos Degollados Etla, two *comisionados de las aguas* are elected every year, one to supervise each of the two main canals. (It is reported that in Santiago Ixtaltepec—or "Santiaguito de los Borrachos," as it is popularly known—water control was also directed by a committee elected specifically for this purpose by the population at large. See Bowerman, 1967.)

In San Miguel Etla, a juez de agua is elected every three years. His assistants, two repartidores, are elected for two-year terms, one being replaced every year, so that, at any one time, one is new and one is experienced. The juez himself decides who gets water and when, while the repartidores supervise the taking of the water in the fields; they are responsible for carrying out the decisions of the juez de agua.

In two villages, Tomaltepec and Teotitlán del Valle, where the SAG has constructed a new dam, villagers must conform to a more or less standard format for water control. Water control is to be supervised by a *junta de aguas* which is elected annually by the *usuarios*—the canal users. The junta consists of a presidente, secretaria, and tesorero and other officials if necessary. Outside advice and supervision comes from the SAG itself. The junta de aguas is to remain separate and apart from the municipal offices. In Tomaltepec, the junta de aguas consists of three officers; in Teotitlán del Valle, it consists of five, but more may be added. I was told in both cases, although it may not have been absolutely true, that the junta was elected by the village at large, not just the canal users. In both villages, the junta had been in existence for less than a year when I visited them. Junta officials not only supervise water use but also may operate the water control devices; they are instructed by the SAG in how to open and close the major sluice gates and the like. They are also responsible for reporting problems in the use or condition of the devices to the SAG.

In Mitla, which does not canal irrigate to any extent but does have the problem of domestic water control, four topiles (low-ranking village officials) alternate weekly in the task of supervising and cleaning the waterworks.

PROBLEMS OF WATER CONTROL AND THEIR SOLUTIONS

TABLE 3
IRRIGATING VILLAGES: SIZE, TYPE, SOURCE AND CONTROL

Village	Population	Type	Source	Control
Teotitlán del Valle	2849	Municipio	Stream	Junta
San Domingo Tomaltepec	1244	Municipio	Stream	Junta
Tlalixtac de Cabrera	2630	Municipio	Stream	Presidente
San Bernardo Mixtepec	1629	Municipio	Río Mixtepec	Presidente
Santa Cruz Mixtepec	935	Municipio	Río Mixtepec	None
Rincón de Tlapacoyan	630	Municipio	Río Mixtepec	None
Emiliano Zapata	302	Agencia (Ejido)	Río Mixtepec	Ejido Consejo de Vigilancia
Santa Ana Tlapacoyan	1698	Municipio	Río Mixtepec	Regidor
San Juan del Estado	1564	Municipio	Stream	5 Suplentes
Magdalena Apasco	1273	Municipio	Stream	Regidor
San Juan Bautista Guelache	663	Municipio	Stream	2 Repartidores
Santos Degollados Etla	566	Agencia	Stream	2 Comisionados
San Gabriel Etla	377	Agencia	Stream	Suplente de Agente
San Miguel Etla	450	Agencia	Stream	1 Juez 2 Repartidores
San Agustín Etla	2389	Municipio	Stream	Regidor
San Sebastián Etla	671	Agencia (Ejido)	Stream	Ejido–2 Jueces de Agua
Santo Domingo Barrio Alto	381	Agencia (Ejido)	Stream	None
San José Mogote	217	Agencia (Ejido)	Stream	None
Santiaguito Etla	740	Agencia (Ejido)	Stream	Ejido–2 Jueces de Agua
Guadalupe Etla	880	Municipio	Río Atoyac	Regidor
San Andrés Zautla	1299	Municipio	Stream	Comisariado 5 Repartidores
Santo Tomás Mazaltepec	1086	Municipio	Stream	Comisariado
San Miguel del Valle	1051	Municipio (Communal)	Stream	Comisariado
Santiago Ixtaltepec	382	Agencia	Stream	Cómite
*San Sebastián Abasolo	1158	Municipio	Wells	Regidor
*San Pablo Mitla	3651	Municipio	Stream	4 Topiles

*These villages do not irrigate with canals.

It is difficult to set up categories of water control officials because the various characteristics of the offices seem to crosscut one another so frequently. Whatever the title of the office, the task to be done is the same. Does the type of office have any effect on the manner in which the task is carried out? Decisions about how much water individuals get are generally made by upper-level or higher-status officials—the presidente, regidores, comisariados, etc. Where special repartidores are appointed by these upper-level officials, they generally seem to carry out higher-level decisions; where the higher-level officials are in charge, they carry out such decisions themselves. The power or control inherent in the task of water allocation lies with higher-level officials and has nothing to do with which particular official directly supervises the taking of water. Whether or not there is more than one official in charge, control seems to be centralized for each major canal, if not for all the canals at once.

Table 3 shows that the ejido communities generally place water control in the hands of ejido officials; communities with government-built dams have government-designed water-control committees; the rest vary more widely. Water control tends to fall under the management of an official representing, as much as possible, the community at large. Where there are small ejidos, for example, control will be in the hands of the ayuntamiento or comisariado or other community officials, not the ejido. The office does not seem to be set apart from the cargo system in general; it is not a function of a special interest group (except where government dams have been built). Variations in population, size, type of water resource, type of irrigation device (except for large government dams) or even village status (municipio, cabecera, or agencia) do not seem to affect the nature of the office in charge of water control. Agencias do not have regidores, of course, but cabeceras do not always use regidores for water control. There does seem to be similarity in types of water control offices for regional clusters; Mazaltepec and Zautla, for example, are similar; Guelache, San Miguel, and Santos Degollados Etla share similarities; Santiaguito Etla and San Sebastián Etla share some—though other villages in their vicinities do not necessarily conform to the patterns.

Water control in this society is a standard administrative task assigned to the community managerial structure. This structure consists of a set of offices rotated among community members. Particular tasks may be divided among the officials in various ways, but the nature of the division is not significant. No matter which official is assigned the task of water control, it will be executed in more or less the same way; and no matter which office controls water, community members rotate the task, like the office, among themselves—just like any other administrative task or office. As long as the administration of water allocation falls within the domain of the cargo system—i.e., is one of the set of offices which must be rotated among all community members equally—then all the variations in the offices supervising water control are basically equivalent. Within certain limits, and with the exception of SAG controlled juntas de agua, all the variations are arbitrary. Unless the offices and tasks are clearly specified by state or federal law, all villages contain variations in the sets of offices they have. They vary not only from one place to the next, but within a single village from one period of time to another. In San Augustín, for example, water control may be in the hands of either a regidor or a special official, whichever the community decides. There is nothing in the administrative tasks themselves (apart from those involving external government control) which requires that they be performed by one particular official or another. Because there are some standard names given by the government to some of the standard officials, such as regidor or comisariado de bienes comunales; it is likely that many of the communities will appear similar to one another in their choice of officials for water control. That is, of the many choices a village has, several likely ones are common to all villages, so many will have made what appears to be the same choice. But a regidor or suplente in one community does not necessarily do everything a regidor or suplente does in another. Also, while one community may have a special repartidor or juez de aguas and another may not, the repartidor and the juez may perform exactly the same activities as the suplente, for example, performs elsewhere.

In other words, in some sense, the set of cargos or offices of a community may be regarded as an undifferentiated administrative body which manages all community public affairs. Within this body are a number of offices among which the tasks are divided up so that no individual has to do everything at once. Responsibilities are also divided up in terms of degrees— greatest responsibility, and greatest power fall to certain offices, while lesser responsibility and manual labor fall to others. It is not the task itself which gives individuals responsibility and power, but the level of his office in the general structure.

CONFLICT OVER WATER

In view of the conclusions of Millon, Hall, and Diaz (1961-62) from a cross cultural study of canal-irrigating societies, and particularly their description of the problems in the valley of Teotihuacán (both of which emphasized the importance of conflict), it is perhaps surprising that in contemporary Oaxaca conflicts over water are rare and tend to be mild if they do occur. Historical records suggest that the same was true in the past; disputes over land were common, but those over water were not. Recent water shortages and population expansion, one would think, might have increased the potential for conflict. But both government hydraulic officials and the villagers themselves assured me that even under present conditions of severe shortage, conflicts over water, whether within or between villages, seldom occur and are never serious. I did hear many expressions of discontent, but almost invariably they were accompanied by total resignation.

Within the village, unfair water distribution through favoritism, special power, or simple cheating, is nearly impossible. On the whole, water-control officials were considered to be responsible individuals. Otherwise, they would not have been elected to office, or if they had managed to deceive the community, they would be quickly removed and replaced. Fair and equitable distribution is a matter of federal law and hence rests on the strongest possible sanctions. Villagers deprived of water, therefore, generally feel that they have only nature or the Deity to blame. It is unlikely that any neighboring community would dare to be responsible for another's deprivation. If an individual suspects unfair treatment, he can easily complain to one or another of the community officials (he is bound to know a few personally) and feel more or less confident that justice will be done. With the combination of careful supervision of the canals by officials and strict sanctions for misbehavior over water use, occasions for conflict and confrontation are minimal. I never once heard of a case of conflict between individuals or groups in a village over water; infractions of the rules had occurred from time to time, but officials invariably intervened before a conflict between individuals ever came about.

Between villages, the same confidence in justice and the same insistence upon cooperation and equity do not exist. But there does seem to be some degree of confidence in the surveillance of the state government on the one hand and the profit motive of upstream villages on the other. That is, if a downstream village starts to get less water or ceases to get water, it is generally believed that there simply is not enough available. If there were enough, the upstream village would certainly sell it if possible; or if the government were apprised of the situation, it would intervene to see that an appropriate portion was allowed to flow downstream. Villages which formerly bought water from upstream seemed to feel that the upstream village had more right to water than they did. Others, who did not formerly buy water, seemed to feel that they had as much right to the water as upstream villages but, on the whole, were resigned to suffering more from the scarcity than did upstream villages. Villagers from Santos Degollados, for example, mildly intimated to me that Guelache was cheating by taking more than its share but were not prepared to do anything about it. On the other hand, Magdalena Apasco and individuals from Santo Domingo Barrio Alto and San José Mogote, who had formerly bought water from upstream villages, seemed not to feel resentful or bitter toward the upstream villages in particular. They were resigned to suffer or look for other alternatives for water, now that the canals they had once used had run dry.

Of the three cases of potential conflict in recent years which I was able to record, two were hearsay and one was officially documented.

1. When the new government dam in Teotitlán del Valle was being built, Macuilxóchitl, the next village downstream, realized that it would soon have no access to water from the stream and would not profit from the building of the dam. The building materials had to be transported by truck on a road which passed through Macuilxóchitl—there was no other passable road. So Macuilxóchitl allegedly tried to prevent the trucks from using the road. Clearly, this was a hostile gesture, but not one which could prevent the building of the dam or obtain water for Macuilxóchitl. It could only be an expression of jealousy and frustration. As it was, most informants were certain that there had never been enough water in the stream for Macuilxóchitl to use in the first place. But

Macuilxóchitl felt somehow that it was unfair that Teotitlán del Valle should profit from the stream through government aid, while it profited not at all.

Tomaltepec was in a similar situation with regard to Santa María del Tule, a village downstream from it on whose road trucks bearing materials for construction would have to pass before reaching Tomaltepec. El Tule did not have enough water for irrigation to begin with. With the construction of the dam, it would have less, at least initially. But it was promised that eventually the dam would provide enough water, to irrigate both towns and that soon El Tule would also have a local junta de aguas just like that of Tomaltepec. Although the benefits to El Tule were not immediate, they were to be realized in the near future. Naturally, El Tule had no objection to the conveyance of materials through the town on the way to Tomaltepec. Reportedly, the reservoir has filled and is stocked with fish and both villages seem content.

2. Santa Ana Tlapacoyan lies near the Mixtepec River from which water is taken to irrigate a large number of towns. A government dam was built for one part of the river, to convey water some distance northward. The remainder went on to Santa Ana. Either because of the dam or because there is just less water in the river now than there has ever been, Santa Ana is getting much less water than it used to. When asked about the situation, the town officials said there was little one could do, since there was so little water in the source. But when it was pointed out that certain upstream villages, such as Rincón de Tlapacoyan and Santa Cruz Mixtepec, had plenty of water even now, the officials said they knew and thought it unfair that the upstream towns were using so much when there was too little left downstream. They added that if the situation did not get much better soon, the villagers had threatened to go after the people upstream (they did not specify exactly whom) with machetes and guns and force them to let more water pass through to Santa Ana. Here there has been no government intervention so far to regulate upstream-downstream allotment, but no doubt there will be in time.

Whether or not intervention would favor Santa Ana as much as Santa Ana would like remains to be seen. As of the summer of 1972, there had been no outbreaks of violence over the water; whether or not Santa Ana's threat was idle is difficult to say. This was the only case in which I heard direct and violent confrontation even mentioned, and it is doubtful that it will ever be carried out.

3. The one recorded case of conflict in recent times was not violent in nature. The village of San Miguel Etla, an agencia of San Juan Bautista Guelache, applied to the SRH for aid in the construction of a small dam across a stream near the village. Soon afterward, the SRH received a letter from the municipio of Guelache stating that San Miguel had been prompted in this endeavor by an outside advisor; that the stream in question belonged rightfully to Guelache, not San Miguel; that Guelache needed the water in the stream for their own purposes; and that part of the town's income came from the sale of some of this water to Etla. The diversion of this water into San Miguel, it stated, would hurt the village economy of Guelache seriously. Taking this complaint into consideration, the SRH decided against building the dam. All this took place a number of years ago; if there was an outbreak of violence or even hard feelings, no mention of this was made to me. San Miguel now denies having any rights to, or interest in, the stream in question.

In the three cases of intercommunity conflict, three alternative paths were followed. In the first, the town that felt unfairly treated for a while attempted to annoy and obstruct the building of the new dam. In the second, the downstream village threatened violence, though it had not carried out its threat by mid-1972. In the third case, objections went directly through government channels and resulted in no conflict at all.

One SRH official mentioned that villagers frequently came to him to settle conflicts but that these arose almost invariably from misunderstandings. Settlement was also almost invariably informal and followed the officials' suggestions, generally by compromise.

On the whole, it appears that conflict is avoided in two ways. First, internal village conflict is avoided because the system of control appears effective and satisfactory and because it conforms more or less with traditional ideology and values. People know that they "ought" to take turns, and officials see to it that they do. The same is true of intervillage water sharing in cases where the downstream village did not formerly buy water. In many, the government performs a function equivalent to that of the village officials. In the other cases, villages simply feel that they have no right to the water beyond that established by short-term contracts. Once the contract elapses, they have no grounds, legal or moral, for complaint. And in this society, people avoid fighting without legal or moral justification at all costs.[5]

CHANGE

Changes which have affected the entire Valley of Oaxaca are also having considerable impact upon canal irrigation at present. Two of the most important causes of change have already been mentioned: government intervention through its development program and gradual diminution of water resources.

Since the revolution, the government has intervened through the SRH to reallocate water resources between villages. Before its intervention—and to a diminished extent even today—downstream villagers had to purchase water by contract or individual sales from upstream villages. In several cases, like that of San Agustín, the government has taken allocation out of the hands of the village, and now redistributes water itself so that many downstream villages are guaranteed equitable proportions of the water supply, as long as it lasts. The advantage of being upstream has, in these cases, been more or less negated. In other cases, however, the government has not intervened, and upstream villages are still favored. One interesting aspect of the government's intervention has to do with the water supply for Oaxaca's urban center, Oaxaca City. The government has appropriated a considerable proportion of the water from a number of sources, particularly on the eastern Piedmont slopes, without compensating the upstream villages in any way. The result is that a number of these villages complain that their agricultural production suffers badly from lack of water.

The decrease in the water supply has, of course, had considerable impact upon most villages dependent upon canal irrigation. Some villages, such as San José Mogote and Santo Domingo Barrio Alto, no longer get any water and complain of a whole series of crop failures in the past few years as a result.

Magdalena Apasco, which formerly contracted to buy water from San Juan del Estado, no longer receives any water at all from upstream. The village once had a regidor de aguas but the position has lapsed—there is no task to go with it. Santa Ana Tlapacoyan did not suffer as severely from the decrease but suffered enough so that it also has dropped the position of regidor de aguas and no longer controls the water used by the few villagers who still get some from the Mixtepec.

San Bernardo Mixtepec, on the other hand, suffered a comparatively slight decrease in water supply. The change which took place here was the opposite of the cases mentioned above. Where there was formerly no control, the presidente has now begun an attempt to regulate at least the sequence in which people use the canal water. The innovation was internal, not inspired by the government or other villages in the area. It seems to be in the experimental stage at this point and may well change again in the years to come. This one case is not enough to support any conclusions in general; but it may be that in cases where there was once a great deal of water and no necessity for control, a slight decrease in the water supply will result in the institution of control procedures.

Too few case histories of community

---

[5]There have in fact, been a number of armed conflicts between villages in colonial and modern times. Some of these, such as the current one between Abasolo and Tlacochahuaya, have taken the form of long-term feuds lasting more than two generations. But, for the most part, these conflicts are over land, not water. They are certainly not restricted to canal-using or water-sharing villages.

responses to a major decrease in water supply (no one remembers ever witnessing an increase) were collected to generalize about or predict changes in local control organization. Generally, however, where the supply diminished sharply, controls tended to weaken or disappear, which was the opposite of what I had expected. Villagers explained it by saying that when there was so little water, so few people used it and it was so unpredictable that it simply was not worth the effort to try to control it or divide it into shares. A partial additional explanation would be that many villagers are now installing deep wells and pumps if they can, rather than relying upon canal water.

III

POLITICAL CONTROL AND ACCESS TO WATER

INTRODUCTION

The last two chapters examined the rules, institutions, and ideals which provide the framework for the management and use of canal water among villagers in the valley. This chapter will show how they apply to actual behavior within communities by examining in detail canal operation in a single village. For comparison, two other villages will be described to illustrate more clearly the types of variation that occur among villages.

The detailed studies of these villages were designed to answer a number of specific questions:

1. Does the ideal of equal opportunity to share the water resource and to play a role in its management obscure real differences among irrigators in access to water and control over its distribution?

2. If there are inequalities among irrigators in access to water or in positions of control, are they related in any way to the geographical positions of the irrigators on the canal? Do upstream irrigators have an advantage over downstream irrigators?

3. If there are inequalities among irrigators, are these differences related to differences in the respective roles which these individuals play in other community affairs? Are those individuals who are favored with better access to water more active in the civil-religious hierarchy? If so, is it the advantage of access to water that gives an advantage in political control or vice versa?

4. If there is no apparent relationship between inequalities in access to water and participation in community leadership, what does underlie differential participation? In what ways, if any, does the existence of canal irrigation affect community political organization?

To answer these questions, I attempted to find out which of the canal irrigators in each village had held public office, which offices they had assumed, how much irrigated land each held, and what additional personal characteristics of each might have influenced his role in politics. The information is not complete and the investigation remains, in a sense, inconclusive. But it represents a first step toward understanding the role of irrigation in village politics and the role of village politics in irrigation.

TLALIXTAC DE CABRERA

Tlalixtac is a relatively large, Zapotec-speaking village in the eastern arm of the valley (Pl. 2a) with a population of 2630 in 1960 and an estimated 440 households.[1] Its land extends from the Río Salado on the valley floor to the high Sierra Juárez mountain range, crosscutting fertile high-water-table alluvium, irrigated and dry piedmont land, and forested mountain land. The mountain terrain, mostly uncultivated, is communal property distributed among villagers by the village comisariado de bienes comunales, which has a presidente, secretaria, and tesorero.

---

[1] See "Index of Populated Places in the Valley of Oaxaca listed in the census of 1960 and shown on the 'Mapa de las Localidades del Valle de Oaxaca'" compiled by Cecil R. Welte (1966). My estimate of average household size at about six individuals is tentative. In a census I took in another village, the average size was about five members per household. The SAG engineers with whom I consulted estimated average household size at about seven. My choice of six for average household size represents a compromise.

None of this land is irrigated. All the rest, irrigated and nonirrigated, is privately owned by villagers and even outsiders. There is no ejido.

The town is entirely agricultural, with no craft specialization for market trade. The main crops are alfalfa and maize. A large proportion of the irrigated and alluvial land is devoted to alfalfa production. Wheat was once a major cash crop; today it is no longer grown and the large wheat mills once run by the local hacendados lie in ruins.

The village is situated on the upper piedmont slope at an altitude of 1548 meters. The residential area, interspersed with small cultivated plots of maize and alfalfa, lies on the eastern side of the Río de los Molinos, which has a flow of nearly 30 liters per second (see Map 5). Most of the irrigated land lies just above, and adjacent to, the village. Both the village and the land around it are divided into three barrios: San Miguel in the center, San Antonio and La Trinidad to either side.[2] From high above the village the Río de los Molinos is channeled into three main canals, one running through (and named for) each of the barrios (see Pl. 3a). The barrio division appears to be related to the three-way canal division: each barrio, like each canal, has two parts, an upper and a lower. The upper and lower parts of each canal irrigate the upper and lower parts of each barrio respectively. There are no barrio officials and no specific administrative tasks associated with the barrios as such. Each barrio has a patron saint, but sponsorship of the saint's mayordomía may come from an individual who lives in another barrio, or it may be barrio-sponsored if no private sponsor can be found. In any case, the celebration is attended and enjoyed by the whole village. The patron saint of the central barrio is the patron saint of the whole village, and if no sponsor is found for his mayordomía, the whole village cooperates to pay for it.

The water used for irrigation is divided among the three canals in equal parts. Although tampering with this division is strictly forbidden,

[2] Recently the village was subdivided into seven sections, but this applies to residences only, not to the land.

my informant and I watched an individual divert water from one canal into another, causing more water to flow in one canal than in the other two. The man explained that since water was scarce, he needed more water than was available in one canal at the time. Ordinarily, however, at least three people could irrigate simultaneously using equal quantities of water. If a person were to observe that one of the others was getting more water than he and felt strongly enough about it, he could complain to the authorities. If the authorities investigated and found that someone had cheated, the guilty person could be fined or even incarcerated. But apparently, at the moment that I observed the tampering, either no one else was irrigating or no one cared. As soon as he had finished irrigating his field, the individual returned to the dam and redirected the water flow so that, once again, it was equal in the three canals.

The rule of equal division of the water supply is not followed consistently for the upper and lower divisions of the canal. When it is plentiful, part of the water in the upper canals is diverted into the lower canal sectors, so that six people have equal access to water at one time. But when water is scarce (from late January through May) there is hardly enough for two people to irrigate simultaneously from the same main canal. The rules, I was told, are as follows: in the dry season there is a charge for water use, while in the wet season there is none. (It was suggested that this might change, and that there might be a charge all year if the presidente so decided.) During the dry season, the lower parts of the canals are not used at all. Those who have land in the upper sector can irrigate all year long, though they have to pay for the water for part of the year; those who have land in the lower sectors can only irrigate during part of the year, but do not have to pay.

If this were true, a basic problem of water control, differential access for those situated upstream, should be reflected directly in the social structure. It is reflected in the division of land into upper and lower, and the difference in real access that accompanies this division. The equality of the barrios is undercut by the in-

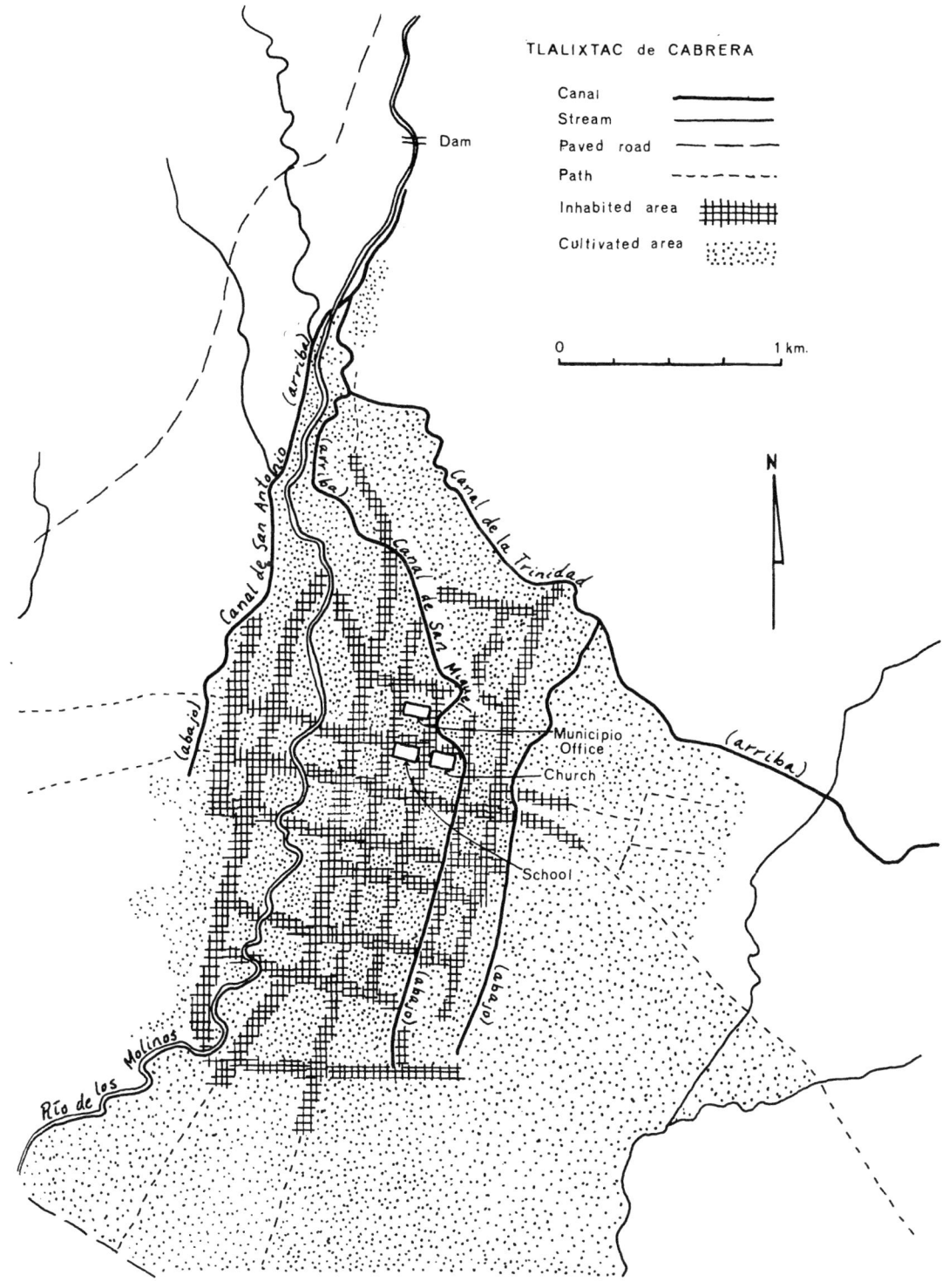

Map 5. Tlalixtac de Cabrera.

equality of the two sectors. However the inhabitants of the upper canal pay for their advantageous access to water during the dry season and the payments become part of the community treasury. Still, their land is more productive, and the water costs are not equal to the potential gain in productivity. Even though the community profits from this essential inequality, it remains an inequality.

Hypothetically those with land in the upper sector should be wealthier, because their land is more productive. And because they are wealthier, they should be more likely to hold political offices for reasons already elaborated upon earlier. As a result, the differential access to water (which is a product of the water flow itself and of seasonal change) should be reflected in the political structure. Those who own land upstream should also hold political power. The village, therefore, would be ruled by the upstream sector. This fact would be obscured partly by the three-way division of the barrios and partly by the ideology of the cargo system itself. So determining the validity of this line of speculation requires determining who the political officers were and where they held land.

Tlalixtac has a traditional political organization combining a civil and a religious hierarchy with offices that are rotated among the community members. At the top of the political hierarchy is the ayuntamiento, consisting of the presidente, a síndico, three regidores, and five suplentes, a tesorero, and a secretaria. The secretaria is an appointed and salaried official. The 10 main members of the ayuntamiento, the consejales (the presidente, síndico, regidores, and their suplentes), are elected every three years and are not paid. In addition, two alcaldes, each with a suplente, serve as judges. These officials are in charge of all community affairs except communal land (whose management has already been described), electricity, the school, and the church, each of which is managed by a separate committee. The school and church committees each have presidentes, secretarias, tesoreros, and seven *vocales* who take turns managing and maintaining the school and church in alternate weeks. These are also elected and unsalaried, like the ayuntamiento. In rank, the presidente comes first, followed by the síndico, then the other ayuntamiento officials, the head comisariado de bienes comunales, the alcaldes, and the presidentes of the other committees. Then come the other officials of these committees, the head of the police force, and various subordinates and suplentes. At the lowest level are the police, who serve as messengers for the officials, caretakers, and custodians. All the young men of the community must serve one year out of every three in these low-level positions until they become eligible for higher office, which may be until they are well into middle age. Thus, of all the men in the village who have not made themselves eligible for higher office, about one-third are serving at any one time as police. Generally this office, like those higher up, does not require full-time service; the officials take turns, alternating work days among themselves.

The primary means of gaining eligibility for office—which is equivalent to freedom from police service—is to sponsor a mayordomía. Any adult male who wants to sponsor such an event and can afford it may do so by stating his intention to the church committee a year in advance. If another community member has already declared his intention to sponsor the same mayordomía, the second in line must either wait one year or choose another mayordomía. Between 15 and 18 mayordomías are celebrated every year, and they are ranked in importance and cost. Every Sunday, all the mayordomos for the coming year gather at the church and line up according to rank. The mayordomo of the patron saint, San Miguel, ranks highest, but sponsorship of any mayordomía qualifies one for higher office. Not all mayordomías are celebrated every year, but that of the patron saint must be; if a sponsor cannot be found the entire village must contribute money to pay for the celebration. Sponsorship is not solicited; for most of the saints' days which are normally celebrated volunteers exist or the celebration is not deemed important enough to be necessary. For many or most mayordomías, two individuals share responsibility for two consecutive years. They need not cooperate, since one pays for one year's celebration, and the other pays for the next. The reason for this pairing of mayordomos seems to have its roots in custom and to have been long forgotten by the community. I thought it might reflect some social division, perhaps even the upper/lower division of the barrios; but informants assured me that this was not the case, and that there were no restrictions on, or special requirements for, who could be cosponsors. Unfortunately, church officials were extremely reticent and refused to produce records of sponsors and co-sponsors, so it was impossible to check on my speculation.

The mayordomía is considered to be strictly voluntary, although "voluntary" has a limited meaning. In the past it was certainly more closely linked to the political offices than it is today. For example, until 18 years ago the alcalde primero (first alcalde) was required to sponsor the mass of Domingo de Pascua (Easter Sunday) and the alcalde secundo, the mass of Espiritu Santu (Holy Spirit). To be eligible for the office of alcalde, one had only to be wealthy enough to afford these mayordomías. Today one must not only be relatively wealthy, but literate in addition. If ambition is not strong enough an inducement to assure voluntary sponsorship, the desire to be free of continual police service is frequently motive enough, not to mention the less formal pressures of public opinion. If fact, it appears that people are more interested in evading office than holding it, particularly the required police service. Frequently people selected for offices at higher levels plead to be excused from service because of illness, poverty, lack of time, etc. Once a person has sponsored a mayordomía, he is *eligible* for office, but he is not required to serve. Only those who are elected are required to serve, an honor most people avoid as long as possible. But mayordomía sponsorship, after an indefinite period of police duty, is the minimum service required of all adult males in the community.

Even the motivation to be free of police duty and the pressure of public opinion are not enough to get some people to volunteer as mayordomos. If the community permitted, these individuals would continue as policemen, even though they have enough money to sponsor a mayordomía. But the community does not permit them to do so. In addition to the voluntary mayordomía, there are three alternative sponsorship positions which are mandatory. If it comes to the attention of the ayuntamiento that an individual is well into middle age, reasonably well off, and still has not been a mayordomo, they may appoint him as either a *mandadero*, a *mayor*, or a *centurión*. These individuals also sponsor religious ceremonies. The four mandaderos appointed annually, for example, sponsor the Easter ceremonies. One may volunteer to serve in these roles, but they may also be filled by people who have not taken them voluntarily. Once appointed one serves, willingly or not, on pain of exile from the village for noncooperation. Like the mayordomía, sponsorship in these positions makes one eligible for higher office and exempt from police duty.

Eventually, then, everyone becomes eligible for higher office. Those who are wealthier and more ambitious or more capable tend to become eligible earlier in life than those who do not have the funds. Sponsorship of only one ceremony is necessary for eligibility, and the rank of the mayordomía is not specified. Even so, some individuals sponsor two or even three mayordomías in their lifetimes, and many choose the more expensive, higher-ranked mayordomías. The rewards (in this world) for such expansiveness are only in esteem.

Tlalixtac was chosen for detailed study because it has a number of characteristics particularly relevant to an investigation of the relationship between canal use and political organization. First, it is a community with a traditional civil-religious hierarchy. Second, it is highly dependent upon canal irrigation, having relatively little alluvial land and no craft specialization. Third, it is not yet affected by modern irrigation techniques; its new cement dam silted up immediately after installation, and was ignored. And fourth, the community was large enough to provide information on a large number and wide range of individuals.

Unfortunately, however, though the village itself seemed ideal for study, the situation was not. The village officials in Tlalixtac were reticent and generally quite uncooperative in providing information about canal users. Finally, after weeks of repeated visits and requests, there came a day when the presidente happened to be out, and the sindico was in an unusually amiable mood. He told me that the irrigation lists were made out once every month, and he would permit me to look at the list for one month, whichever month I chose. And, he hinted, the month with the longest list would be January, since that was the beginning of the year, and nearly everybody would be on it. Naturally, I chose the January list. Near the names of many of the individuals on the list were figures which I took to represent quantities of land irrigated and, sometimes, payments for the use of the water. But I could not obtain complete information about amounts of land irrigated, amounts of money paid, or any other information about the persons listed, at least from the officials of the ayuntamiento.

However, I was able to find one truly useful and cooperative informant, one of the policemen, who, with the help of his family—his wife, father, and mother-in-law—was able to tell me something about nearly everyone on the lists and even add a few names. The information he gave me was probably reliable, although there was no way to determine what he left out—if, indeed, he left out any information. Therefore, I consider my figures to represent minima, not absolutes or real quantities. If they cannot be used to demonstrate relationships, they can be used to suggest them.

Information was available on 273 individuals. How many of these are heads of households is not known, but it is likely that the vast majority are or at least are the only members of their households represented on the list. Since there are an estimated 440 households in the community at least two-thirds of the households in the community use canal water for irrigation. These households are situated in every one of the six barrio sections.

The information collected and analyzed covers a number of different characteristics of the individuals on the irrigation list: age, political career, location of residence and canal use, and amount of land held. Age is an important variable because it figures into political career; younger men have only begun their climb up the political ladder. Furthermore, a consideration of different age groups might also give some indication of change through time. Locations of residence and canal use are also important, because they might influence relative degree of access to water and, indirectly, political power. Amounts of irrigable land held might serve to indicate wealth, which, in turn, might influence relative political power.

Of the 273 person on my list, four are women and five are newcomers or live out of town; and for 23 no further information was available. Information was collected on the public careers of the remaining 241 individuals, although, unfortunately it was not always complete (see Tables 4 and 5).

Of the 241 individuals for whom information was obtained, more than one-half (136 = 56.4%) were eligible for political office (i.e., were literate and had sponsored mayordomías): one-third of these individuals had held a political office above the level of policeman and the remainder had not. Of the 105 persons not eligible for political office, 52.3% were illiterate (although 43.8% had sponsored mayordomías) and 47.6% were literate but had not yet served in ceremonial office. Forty-six of the 105 ineligible individuals were illiterate but had served in political office before

TABLE 4

POLITICAL CAREERS: TLALIXTAC DE CABRERA SAMPLE

Status	Number	Percent
Eligible for Office		
Had held office	75	31.1
Had not held office	61	25.3
Ineligible		
Illiterate, but had		
sponsored a ceremony	46	19.1
Illiterate, had not		
sponsored a ceremony	9	3.7
Literate, but had not		
sponsored a ceremony	50	20.8
Total	241	100.0

Note: Total sample contains 273 persons. Political career information was unavailable for 32 of them.

TABLE 5
PUBLIC OFFICES HELD:
TLALIXTAC DE CABRERA SAMPLE

Type of Office	Number Having Held That Office
Presidente	7
Presidente + Síndico	3
Presidente + Regidor	1
Presidente + 3 Other Offices	1
Síndico	3
Síndico + Alcalde	1
Síndico + Regidor	1
Síndico + Presidente de Bienes Comunales	1
Alcalde	16
Alcalde + Regidor	4
Alcalde + Church Committee	2
Regidor	18
Regidor 3 times	1
Tesorero	2
*Presidente of Major Committee	5
Other Committee Member	9
Total	75

*Committees include: Bienes Comunales, church, school, electrification.

the literacy requirement became law. It is possible, although not common, to hold political office more than once. One-fifth of those individuals who had held political office had done so more than once: 13 had held two offices; one had held three offices; and one man had held four.

Holding ceremonial office is a prerequisite not only for holding higher political office, but for release from service as a policeman. Thus, even those who have no hope of holding higher political office (those who are illiterate) are motivated to hold ceremonial office, whether as mayordomo (voluntary) or as mandadero, centurión, or mayor (appointed). Table 6 summarizes the patterns of ceremonial officeholding among the Tlalixtac sample. There is no limit on the number of times an individual may serve in ceremonial office, but individuals rarely choose to serve more than once. Four of the mayordomos who were political officeholders had served twice in ceremonial office, three of those who were ineligible for office had served twice, and one of those who were eligible for political office had served three times in ceremonial office.

TABLE 6
SERVICE IN CEREMONIAL OFFICE: TLALIXTAC DE CABRERA SAMPLE

Type of Ceremonial Office	Had Held Political Office						Had Not Held Political Office						Total	
	Literate		Illiterate		Total		Literate		Illiterate		Total			
	Number	Percent	Number	Percent	Number	Percent	Number	Percent	Number	Percent	Number	Percent	Number	Percent
Mayordomo	31	54.4	2	3.5	33	57.9	27	25.2	35	32.7	62	57.9	95	57.9
Mandadero	12	21.0	—	—	12	21.0	23	21.5	8	7.5	31	29.0	43	26.2
Centurión	2	3.5	1	1.8	3	5.3	7	6.5	2	1.9	9	8.4	12	7.3
Mayor	7	12.3	2	3.5	9	15.8	4	3.8	1	.9	5	4.7	14	8.6
Total	52	91.2	5	8.8	57	100.0	61	57.0	46	43.0	107	100.0	164	100.0

The age distribution of the listed individuals about whom such information was available is summarized in Table 7a and Figure 1. Those who used canal irrigation most fall mainly into the 30-50 year age groups. Age distribution among the categories of officeholders and non-officeholders differed in predictable ways. Officeholders fall mainly in the 31-60 year groups, the greatest number falling between 41 and 50 years old. Illiterate officeholders are somewhat older. Those who are eligible but have not yet held office fall almost equally into the 31-40 year and under-30 age groups. Those who are ineligible due to illiteracy, but have held ceremonial offices, fall mainly in the 51-60 year age group, though the illiterates who have not held ceremonial office are distributed among all the age groups.

Age groupings of those who have held office varied by the type of office held. Those who have served in higher offices are, again predictably, older than those who have served in lower offices. Those who have served as regidores are comparatively young, mainly between the ages of 31-50. The treasurers and various committee members are quite young, mainly in the under-40 age groups (see Table 7b).

Residential data were collected for 252 of the 273 individuals on the irrigation list (see Table 8). Less than one-third of the community (31.3%) live in the upper sectors of the village; more than two thirds (68.6%) live in the lower sectors. The largest proportion (40%) live in Barrio San Miguel. La Trinidad follows close behind with a total of 38.4 percent, while Barrio San Antonio is smallest, with only 21.3 percent of the community, as represented by the sample collected. It may be that the sample is distorted and does not represent the total village distribution, because the sample includes only irrigators. Because the upper/lower division of the village might prove to be significant, the breakdown by percentages of the populations within each barrio is also shown. This breakdown indicates that slightly more than one-third of the residents of Barrio San Miguel live in the upper sector, slightly fewer than one-third of those in La Trinidad live in the upper sector, and about one-quarter of the San Antonio residents live in the upper sector of their barrio.

Information about both residence and political career was available for a total of 236 individuals. Residential distributions of officeholders and non-officeholders seem to follow a pattern. Analysis of residence was done for the barrios and for the upper/lower division of the village. While most of those on the January irrigation lists live in the lower part of the barrios, a larger proportion of the officeholders than of the non-officeholders live in the upper part of the village. On the other hand (see Table 9), a smaller proportion of those who are eligible but have not yet held political office live in the upper sector than of the other two categories. This suggests that the residents of the upper sector of town hold more political power than their numbers would seem to warrant. Similarly, a breakdown by sector shows that a higher proportion of eligible non-officeholders live in the lower sector of the town than in the upper, while a higher proportion of officeholders live in the upper sector than in the lower sector of the town. This suggests that living in the upper sector of town gives one a better chance of holding office than living in the lower sector does. Indeed Table 9 indicates that residence in the upper sector of the village correlates with officeholding. Among those who are eligible for political positions, those who live in the upper sector are more likely to serve in public office than those who live in the lower sector.

Distribution of officeholders among barrios also showed that of those who live in Barrio San Miguel, 35.8 percent are officeholders, as compared to only 29.6 percent of those who live in La Trinidad, and 24.5 percent of those who live in San Antonio. Those living in San Miguel who are eligible but have not yet served in office comprise a smaller proportion than that of the population of those living in La Trinidad or San Antonio (see Table 10).

As would be expected, then, the group that has held political office is composed of more San Miguel residents than residents of either of the other two barrios: 45.2 percent lived in Barrio San Miguel, while 36 percent lived in Barrio La Trinidad, and only 17.8 percent lived in Barrio

TABLE 7
AGE GROUP AND POLITICAL CAREER: TLALIXTAC DE CABRERA SAMPLE

a. Age Group and Eligibility for Political Office

Age Group	Had Held Political Office				Eligible But Had Not Held Office		Had Not Held Political Office						Total	
	Literate		Illiterate				Literate		Illiterate, no Ceremonial Sponsorship		Illiterate, had Sponsored Ceremony			
	Number	Percent	Number	Percent	Number	Percent	Number	Percent	Number	Percent	Number	Percent	Number	Percent
Under 30	4	6.0	—	—	10	16.9	22	44	1	11.1	—	—	37	15.6
31-40	15	22.4	—	—	37	62.7	21	42	2	22.2	8	17.4	83	35.0
41-50	23	34.3	3	50	9	15.3	5	10	3	33.3	7	15.2	50	21.1
51-60	14	20.9	1	16.7	2	3.4	1	2	2	22.2	17	37.0	37	15.6
61-70+	11	16.4	2	33.3	1	1.7	1	2	1	11.1	14	30.4	30	12.7
Totals	67	100.0	6	100.0	59	100.0	50	100	9	100.0	46	100.0	237	100.0

b. Age Group and Type of Political Office

Age Group	Presidente	Síndico	Alcalde	Regidor	Tesorero	Presidente of a Committee	Other Committee Member	Total
Under 30	—	—	—	—	1	1	2	4
31-40	—	—	2	8	1	2	2	15
41-50	2	4	9	8	—	—	3	26
51-60	2	2	8	1	—	2	—	15
61-70+	6	—	3	2	—	—	2	13
Unknown	2	—	—	—	—	—	—	2
Total	12	6	22	19	2	5	9	75

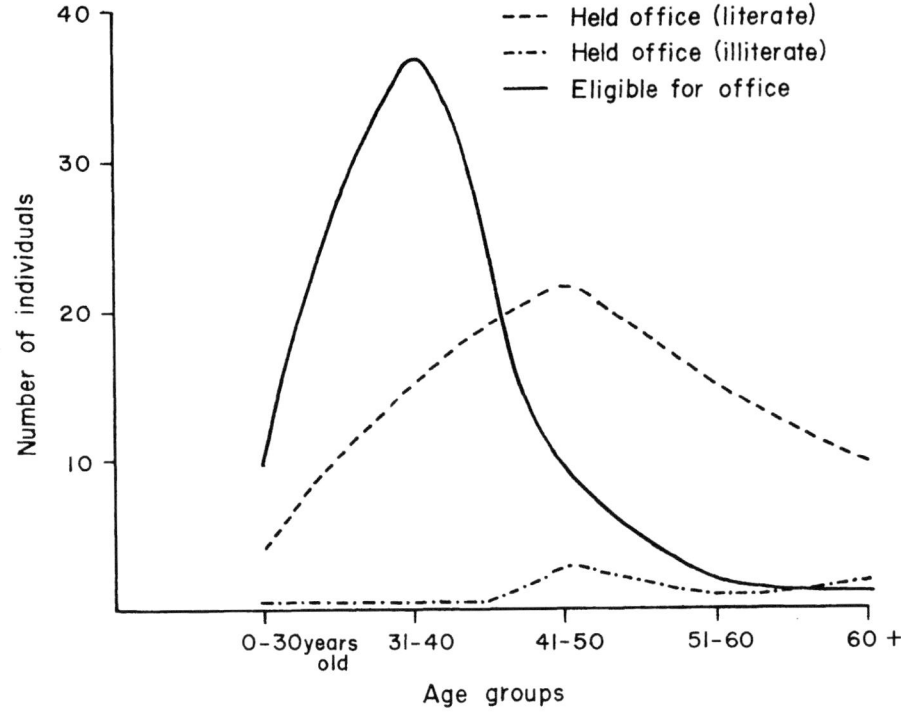

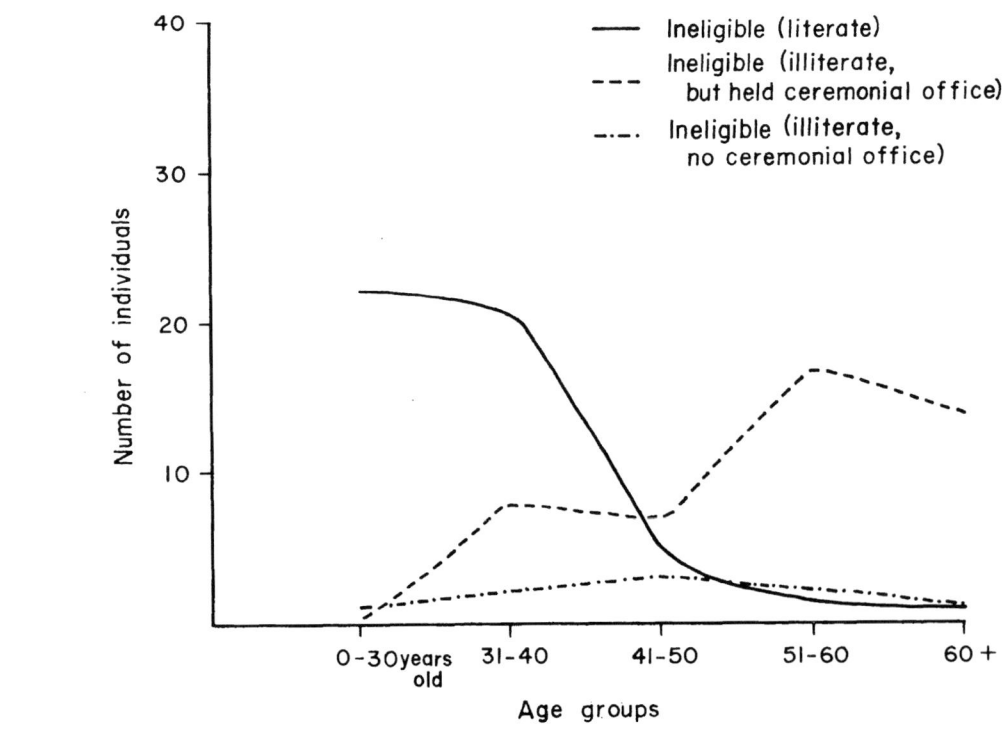

Fig. 1a & b. Age breakdown by political career.

TABLE 8
RESIDENTIAL DISTRIBUTION: TLALIXTAC DE CABRERA SAMPLE

Barrio	Upper Sector			Lower Sector			Total	
	Number of Residents	Percent of Total Population	Percent of Barrio Population	Number of Residents	Percent of Total Population	Percent of Barrio Population	Number of Residents	Percent of Total Population
San Miguel	35	13.8	34.6	66	26.1	65.3	101	40
La Trinidad	30	11.9	30.9	67	26.5	69.0	97	38.4
San Antonio	14	5.5	25.9	40	15.8	74.0	54	21.4
Total	79	91.4	31.3	173	67.4	?	252	99.8

TABLE 9
POLITICAL OFFICE AND RESIDENCE BY SECTOR: TLALIXTAC DE CABRERA

Political Career Status	Upper Sector			Lower Sector			Total	
	Number of Persons	Percent of Status Type	Percent of Sector Population	Number of Persons	Percent of Status Type	Percent of Sector Population	Number of Persons	Percent of Sector Population
Had Held Office	28	38.3	40.0	45	61.6	27.1	73	30.9
Eligible, But Had Not Held Office	12	20.6	17.1	46	79.3	27.7	58	24.5
Ineligible	30	28.5	42.8	75	71.4	45.1	105	44.4
Total	70	29.6	99.9	166	70.3	99.9	236	99.8

TABLE 10
POLITICAL OFFICE AND RESIDENCE BY BARRIO: TLALIXTAC DE CABRERA SAMPLE

Political Career Status	San Miguel			La Trinidad			San Antonio			Total	
	Number of Persons	Percent of Status Type	Percent of Barrio Population	Number of Persons	Percent of Status Type	Percent of Barrio Population	Number of Persons	Percent of Status Type	Percent of Barrio Population	Number of Persons	Percent of Barrio Population
Had Held Office	33	45.2	35.8	27	36.9	29.6	13	17.8	24.5	73	30.9
Eligible But Has Not Held Office	21	36.2	22.8	23	39.6	25.2	14	24.1	26.4	58	24.5
Ineligible	38	36.1	41.3	41	39.0	45.0	26	24.7	49.0	105	44.4
Total	92	38.9	99.9	91	38.5	99.8	53	22.4	99.9	236	99.8

San Antonio. San Antonio had the smallest proportion of individuals eligible for office who had not served, but then, only 22.4 percent of the total population represented by the sample, lived in this barrio (see Table 10).

In sum, the analysis suggests that there is a difference in residence among officeholding and non-officeholding groups. Civil officials tend to live in the central barrio, Barrio San Miguel. This may be connected with the fact that, traditionally throughout this region of Mexico, the wealthier and more prestigious individuals of a town have tended to congregate at its center. But the fact that a higher proportion of officeholders than non-officeholders live in the upper section of town is not accounted for by this tradition. Some other explanation must therefore be sought for this unequal residential distribution.

There were 300 irrigation requests on the January list supplied by town officials. Some of the population were listed more than once, since they had requested rights to irrigate from more than one canal. The largest single group of irrigators was from the upper sector of the La Trinidad canal (22.6% of the total population), and the La Trinidad canal was as a whole the most used (see Table 11). Irrigation requests of the other two canals were almost equally distributed: 30.6 percent for San Miguel and 29.6 percent for San Antonio. In each case, canal users are nearly equally divided between the upper and lower sectors of the canals.

A comparison of canal use between officeholders and non-officeholders shows that a larger proportion of officeholders use the lower sectors of the canals than non-officeholders, and that a larger proportion use the San Miguel canal than non-officeholders. The fact that a larger proportion of officeholders use the San Miguel canal may be explained by the high degree of correlation between residence and canal use (see below); a higher proportion of officeholders live in Barrio San Miguel than elsewhere. But the high proportion of lower-sector canal users among political officeholders cannot be accounted for in this way (see Table 12).

It is not known where all of the 75 persons who are listed as having held political office

TABLE 11

CANAL USE AND POPULATION BY BARRIO: TLALIXTAC DE CABRERA SAMPLE

Barrio	Use Upper Sector			Use Lower Sector			Total	
	Number of Persons	Percent Barrio Population	Percent Total Population	Number of Persons	Percent Barrio Population	Percent Total Population	Number of Persons	Percent Total Population
San Miguel	44	47.8	14.6	48	52.1	16.0	92	30.6
La Trinidad	68	57.1	22.6	51	42.8	17.0	119	39.6
San Antonio	39	43.8	13.0	50	56.1	16.6	89	29.6
Total	151	–	50.2	149	–	49.6	300	99.8

irrigated, and of those for whom information was available, several used more than one canal. Of political officeholders 46.6 percent used the upper sectors of the canals, while 72.0 percent used the lower sectors. Nearly half of the officeholders used the San Miguel canal, 44 percent used the Trinidad canal, while only 25.3 percent used the San Antonio canal. Among those who had not held office, the distribution of canal use was somewhat different. Over 58 percent used the upstream sectors of the canals, while 48.1 percent used the downstream sectors. Also, 22.2 percent fewer non-officeholders irrigated from the San Miguel canal than officeholders; the same proportion of each used the Trinidad canal, while 10 percent more non-officeholders used the San Antonio canal than officeholders (see Table 12).

A breakdown by sector shows that a higher proportion of downstream irrigators held office than upstream irrigators. Of those who used the upper sectors of the canals, only 26.5 percent had held office, while 73.4 percent had not held office. Of those who used the lower sectors of the canals, on the other hand, 40.2 percent had held office, and only 59.7 percent had not. The totals for canal use show that 33.4 percent had held office and 66.5 percent had not; it appears that a much larger proportion of the downstream users had held office (see Table 13). Of those who had held office, only 39.3 percent irrigated from the upper sectors of the canals, as compared with 54.8 percent of the non-officeholders.

Contrary to expectations, then, it appears that those who hold the most political power in the town have a greater tendency to irrigate downstream than do those who do not hold political power. This evidence clearly puts into question any hypothesis that political power in this area is directly associated with upstream control of water resources, or any suggestion that upstream irrigators can make use of their geographical location to exert special political control. These data, however, require further explanation. It is not simply that location of canal use has no relation to political power; rather, the most active participants in the political system actually seem to cluster along the lower sectors of the canals. At this point, I have no explanation for this tendency. However, further evidence, which will be presented below, indicates that the correlation between downstream irrigation and a higher degree of political participation is not accidental.

Individuals are not restricted to cultivating or irrigating land in the barrio or sector in which they live. However, there is a high degree of correlation between residence and canal use. Individuals who do not irrigate in the barrio and sector in which they live tend to irrigate at least within the same barrio, or in the adjacent sector of another barrio. Thus, an individual living in the lower sector of La Trinidad might irrigate in the upper sector of La Trinidad, or in the lower sector of San Miguel (see Table 14).

In view of this apparent relationship between residence and location of canal use, it is interesting to note that while a higher proportion of officeholders than non-officeholders reside in the upper sectors of the town, the officeholders also tend to irrigate downstream. That is, even

TABLE 12
POLITICAL CAREER AND CANAL USE BY BARRIO: TLALIXTAC DE CABRERA SAMPLE

Barrio	Had Held Political Office (n=75)						Had Not Held Political Office (n=166)					
	Upper Sector		Lower Sector		Total		Upper Sector		Lower Sector		Total	
	Number of Persons	Percent of Sample	Number of Persons	Percent of Sample	Number of Persons	Percent of Sample	Number of Persons	Percent of Sample	Number of Persons	Percent of Sample	Number of Persons	Percent of Sample
San Miguel	15	20.0	22	29.3	37	49.3	21	12.6	24	14.4	45	27.1
La Trinidad	15	20.0	18	24.0	33	44.0	47	28.3	26	15.6	73	43.9
San Antonio	5	6.6	14	18.6	19	25.3	29	17.4	30	18.0	59	35.5
Total	35	46.6	54	71.0	+89	+	97	58.4	80	48.1	+177	+

+Because some people irrigated in both sectors, totals will exceed number in sample and 100%. Figures are for comparative purposes only.

though the officeholders reside more frequently in the upper sectors, they contradict the pattern of irrigating in the place of residence by irrigating downstream. This pattern of preference among political officials for downstream irrigation requires some explanation.

Of the 273 individuals on the irrigation list, four were women, which suggests that women are generally not involved in canal irrigation in Tlalixtac as they are in some other villages (see below). Since women do not work in the fields, this is not surprising. But many women own land, which is cultivated by men—their sons, sharecroppers, and the like. Land ownership, then, is not a criterion for water use or water rights. Water can be requested, paid for, and used by those who cultivate the fields, not necessarily by those who own them.

Water can also be obtained by individuals who neither own nor sharecrop the land through arrangements with owners or sharecroppers who have access to canals. The latter request water for these fields in return for a part of the crops produced in the fields—apparently invariably alfalfa. Whether such arrangements enable landowners or sharecroppers to avoid payment for water (which seems unlikely, since payment could be made from the sale of the alfalfa) or provide water to individuals who for some reason have no right to the water themselves or merely want an extra turn to irrigate could not be ascertained. However since who owned what land is common knowledge, if obtaining extra water in this way were cheating, it probably would not be permitted. From observation and conversation, taking turns at irrigation appears to operate as follows (except in the dry season): every individual who requests water is entitled to some, providing he waits his turn. To irrigate more often, he can exchange some of his produce for another man's turn. Thus, individuals who have no land can still profit from their rights to water by exchanging their right for produce; they have an interest in the field and the produce, even though they neither own nor cultivate it, because they provide part of the water it needs. At least 30 of the individuals on the irrigation list had made such an arrangement.

TABLE 13
POLITICAL CAREER AND CANAL USE BY SECTOR: TLALIXTAC DE CABRERA SAMPLE

Career Status	Upper Sector			Lower Sector			Total	
	Number of Persons	Percent of Sector Population	Percent of Status Type	Number of Persons	Percent of Sector Population	Percent of Status Type	Number of Persons	Percent of Total Population
Had Held Office	35	26.5	39.3	54	40.2	60.6	89	33.4
Had Not Held Office	97	73.4	54.8	80	59.7	45.1	177	66.5
Total	132	99.9	49.6	134	99.9	50.3	266	99.9

TABLE 14
RESIDENCE AND CANAL USE: TLALIXTAC DE CABRERA SAMPLE*

Canal Used	Residence of Canal User							
	Same Barrio and Sector		Same Barrio Different Sector		Adjacent Barrio Same Sector		Nonadjacent Barrio and Sector	
	Number of Persons	Percent of Sector Using Canals	Number of Persons	Percent of Sector Using Canals	Number of Persons	Percent of Sector Using Canals	Number of Persons	Percent of Sector Using Canals
San Miguel								
Upper	23	56.0	10	24.4	4	9.7	4	9.7
Lower	32	68.0	–	–	12	25.0	3	6.3
La Trinidad								
Upper	24	36.9	29	44.6	6	9.2	6	9.2
Lower	33	68.7	7	14.5	5	10.4	3	6.2
San Antonio								
Upper	9	25.0	19	61.1	5	13.8	3	8.3
Lower	17	40.4	3	7.1	19	45.2	3	7.1

*Figures represent only those individuals for whom reliable information was available.

Such arrangements are most common among persons ineligible for political office, probably because their group contained the largest proportion of very young men, many of whom had not yet had a chance to acquire irrigable land of their own. Only half as many of the eligible group had made this arrangement, and less than one-sixth as many of the officeholding group had done so (see Table 15).

Most individuals in each category own the land they irrigate and the proportion of those owning land increases from the ineligible group to the eligibles to the officeholders. The proportion of sharecroppers also increases with regard to access to political power although not as steeply. Land ownership may be related to difference in age among the groups and therefore may be significant only in the sense that political power is related to age.

It is interesting that a number of officials who had served in higher offices were sharecroppers or had exchanged water rights for produce. Several of the síndicos, alcaldes, and regidores did not own irrigable land, according to my information. More than half of those who had served in the lower ranks as committee members were sharecroppers, but these were generally younger men.

At least 13 percent of the individuals in my sample owned more than one irrigated plot, and

TABLE 15

LAND TENURE AND POLITICAL CAREER: TLALIXTAC DE CABRERA SAMPLE

a.   Political Career Status and Land Tenure

Career Status	Owns Land		Sharecrops		Other Arrangement		Total
	Number of Persons	Percent of Status Type	Number of Persons	Percent of Status Type	Number of Persons	Percent of Status Type	Number of Persons
Had Held Office	58	79.5	12	16.4	3	4.1	73
Eligible, But Has Not Held Office	40	71.4	8	14.3	8	14.3	56
Ineligible	71	68.9	13	12.6	19	18.5	103
Total	169	72.8	33	14.3	30	12.9	232

b.   Political Office Held and Land Tenure

Land Tenure	Presidente	Síndico	Alcalde	Regidor	Tesorero	Presidente of Committee	Other Committee Member	Total
Owns Land	10	4	17	16	2	5	4	58
Sharecrops	–	2	3	2	–	–	5	12
Other Arrangement	–	–	2	1	–	–	–	3
Total	10	6	22	19	2	5	9	73

the proportion of the eligibles holding more than one plot was greater than that of the ineligibles. Thus, though few had access to more than one irrigated plot (32 of 238 for which information exists), those who did tended to have held public office. Once again, the influence of the age factor applies in this case; an increase in number of plots held may correlate with age (see Table 16a). At least 23.3 percent of the officeholders in the sample use canal water for two or more different plots of irrigated land. The largest proportion of these fell into the higher ranked offices (see Table 16b).

However, owning more than one plot of land does not necessarily mean owning more land than average. Of the 20 individuals who owned two plots of land of known size, only four owned more than six almudes (one almud equals one-fourth hectare). The two who held three plots of known size had eight and 15 almudes, respectively (see Table 16c).

The January lists gave quantities of land to be irrigated in 265 cases. The total amount of land involved was 737.5 almudes, or nearly 185 hectares. It was distributed in parcels as shown in Table 17. The average size of individual irrigated plots varied somewhat from canal to canal. As a group, the plots irrigated from the San Antonio canal were slightly larger, on the average, than those irrigated from the other canals, although the largest individual plots on the average, were irrigated from the lower portion of La Trinidad canal (see Table 18). Exactly what this signifies is not clear, but it is possible that the land around San Antonio and the lower sector of La Trinidad either were more recently opened up for cultivation or more recently redistributed since the revolution, and hence not as often subdivided through sale and inheritance as the rest of the land in the village.

It is difficult to interpret the significance of amount of land owned because the data indicate only minima. The average amount of land owned does not seem to vary much among the various categories of officeholders and non-officeholders (see Table 19a). Those still serving as police, by and large the youngest group, averaged less than others, probably for reasons given above. Al-

TABLE 16

MULTIPLE PLOTS OF IRRIGATED LAND: TLALIXTAC DE CABRERA SAMPLE

a. Political Career Status and Number of Irrigated Plots

Career Status	One Plot		Two Plots		Three Plots		Total	
	Number of Persons	Percent of Status Type	Number of Persons	Percent of Status Type	Number of Persons	Percent of Status Type	Number of Persons	Percent of Status Type
Officeholder	56	76.7	13	17.8	4	5.5	73	
Eligible, But Had Not Held Office	51	85.0	8	13.3	1	1.6	60	
Ineligible	99	94.2	5	4.7	1	.9	105	
Total	206	86.5	26	10.5	6	2.9	238	

b. Political Office Held and Number of Irrigated Plots

Number of Plots	Presidente	Síndico	Alcalde	Regidor	Tesorero	Presidente of Committee	Other Committee Member	Total
1	7	4	18	14	2	4	7	56
2	1	2	2	5	–	1	2	13
3	3	–	1	–	–	–	–	4
Total	12	6	22	19	2	5	9	75

c. Number and Size of Irrigated Plots (in Almudes)

Size	<1	1<2	2<3	3<4	4<5	5<6	6<7	7<8	8<9	9<10	10<11	11<12	12<13	13<14	14<15	15<16	Total
Number of Plots																	
2		1	3	7	4	1		1	1		1		1				20
3									1							1	2

TABLE 17

PARCEL SIZE OF IRRIGATED LAND: TLALIXTAC DE CABRERA SAMPLE

Size of Parcel (almudes)	Number of Parcels	Amount of Land (almudes)	Percent of Irrigated Land
<1	11	5.75	4.1
1- 1<2	55	70.25	20.8
2<3	70	144.50	26.4
3<4	58	178.50	21.9
4<5	39	156.50	14.7
5<6	18	91.00	6.8
6<7	11	66.00	4.1
7	1	7.00	.4
8	1	8.00	.4
10	1	10.00	.4
Total	265	737.50	100.00

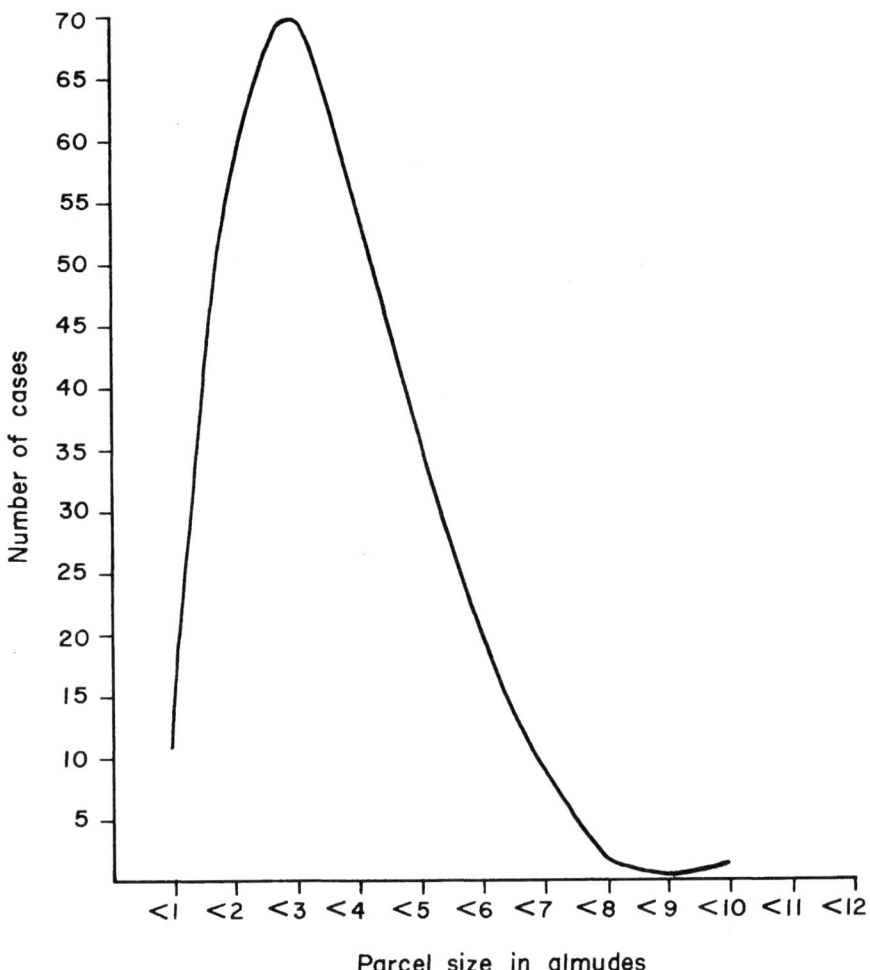

Fig. 2. Size of irrigated plots in Tlalixtac de Cabrera.

though presidentes and síndicos do appear to use more irrigated land than others, so do tesoreros and various committee presidentes who have a lower rank; thus, amount of land can not be correlated directly with political rank (see Table 19b).

A number of individuals not only own several parcels of land, but act as landlords in addition. Of the 15 landlords in the town, at least two are outsiders and four are women. Three have only one piece of land, three have two pieces, one has three pieces, and one has four pieces. Two of the remaining male landlords have eight and 10 plots of land respectively, but no further information was available. The four remaining are described as follows:

1. The wealthiest, 68 years of age, has between 25 and 30 pieces of land. He has been mayordomo of the patron saint of the village (San Miguel) twice and has served as municipal presidente.
2. The next wealthiest, aged 54, has 15 pieces of land, has served as mayordomo of the patron saint once and as centurión, and has been municipal presidente and síndico.
3. The third, aged 42, has about eight sharecroppers working his lands, owns a prosperous general store in the village center, has been mandadero, regidor, and is the current municipal presidente.
4. The fourth, aged only 27, has about six pieces of land, has already been mayor-

TABLE 18
SIZE OF IRRIGATED PLOTS BY CANAL USED: TLALIXTAC DE CABRERA SAMPLE (almudes)

Canal Used	Amount of Land Irrigated	Number of Irrigators	Average Size of Plot
San Miguel			
Upper Sector	77.5 ⎫ 182.5	35	2.24
Lower Sector	105.0 ⎭	42	2.50
La Trinidad			
Upper Sector	127.0 ⎫ 285	59	2.15
Lower Sector	158.0 ⎭	45	3.51
San Antonio			
Upper Sector	129.0 ⎫ 270	39	3.30
Lower Sector	141.0 ⎭	45	3.13
Total	737.5	265	2.78

TABLE 19
POLITICAL CAREER AND AMOUNT OF IRRIGATED LAND OWNED: TLALIXTAC DE CABRERA SAMPLE

a. Political Status and Amount of Irrigated Land Owned (in almudes)

Political Status	Total Land Owned	Number of Landowners	Average Amount of Land Owned
Held Higher Office	151.0	46	3.28
Police	93.5	36	2.6
Eligible, But Had Not Held Office	136.75	39	3.5
Ceremonial Office	95.0	34	2.8
Total	476.25	155	3.07

b. Political Office and Amount of Irrigated Land Owned (in almudes)

Amount of Land	Presidente	Síndico	Alcalde	Regidor	Tesorero	Presidente of Committee	Other Committee Member	Total
<1	–	–	1	–	–	–	–	1
1-<2	1	–	2	4	–	1	1	9
2-<3	–	1	4	4	–	–	–	9
3-<4	1	–	3	1	–	1	–	6
4-<5	1	–	2	1	2	1	3	10
5-<6	1	1	2	–	–	–	–	4
6-<7	3	–	–	–	–	–	–	3
7-<8	–	1	–	–	–	–	–	1
8-<9	–	–	–	1	–	–	–	1
12	–	–	–	–	–	1	–	1
15	1	–	–	–	–	–	–	1
Total	8	3	14	12	2	4	4	46
Total Owned	34.0	14.0	35.5	28.5	8.0	19.5	13.5	151.0
Average Owned	4.25	4.67	2.54	2.38	4.0	4.88	3.38	3.28

domo, and has served as municipal tesorero.

The extensive participation of these individuals does suggest that wealthier landowners tend to be active as municipal officials. Other active officeholders were:

1. A town musician, aged 66, who has been regidor and alcalde, and owns one piece of irrigated land.
2. A man, aged 54, who has been mayordomo, alcalde, and síndico, and owns one piece of irrigated land.
3. Another, aged 60, who has been mayordomo, síndico, and presidente, and owns about three pieces of irrigated land.
4. Another, aged 60, who has been mayordomo, has served as regidor three times, owns one and sharecrops another piece of irrigated land.
5. A man, aged 48, who has been mayor, regidor, and alcalde, and sharecrops one piece of irrigated land.
6. Another, aged 50, who has been centurión, regidor, and síndico and sharecrops two pieces of irrigated land.
7. Another, aged 50, who has been mayordomo, regidor, síndico, municipal secretaria and presidente, and owns one piece of irrigated land.
8. And finally, a man, aged 50, who has not been mayordomo or sponsor of any religious ceremony, but has been regidor, síndico, and presidente. He owns one piece of irrigated land.

Some of these individuals might have owned some good nonirrigated land near the river (there is very little such land available), but none are major landlords. The fact that at least three are sharecroppers suggests that the poorer farmers of the town can be quite active in civil affairs. The last two, clearly more active than the others, are special cases. Neither is considered outstandingly wealthy, but both are considered outstandingly well-educated and competent. The latter, who has not served as religious sponsor, is interesting: he is a headstrong and outspoken community leader, apparently making a conscious effort to be different. Although aware that he has not followed the traditional paths to office through ceremonial sponsorship, the community was sufficiently impressed by his education and capability to elect him presidente. But his eccentricity finally proved intolerable. After he had been presidente for several months, community members were so dissatisfied that they threatened to kill him. Finally, he was impeached and was succeeded by his síndico. As this story illustrates, education and capability are important qualifications in this village, but they also have their limitations. Observance of traditional ways, including a certain degree of conformity to the tenor of the population at large, are at least as important in community leadership. Personal power arising from such personal qualities as capability is a relatively minor factor in village leadership. Individuals obtain power either through conformity to specified roles, where power is invested in the roles themselves by the community, or through personal wealth; both together are the strongest possible combination.

Relative age is an important factor influencing political participation. Two age groups—men aged 36 to 40 and men aged 46 to 50—were compared. They were divided into four categories: (*a*) those who have held political office; (*b*) those who are eligible; (*c*) those who are ineligible because they are illiterate, but have served in ceremonial office; and (*d*) those who are still serving as policemen because they have not served yet in ceremonial office.

Only one-quarter of the younger group have held office, while nearly 60 percent of the older group have been officeholders. The largest proportion of the younger group are in the eligible category; only a small proportion of the older group are represented there, indicating that most individuals who are eligible will have served in political office by the time they are 46 to 50 years old (see Table 20).

Patterns of residence are not strikingly different in the two age groups (see Table 21). A larger proportion of the younger men live in Barrio San Antonio than older men, suggesting that this barrio has been more recently settled, and is being expanded by younger families. The

TABLE 20

POLITICAL STATUS BY AGE GROUP: TLALIXTAC DE CABRERA SAMPLE

Political Status	36-40 Years Old (%)	46-50 Years Old (%)
Had Held Office	14 (25.0)	16 (59.2)
Eligible But Has Not Held Office	20 (35.7)	4 (14.8)
Ceremonial Office	13 (23.2)	4 (14.8)
Police	9 (16.1)	3 (11.1)
Total	56	27

TABLE 21

RESIDENCE BY AGE GROUP: TLALIXTAC DE CABRERA SAMPLE

a.   Age Group and Residence by Barrio

Barrio	36-40 Years Old (%)	46-50 Years Old (%)
San Miguel	19 (33.9)	11 (37.0)
La Trinidad	20 (37.5)	11 (37.0)
San Antonio	17 (30.4)	5 (18.5)
Total	56	27

b.   Age Group and Residence by Sector

Sector	36-40 Years Old	46-50 Years Old
Upper	17 (30.4)	8 (29.6)
Lower	39 (69.6)	19 (70.4)
Total	56	27

same proportion of individuals live in the upper and lower sectors in both groups.

Patterns of irrigation vary more between the two groups than does place of residence. The older group is concentrated on the San Miguel canal while the younger group is more evenly distributed among the three canals. In the older group, almost the same proportion irrigate from the upper parts of the canals as the lower parts; in the younger group, two-thirds irrigate from above, and only one-third from below (see Table 22). Like the evidence on residence, these data may indicate that the upper part of the town has been developed more recently for irrigation than the lower, which might account for the concentration of the younger men in the upper areas. Since a larger proportion of the older men have been officials, this factor may account for the fact that officials in general seem to irrigate more in the lower sectors than the upper sectors and to a greater degree than do other groups.

In reference to land ownership and relative amounts of land owned, there does appear to be some difference between the two groups. While the pattern of multiple parcel ownership is comparable in both groups, the proportion of sharecroppers is twice as great in the older group as in the younger, and the proportion of individuals allowing others to use their irrigation rights is twice as great in the younger group as in the older (see Tables 23 and 24). This pattern is probably due to the fact that younger men who have no land tend to find sources of income through wage labor (often in the city, which is within commuting distance), while older men with no land tend to turn to farming by sharecropping. Although there is no direct evidence to support this claim in Tlalixtac de Cabrera, it

TABLE 22
LOCATION OF CANAL USE BY AGE GROUP: TLALIXTAC DE CABRERA SAMPLE

a. Age Group and Canal Use by Canal

Canal	36-40 Years Old		46-50 Years Old	
	Number of Persons	Percent of Age Group	Number of Persons	Percent of Age Group
San Miguel	17	30.4	16	59.2
La Trinidad	21	37.5	7	25.9
San Antonio	18	32.1	4	14.8
Total	56	100.0	27	99.9

b. Age Group and Canal Use by Sector

Sector	36-40 Years Old		46-50 Years Old	
	Number of Persons	Percent of Age Group	Number of Persons	Percent of Age Group
Upper	37	66.1	13	48.1
Lower	19	33.9	14	51.9
Total	54	100.0	27	100.0

TABLE 23
LAND TENURE BY AGE GROUP: TLALIXTAC DE CABRERA SAMPLE

Tenure	36-40 Years Old		46-50 Years Old	
	Number of Persons	Percent of Age Group	Number of Persons	Percent of Age Group
Landowner	45	80.3	20	74.1
Sharecropper	6	10.7	6	22.2
Other Arrangement	5	8.9	1	3.7
Total	56	99.9	27	100.0

does appear to be a general pattern in the Valley of Oaxaca and elsewhere in Mexico.

In average amount of land owned, the groups differ slightly. In total average, the older group hold somewhat more: 3.32 almudes per person compared to 2.95 almudes per person in the younger group. Comparing the groups in terms of political career, members of the older group with successful political careers own considerably more land than those with no such careers; the same discrepancy does not appear in the younger group. These figures suggest that those in the older group who have been unsuccessful in political careers have also not been successful in other ways, whereas in the younger group, individuals with economic potential may not yet have fulfilled their political potential (see Table 25).

Conclusions

Control of the canal system in Tlalixtac de Cabrera lies with the ayuntamiento, specifically with the presidente. The individual who controls water, then, is the same individual who has the greatest power in other public affairs. He need not use one to gain control of the other. Individuals who own a great deal of land, and thus are likely to own quite a bit of irrigated land, are likely to hold the highest office as well. But they only do so by conforming to traditions and community demands; they are subject to a greater power, that of the community at large.

TABLE 24

MULTIPLE PARCEL-HOLDING BY AGE GROUP: TLALIXTAC DE CABRERA SAMPLE

Number of Parcels	36-40 Years Old		46-50 Years Old	
	Number of Persons	Percent of Age Group	Number of Persons	Percent of Age Group
1	37	82.2	17	85.0
2	7	15.6	3	15.0
3	1	2.2	–	–
Total	45	100.0	20	100.0

Although poor individuals rarely serve in the highest office, neither do individuals who are illiterate or less than unusually capable. The most important differentiating factor among individuals, in terms of both participation in higher political office and landholding, is age. Older men are more politically and economically powerful, on the whole, than younger men.

The right to use canal water is not restricted to land ownership or even cultivation, or to any particular participation in community management. Any villager who requests permission to irrigate may have water, for his own land or someone else's. The presidente does not, at least legally, have the right to give or deny water without just cause; he merely administers distribution to enable everyone to have a turn. It is said by some that the officials may favor certain individuals in distribution, particularly the wealthy, by allowing them to take a little more a little more often. But so many people participate in the water sharing that the advantage must be minor.

TABLE 25

SIZE OF LANDHOLDING AND POLITICAL STATUS BY AGE GROUP: TLALIXTAC DE CABRERA SAMPLE

Political Status	36-40 Years Old	46-50 Years Old
Had Held Office	2.75*	4.28*
Eligible But Had Not Held Office	3.64	4.25
Ceremonial Office	2.35	2.0
Police	2.35	1.58
Total	2.95	3.32

*In almudes

Tlalixtac is clearly governed by a traditional cargo system and all that it implies: power and ultimate control lie with the community and are concentrated in certain offices which are rotated among the community members so that a large proportion of villagers eventually participate as officeholders. The system, by requiring an expenditure of wealth for eligibility to office, tends to favor the wealthier citizens; and by demanding a high degree of conformity, it tends to ignore or sometimes disfavor personal leadership qualities.

The system by which wealth is obtained lies outside the cargo system. The two systems meet only where the slight advantage of the wealthy is concerned, in the selection of officials. But water control and water rights fall, not into the system by which wealth is obtained, but into the cargo system of community control, where rotation and equality are the primary characteristics. The fact that individuals may own land anywhere and may accumulate as much anywhere as they can negates the upstream/downstream division. Any one individual may have land upstream, downstream, in both places, or in neither. Wealthy people tend to have land everywhere. Poor people have rights to water whether they have land or not.

Access to water is thus separated from wealth at the receiving end; at the administrative end it is only to a very limited extent related to wealth. But the power to administer water use does not increase the wealth or access to water of the administrator; neither does access to water enable one person to become administrator rather than another.

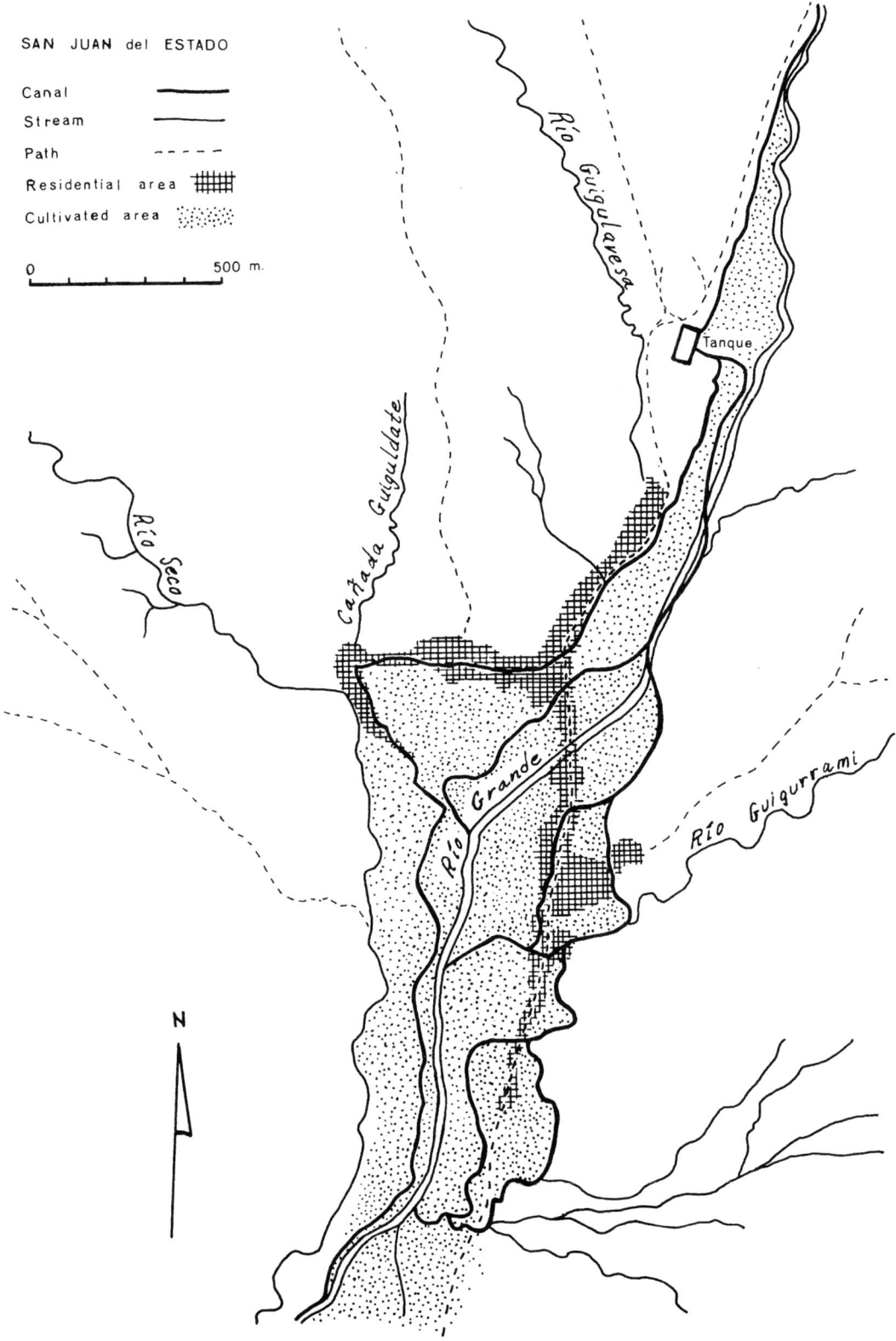

Map 6. San Juan del Estado.

SAN JUAN DEL ESTADO

The village of San Juan del Estado is located in the northern arm of the valley, at the upper edge of the piedmont zone at an altitude of approximately 1750 meters above sea level. It has a population of about 1560, with approximately 260 families. The town is divided into five barrios, each of which has a canal running through it. As in Tlalixtac, the residences are more dispersed than in towns which do not canal irrigate, with irrigated plots near and between the houses. The canals are fed from the village tanque or reservoir (Pl. 4a,b), whose source is a large stream (the Río Grande or Río de los Molinos) which flows from the eastern side of town carrying over 30 liters of water per second. The two smaller canals on the south side of town are fed from one of the larger canals. The irrigable land is all privately owned; there is no ejido. Communal land, which is used mainly for pasture and forest, is under the management of the comisariado de bienes comunales.

My main informant was the village síndico. With his help I was able to obtain lists of the users of the five canals, indicating the names of the users and the amount irrigated by each. The village officials also told me who had filled the main village offices over the past 10 years, from 1960 to 1969. The officials were reluctant to give more information about the canal users, and since my informant was one of the group, he felt obliged to follow their decision. Therefore, I could find out neither which of the canal users had held office before 1960, nor what other land was owned by them or by the officials on the lists.

The offices about which information was obtained were: presidente, regidor, síndico, suplente, and comisariado de bienes comunales. There is one presidente, síndico, and comisariado, and there are three regidores and five suplentes. The five suplentes are substitutes for the main council members when needed, and, in addition, they are responsible for allocation of water in the canals, one suplente to each of the five canals. There is no charge for water use, but the users must take turns and check with the suplente to see if anyone else is using the canal at the same time.

Out of the total population of about 260 families, at least 184, or about 71 percent, are canal users. The five canals are used by 76, 57, 65, 25, and 12 persons respectively. A total of 113.4 hectares of land is irrigated, and it is distributed among the canals in amounts of 29.53, 30.69, 38.12, 8.06, and 7 hectares respectively (see Table 26). This comprises most, if not all, of the cultivated village land.

The size of the irrigated plots ranges from one-eighth almud to 10 almudes (not including a 20-almud *rancho*). Most individuals own only one plot of land, but some have several plots irrigated by several canals; 33 individuals irrigate from two canals, seven irrigate from three canals, and one person from four different canals. The

TABLE 26

SIZE OF PLOT AMOUNT OF IRRIGATED LAND AND LOCATION OF CANAL USE: SAN JUAN SAMPLE

a. Amount of Land Irrigated by Canal

Name of Canal	Number of Users	Average Plot Size (almudes)	Total Amount of Land (almudes)	Total Amount of Land (hectares)
Principal	76	1.55	118.125	29.53
Paraje	57	1.83	122.75	30.69
Medio	65	2.35	152.50	38.12
Guigulavesa	25	1.30	32.25	8.06
Number 4	12	2.33	28.00	7.00
Total	235	1.85*	453.625	113.4

*Does not include 20-almud rancho irrigated from Paraje canal.

TABLE 26 (Continued)

b. Parcel Size and Location of Canal Use (almudes)

Parcel Size	Canal										Total	
	Principal		Paraje		Medio		Guigulavesa		Number 4			
	Number of Parcels	Percent of Land Irrigated	Number of Parcels	Percent of Land Irrigated	Number of Parcels	Percent of Land Irrigated	Number of Parcels	Percent of Land Irrigated	Number of Parcels	Percent of Land Irrigated	Number of Parcels	Percent of Land Irrigated
>1	17	22.36	13	23.21	1	1.53	11	44.0	4	33.33	46	19.65
1<2	30	39.47	15	26.78	27	41.53	5	20.0	2	16.66	79	33.76
2<3	13	17.10	15	26.78	17	26.15	6	24.0	1	8.33	52	22.22
3<4	9	11.84	8	14.28	9	13.84	2	8.0	2	16.66	30	12.71
4<5	3	3.94	2	3.57	4	6.15	1	4.0	2	16.66	12	5.12
5<6	3	3.94	1	1.78	1	1.53	—	—	—	—	5	2.13
6<7	—	—	1	1.78	2	3.07	—	—	—	—	3	1.28
7<8	1	1.31	—	—	1	1.53	—	—	—	—	2	.85
8<9	—	—	1	1.78	—	—	—	—	1	8.33	1	.42
9<10	—	—	—	—	—	—	—	—	—	—	1	.42
10<11	—	—	—	—	2	3.07	—	—	—	—	2	.85
12	—	—	—	—	1	1.53	—	—	—	—	1	.42
Total	76	100.0	56*	99.9	65	99.9	25	100.0	12	100.0	234	99.9
Total Amount Land	118.125		102.75*		152.50		32.25		28.0		433.625*	
Average Plot Size	1.55		1.83*		2.35		1.30		2.33		1.85*	

*Does not include a 20-almud rancho.

TABLE 27

POLITICAL STATUS AND AMOUNT OF LAND OWNED: SAN JUAN SAMPLE

(in almudes)

Parcel Size	Political Status				Total	
	Officials		Nonofficials			
	Number of Parcels	Percent of Total Land	Number of Parcels	Percent of Total Land	Number of Parcels	Percent of Total Land
<1	3	13.6	33	20.5	36	19.7
1-<2	2	9.1	55	34.2	57	31.1
2-<3	5	22.7	29	18.0	34	18.6
3-<4	5	22.7	20	12.4	25	13.7
4-<5	1	4.5	6	3.7	7	3.8
5-<6	1	4.5	9	5.6	10	5.5
6-<7	1	4.5	–	–	1	.5
7-<8	1	4.5	2	1.2	3	1.6
8-<9	1	4.5	2	1.2	3	1.6
9-<10	1	4.5	2	1.2	3	1.6
10-<11	–	–	1	.6	1	.5
14-<15	–	–	1	.6	1	.5
15-<16	–	–	1	.6	1	.5
27	1	4.5	–	–	1	.5
Total	22	99.6	161	99.8	183	99.7
Minimum Land	94		345*		439	
Average Parcel Size	4.22**		2.14*		2.40	

*Does not include a 20-almud rancho.
**This average is probably too high. It includes one individual who has an unusually large landholding—27 almudes. If this individual is not included in the calculation the average for officials is 3.19.

amount of land irrigated by individuals ranges from one-eighth almud to 27 almudes (not including the rancho). It is distributed among the officeholders and non-officeholders as shown in Table 27.

Eleven official positions are considered here over a period of four terms, a total of 44 possible official positions. These positions are filled by 35 individuals; eight individuals serve twice (one officeholder was not known), in different years and positions (see Table 28 and Fig. 3). Of the 35 individuals, only 22, or about 63 percent, are currently listed as canal users (see Table 29). Although this percentage is somewhat below the proportion of canal irrigators to non-irrigators for the town as a whole, the difference is probably not important. In other words, the proportion of canal users to nonusers is the same or somewhat larger for the population at large, compared with the town officials. Use of canals or possession of irrigable land is not a factor favoring election to political office; it would appear irrelevant at best.

Irrigated land is distributed among the 22 officials who do irrigate, as shown in Table 30. Higher officials appear to hold more land than do lower ones (suplentes). This is probably accounted for by the age differential. Although information about the exact ages of these individuals was not available, it is most likely that here, as elsewhere, lower-level positions are held by younger men; and younger men generally hold less land, on the average, than older men.

Among those who owned seven or more

TABLE 28
POLITICAL OFFICE AND LOCATION OF CANAL USE: SAN JUAN SAMPLE

Office Held	Number of Office-Holders	Number of Irrigators	Percent Who Are Irrigators	Location of Canal Use				
				Principal	Paraje	Medio	Gui.	Number 4
Presidente	4	3	75	2	–	2	–	–
Síndico	4	4	100	2	2	3	1	1
Regidor	12	7	58.4	6	2	3	1	–
Comisariado	4	2	50	2	–	1	1	–
Suplente	19	10	52.6	–	5	6	–	–

Note—Landownership was unknown for one suplente. Eight individuals have held office twice.

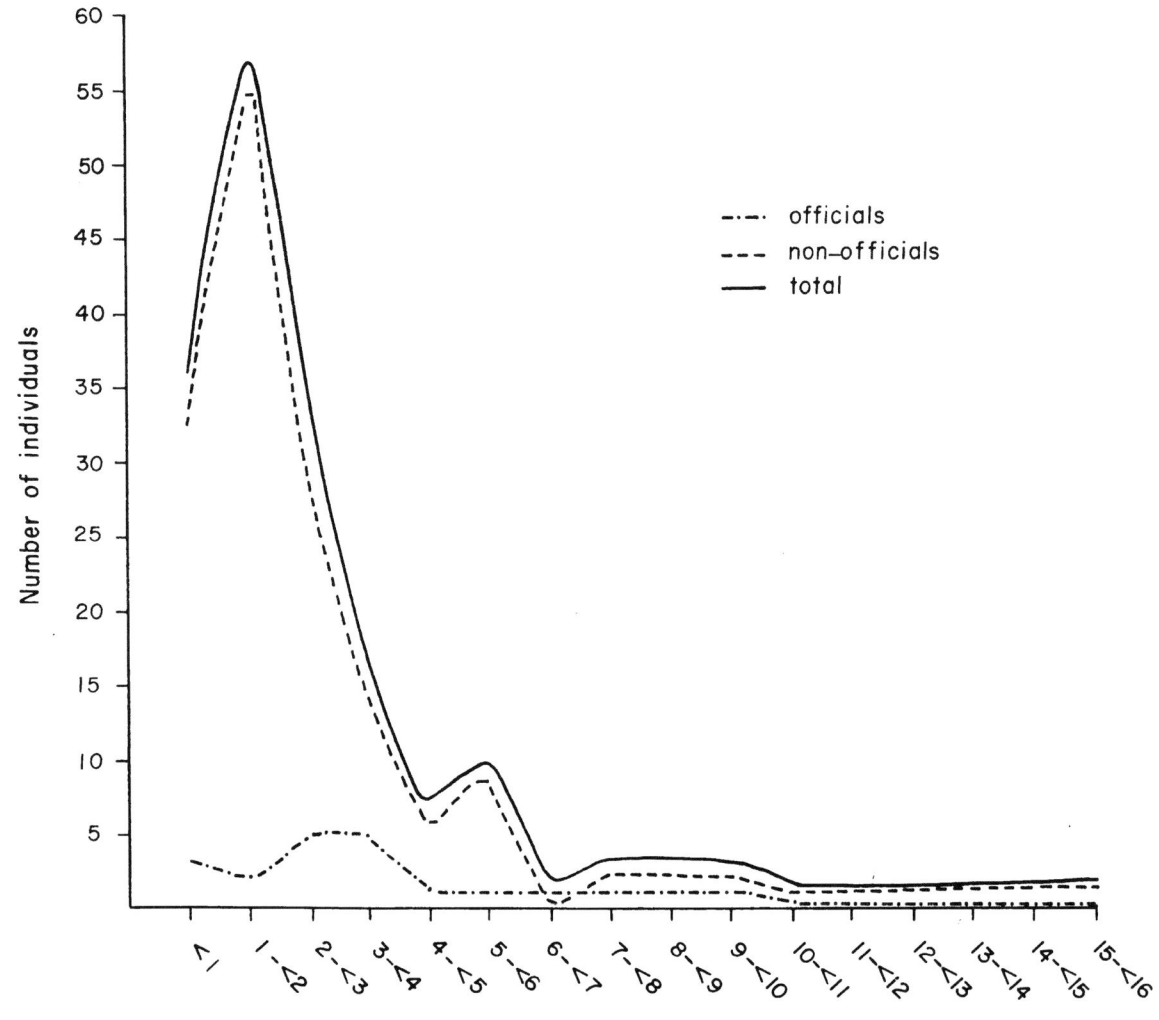

Fig. 3. Amount of land and political career in San Juan del Estado.

TABLE 29
POLITICAL OFFICE AND OWNERSHIP OF
IRRIGABLE LAND: SAN JUAN SAMPLE

Official	Year Office Was Held			
	1960	1963	1966	1969
Presidente	+	+	+	−
Síndico	+	+	+	+
Regidor	+	−	−	+
	+	−	−	−
	+	+	+	+
Suplente	−	−	−	+
	−	+	+	+
	+	+	−	+
	−	−	+	+
	?	−	+	−
Comisariado	−	−	+	+

Note—+ = owns irrigable land, − = does not own irrigable land.
Over the past ten years, there has been a gradual increase in the proportion of irrigated land holders among the town officials, but the year of the study (1969) the most important official, the presidente, was reported not to be a canal user.

almudes of irrigated land in the village, one was an outsider. This left 13 persons, of whom only four had held office, two as suplente, one as comisariado, and one as both presidente and regidor. The major holders of irrigated land are not predominantly the ones who hold office, and officials are not chosen more frequently from this group.

In San Juan del Estado, there is no direct and necessary correlation between use of irrigation water and high official position. Officials did not tend to own irrigable land in a greater proportion than did others in the village. Those who did have irrigable land appeared to hold greater quantities, on the average, than nonofficials. This difference may be related to some extent to age, as elsewhere noted. Even those officials who did hold more than average amounts of irrigable land were not among the persons who owned the *most* irrigable land. Those who were in control of water frequently did not even use the canal over which they had control.

This village, like Tlalixtac, has a cargo system but not of the traditional variety. There are no mayordomías, hence no requirement of ceremonial sponsorship for eligibility. This may partly explain why there is less of a tendency for wealthy individuals to hold important office. Where tradition is not strong, personal qualifications may count more than wealth or conformity for officeholders.

SAN AGUSTÍN ETLA

San Agustín Etla is situated in the upper piedmont zone, near the base of the mountains, at 1702 meters above sea level. It is a hilly area with very little flat land. The large tributary

TABLE 30
POLITICAL OFFICE AND IRRIGABLE LAND HELD: SAN JUAN SAMPLE
(in almudes)

Amount of Land	Highest Office Held					Total
	Presidente	Síndico	Regidor	Comisariado	Suplente	
<1					3	3
1-<2			1	1	2	4
2-<3	1		1		1	3
3-<4	1	1	1		2	5
4-<5			1			1
5-<6		1				1
6-<7					1	1
7-<8		1				1
8-<9				1		1
9-<10	1					1
27		1				1
Total	3	4	4	2	9	22

stream which provides the village with irrigation water, the Río de San Agustín, has a flow of over 30 liters per second. Its source, called El Cárcamo or Mano de León, lies some 20 kilometers away in the mountains. About four kilometers above the town the stream is tapped by a single main canal (Pl. 5b), but nearly all the irrigated land lies below the village and is watered by smaller canals which branch off from the main canal near the center of the village. Houses with irrigated plots line the canals, forming the spread-out pattern found in both San Juan del Estado and Tlalixtac (see Map 7).

San Agustín once controlled all the water in the stream, whose outlet into the valley lies very close to the village. The town once had enough water, after irrigating its own fields, to sell to 400 individuals from other villages, particularly Santo Domingo Barrio Alto. Recently, the government divided up the water so that San Agustín receives only one-fourth of the flow. In the years following, water from San Agustín was sold to only 20 people, and in 1968 no water was sold to outsiders. Because of the water source, two large textile mills (Fábricas San José and Vista Hermosa) were built in the town, and many of the villagers are employed there. But, due to government intervention, the water used by the factories and the other towns downstream (San Sebastián, Santiaguito Etla, and Oaxaca City) is set completely apart from the water used by San Agustín. San Agustín itself has four canals, which originate at the point (the caseta de distribución) where the government has divided up the water between San Agustín and points below (see Plate 5d). The main canal from the initial diversion point, which is four kilometers from the village, runs through the village lands but is not under village control.

There are approximately 2400 inhabitants in San Agustín, or about 400 households. Of these, 114 are listed as canal irrigators. I could not get the exact quantity of irrigated land, but it came to a minimum of about 58 hectares. This quantity is much lower than that of the other villages in the study, which is interesting because the water source is certainly the largest of the three. But the quantity of land irrigated here has probably diminished because of the scarcity of water in recent years, and because the government has diverted a large proportion of the available water for use elsewhere.

Among the 114 irrigators, 14 are women. Of the 100 remaining, 45 have served in public office. The offices which had been held by those on the irrigation lists were given to me as:

presidente	11	jefe de policía	2
síndico	5	tesorero	1
regidor	14	comisariado de	
suplente	8	bienes comunales	1
alcalde	6		

with 3 individuals having held office twice.

One presidente, one síndico, three regidores, five suplentes, two alcaldes, one jefe de policía, one tesorero, and one comisariado are elected every three years. The frequent appearance of presidente and regidor on the list may mean either (1) that this position is remembered better by my informants (and while many others had served in other offices, their careers were forgotten), or (2) that presidentes and regidores tend to be canal users more often than those who fill other official positions, and the latter would therefore not be on the list. Unfortunately, no information was available about people not on the list. The official in charge of irrigation in the village is a regidor, each of the three regidores serving in this capacity for one year.

The figures concerning canal irrigation and political career, parcel size, source of water, etc., are given in Tables 31-36 and Figures 4 and 5.

Irrigated parcel size averages about 2.36 almudes, a little more than half a hectare for the population as a whole. Thirty-seven percent of the parcels were less than two almudes, and 36 percent of the parcels were more than three almudes (Table 31). The average parcel size is less than that of Tlalixtac (2.78 almudes) and more than that of San Juan (1.85 almudes). The amount of irrigated land held by officials averages somewhat greater than for the population at large (Table 32), indicating some bias toward those with more land, particularly in the

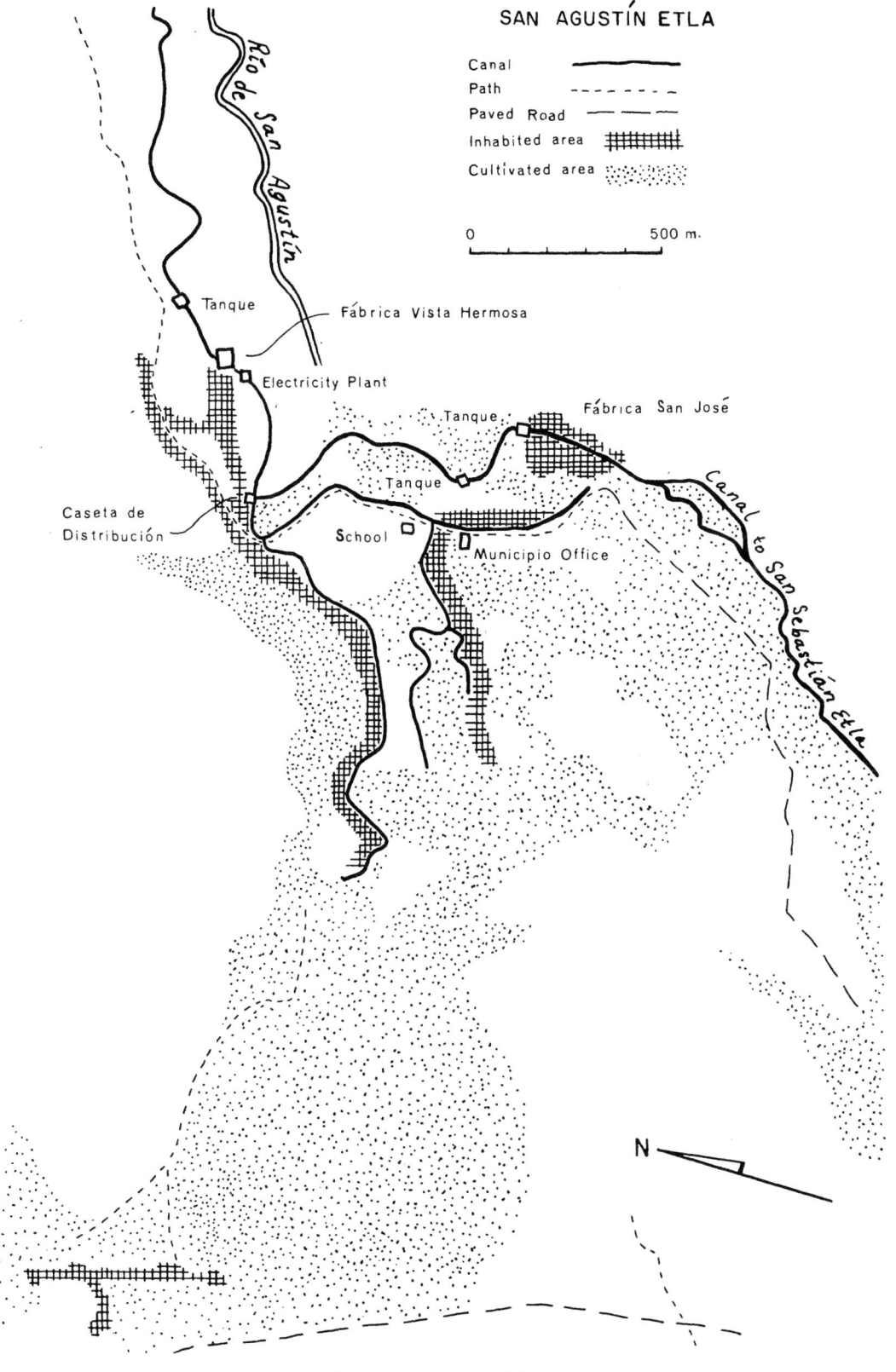

Map 7. San Agustín Etla.

TABLE 31

SIZE OF IRRIGATED PARCELS AND LOCATION OF CANAL USE: SAN AGUSTIN SAMPLE
(in almudes)

Parcel Size	Canal #1		Canal #2		Canal #3		Canal #4		Total	
	Number of Parcels	Percent	Number of Parcels	Percent	Number of Parcels	Percent	Number of Parcels	Percent	Number of Parcels	Percent Total Canal Use
<1	–	–	1	5.3	3	9.7	2	6.9	6	6.0
1-<2	3	15	7	36;8	13	41.9	4	13.8	27	27.0
2-<3	10	50	5	26.3	6	19.4	9	31.0	31	31.0
3-<4	2	10	2	10.6	5	16.1	5	17.2	14	14.0
4-<5	4	20	4	21.2	4	12.9	4	13.8	16	16.0
5-<6	1	5	–	–	–	–	4	13.8	5	5.0
8	–	–	–	–	–	–	1	3.4	1	1.0
Total Parcels	20		19		31		29		100	
Total Land	50.5		41.0		61.0		83.5		236	
Average Parcel Size	2.52		2.15		1.97		2.88		2.36	

TABLE 32

POLITICAL STATUS AND AMOUNT OF IRRIGATED LAND: SAN AGUSTIN SAMPLE
(in almudes)

Parcel Size	Political Status						Total	
	Women		Nonofficials		Officials			
	Number of Parcels	Percent	Number of Parcels	Percent	Number of Parcels	Percent	Number of Parcels	Percent of Land Held
<1	–	–	4	8.2	2	5.4	6	6.1
1-<2	5	38.5	15	30.6	7	18.9	27	27.3
2-<3	4	30.8	17	34.7	9	24.3	30	30.3
3-<4	1	7.7	5	10.2	8	21.6	14	14.1
4-<5	3	23.1	6	12.2	7	18.9	16	16.2
5-<6	–	–	2	4.1	3	8.1	5	5.0
8	–	–	–	–	1	2.7	1	1.0
Total Parcels	13		49		37		99	
Total Land	29.5		103.0		103.5		236.0	
Average Parcel Size	2.27		2.10		2.80		2.38	

TABLE 33
LOCATION OF CANAL USE AND POLITICAL STATUS: SAN AGUSTIN SAMPLE

Political Status	Canal								Total
	Canal #1		Canal #2		Canal #3		Canal #4		
	Number of Persons	Percent of Status Type	Number of Persons	Percent of Status Type	Number of Persons	Percent of Status Type	Number of Persons	Percent of Status Type	Number of Persons
Women	2	14.3	5	35.7	3	21.4	4	28.6	14
Non-Officials	13	23.6	11	20.0	14	25.5	17	30.9	55
Officials	14	31.1	7	15.6	15	33.3	9	20.0	45
Total Number of Persons	29		23		32		30		114

TABLE 34
AGE AND POLITICAL STATUS, IRRIGABLE LAND HOLDERS: SAN AGUSTIN SAMPLE

Age Group	Political Status									Total
	Women			Officials			Nonofficials			
	Number of Persons	Percent of Status Type	Percent of Age Group	Number of Persons	Percent of Status Type	Percent of Age Group	Number of Person	Percent of Status Type	Percent of Age Group	Number of Persons
Young	–	–	–	3	6.7	17.6	14	25.9	82.4	17
Middle-Aged	6	50	17.1	17	37.7	48.6	12	22.2	34.3	35
Old	6	50	10.2	25	55.6	42.4	28	51.9	47.4	59
Total	12	100	–	45	100	–	54	100	–	111

higher offices of presidente, síndico, and regidor (though not suplente, as is the case in San Juan del Estado).

The population at large appears to be more or less evenly distributed along the four major canals. Officials appear to irrigate more frequently than others from canals one and three and less frequently than others from canals two and four (see Table 33), but the significance, if any, of this slight differential in distribution is not clear.

The age distribution of the sample in San Agustín is interesting (Table 34). A very small proportion of younger men are involved in irrigation, much smaller than in Tlalixtac. This may indicate that younger men turn more often to occupations outside of agriculture. The trend may be stronger here than elsewhere because the factories provide nearby alternatives for the residents of San Agustín. Only a small proportion of the younger men have served as officials, as might be expected. However, 48% of the men in the "middle-aged" category have served as officials as compared with 42% of the "old" men. This is particularly surprising in view of the weighting in favor of age in the sample as a whole. However, this difference may be due in part to faulty memory on the part of my

TABLE 35
POLITICAL OFFICE HELD AND AGE: SAN AGUSTIN SAMPLE

Age Group	Office Held								Total
	Presidente	Síndico	Regidor	Alcalde	Suplente	Jefe	Tesorero	Comisariado	
Young	—	—	—	—	3				3
Middle-Aged	2	3	7		3	2	—	—	17
Old	9	1	6	6	1	—	1	1	25
Total	11	4	13	6	7	2	1	1	45

TABLE 36
POLITICAL OFFICE AND IRRIGABLE LAND HELD: SAN AGUSTIN SAMPLE
(in almudes)

Amount of Land	Office Held								Total
	Presidente	Síndico	Regidor	Alcalde	Suplente	Jefe	Tesorero	Comisariado	
<1	1				1				2
1-<2	1	1	3	1	1				7
2-<3	2	1		2	3	1			9
3-<4	2	2	3					1	8
4-<5	2		2	2	1				7
5-<6	1		2						3
6-<7									
7-<8									
8-<9							1		1
Total	9	4	10	5	6	1	1	1	37

informants: older men who have served in public office many years ago might have been forgotten, while middle-aged men, having served more recently, would be fresher in my informants' memories.

The younger men have served as suplentes, the public office with the lowest rank (and status) in this sample (Table 35). Although officials do tend to hold more land, on the average, than nonofficials, there is still a considerable spread in amount of irrigated land held. Land held by presidentes ranges from less than one almud to more than five almudes. Similarly, land held by regidores ranges from one to less than five almudes. As shown in Table 36, the official holding the most irrigated land in this sample is the tesorero (see also Fig. 4).

Perhaps since only approximately one-fourth of the village members are irrigators, irrigation plays a smaller role in the structuring of community relations than in the other villages studied. Nearly one-half of the irrigators have served in office; what proportion of the non-irrigators have served is not known, but such information is essential before any conclusions can be drawn.

In San Agustín, there is no charge for water use among community members. However, community members are expected to contribute voluntarily to village funds, and I was told that villagers receive water in proportion to the amount of money they contribute. This was not conceived of as payment for water; contributions are considered informal and voluntary, even though they are carefully accounted for on the irrigation list kept in the municipal offices.

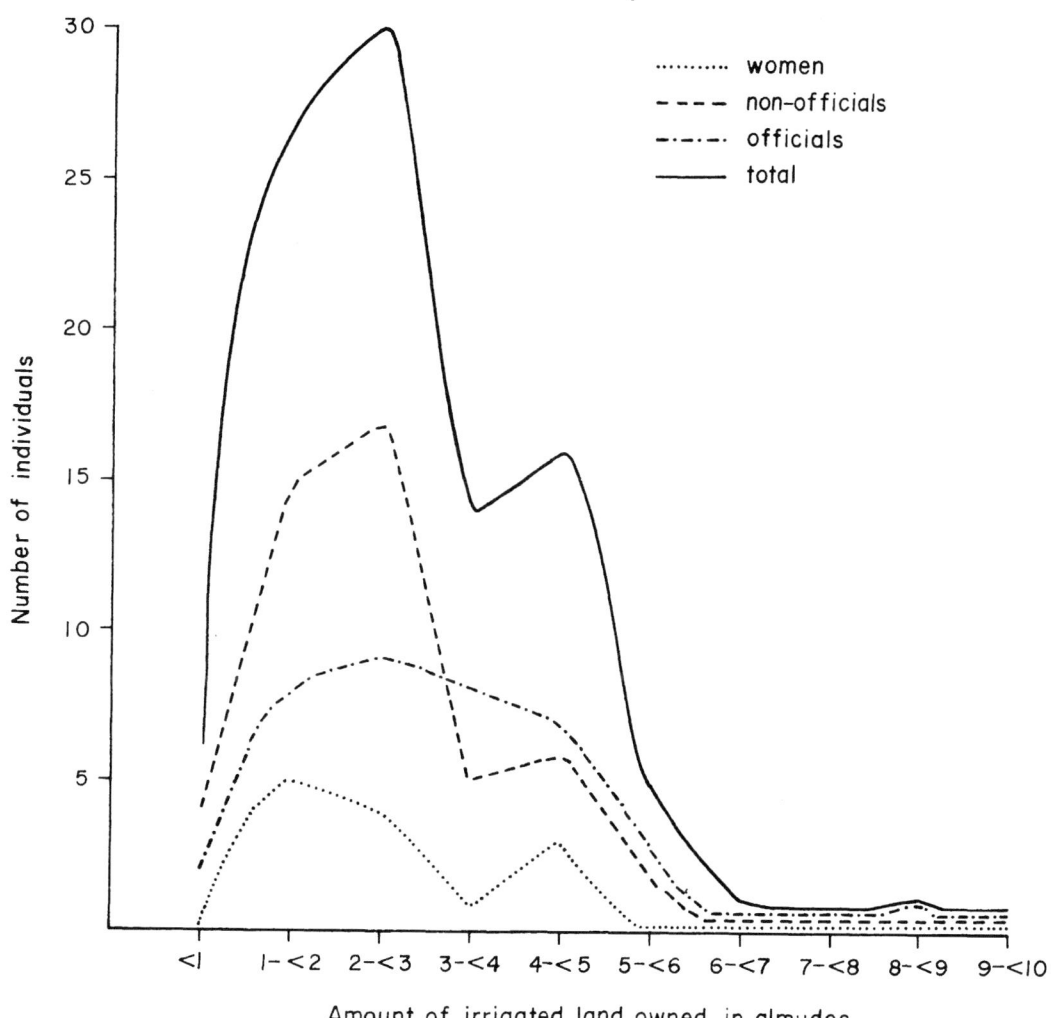

Fig. 4. Amount of irrigated land and political status in San Agustín Etla.

Separation of the process of contribution from access to water in this way merely obscures the reality that contributing money and receiving water are two parts of one operation. We might interpret this behavior as being necessary because of the "ideal versus reality" conflict discussed before. The system is founded upon a principle of equality in both contributing and receiving in all village matters. This ideal must be dealt with in terms of the real inequalities in capabilities and needs which are the result of another system in which equality does not exist.

San Agustín has a cargo system but no mayordomía or sponsorship requirement. Education and capability are considered important factors in the selection of higher-ranking village officials. The task of administering canal water is rotated among the regidores, but sometimes a special repartidor is elected or appointed by the ayuntamiento to do the job. This is only one of the many administrative tasks of the village officials; it confers no special privilege, nor do any special qualifications lead to the selection of one individual to be in charge of water rather than another.

SUMMARY AND CONCLUSIONS

Detailed observations of irrigation, water control, and selection of public officials in Tlalixtac

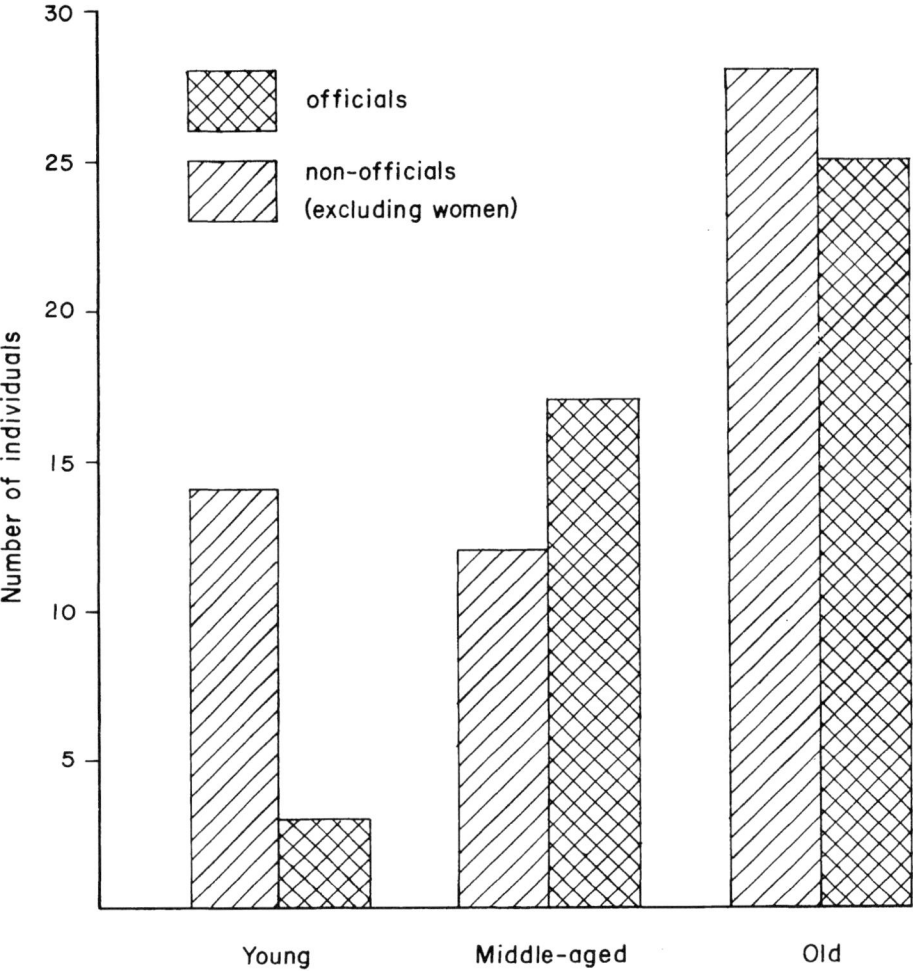

Fig. 5. Bar graph of officeholders by age group.

de Cabrera, San Juan del Estado, and San Agustín Etla suggest that if there is an inherent difference in control of power involved in a canal irrigation system, the special potential advantage of upstream irrigators is almost completely obliterated by the cargo system and by private property ownership.

First, there is no political advantage to owning land or irrigating upstream and no possibility of controlling others through controlling their water supply, since the use of the canal is supervised by village officials who guarantee that everyone, including downstream irrigators, can take a turn at using the canal. Second, there is no economic advantage in an upstream position, since relative wealth depends not only on access to water, but also upon ownership of greater quantities of land. A downstream irrigator with a great deal of land will certainly be wealthier than an upstream irrigator with very little land. Furthermore, the fact that sharecroppers may also have rights to water, in a sense, separates the advantage of access to water from ownership of land (and thus wealth) altogether.

While there is no particular advantage to an upstream location on the canal, private ownership of irrigated land permits a sort of by-passing of the rule of equal access to water, since access is useful only to those who have land. Thus the rule of equal access does not create any sort of economic equality among irrigators or community members in general, since those who have more land, get more water. On the other hand, the limitations on personal initiative among the public officials as such, combined with the insurance of access to water for all who apply, mean that there is no incentive and no advantage for those who require a great deal of water to have the responsibility of distributing it.

It is important to understand the relationship between personal power and public power in this society. There is little in the social system to motivate one to want to hold office in the first place; it is not a profession; it is a drain on one's resources; and it is not a very effective means of exerting personal influence, particularly when conformity is required of the officials. Holding public office is a responsibility which is rotated among many individuals. It cannot become attached to an individual in this system. Personal power is associated almost exclusively with wealth. And wealth may be obtained only by using private resources. An individual, therefore, cannot become wealthy or powerful by using public resources. Since water is a public resource, it cannot be used as a basis for individual power. The only power associated with water is that of the community at large over individual canal irrigators.

The fact that the power associated with control over water resources rests with the community at large is very much in keeping with the traditional subordination of the interests of the individual to those of the community in this social system. And yet, as this chapter hopefully has shown, this is only one part of the picture. Private wealth does play a role in community organization, though its relationship to public office and the management of public resources tends to be indirect. On the whole, personal power tends to be relegated to the private sphere of life and kept apart from the public sphere.

In sum we might conclude, at least on the preliminary basis, that canal irrigation itself has little, if any, effect upon community political organization. Although the presence of canals creates the administrative tasks of distributing water and organizing labor for maintenance, the nature of public offices in general is not affected. Furthermore, the rules for sharing the resource and administration of water distribution and canal maintenance are the same as those for public administration and participation in general. In other words, water control is completely incorporated into the larger system of public administration.

But the final test of the relative influence of canal irrigation upon community political organization would be a detailed comparison of canal irrigating communities with other communities of the same area which do not have canals. At present, although no adequate information is available for such a comparison, more ethnographic reports from ongoing and future studies should eventually make such a test possible.

IV

THE ROLES OF THE VILLAGE AND THE STATE IN WATER CONTROL

INTRODUCTION

In this chapter the respective roles of the community and the state with regard to water control will be discussed in detail. Chapters II and III indicated that the organization of water control at the village level is incorporated into a larger system of public administration, which has little if anything to do with the nature of the resource itself; the possibility that other types of organization might be applied to water control has not yet been considered. This chapter, then, will discuss alternative types of organization, how they might be established, and what the implications of such changes might be for the Valley of Oaxaca.

In addition, this chapter will address itself to a question implicit throughout this study: Are there aspects of water control or the use of canal irrigation that significantly affect political organization or social interaction? Although a negative answer was tentatively suggested in the last chapter, there are qualifications that need to be examined: the first rests on a distinction between the internal and the external relationships of the community; and the second rests on a distinction between periods of stability and times of change.

INTRAVILLAGE AND INTERVILLAGE WATER CONTROL

The potential differences in control and access between upstream and downstream irrigators could theoretically provide a power imbalance among individuals who use the same resource. But this potential power imbalance is never realized within the rural community in the Valley of Oaxaca today because the community itself offers alternative means of organizing relationships among canal users. The community power structure permits, even necessitates, the circumvention of the potential differences among irrigators, by the more general rules which organize social relationships for the society as a whole. Thus, water control, which is assigned to the public sphere of social organization, is consistent with other types of control: centralized responsibility and leadership through public offices, rotation of these offices among community members, equal rights to hold office and to have access to public resources, and cooperation in participation through taking turns.

The same rules which regulate social organization within the community do not operate at the intercommunity level. Community organization imposes no constraints upon relationships among communities. At the intercommunity level, the potential differences between upstream and downstream villages are often realized; no alternative basis for their relationship is provided by the social system. These differences are reflected in the buyer-seller relationship or perhaps even a form of patron-client relationship, since the sale of water by an upstream community to a downstream community is by no means a market exchange relationship. The upstream community is generally the sole source of water for the downstream community, and the downstream community is generally the only customer. In this relationship, the upstream community is dominant; though it cannot always choose its customer, it can choose whether, when, and how much to sell. The downstream community can only choose whether to buy or not to buy and go thirsty and hungry. The only cases in which this dominant-subordinate relationship does not appear are those in which the two communities consider themselves in one sense or another as one community, or the state government has intervened, appropriating the dominant position to itself.

Neither the buyer-seller relationship nor the patron-client relationship, where these govern intercommunity relations over the sharing of water, is consistent with the rules of social organization in the public sphere at the community level. Such relationships are consistent with the private sphere of social interaction. Similarly, the fact that the resource is owned by one community and not another is consistent with the rules which apply to private property ownership at the community level, such as the notion that private property is to be used for personal profit. Since the conquest, both the nature of organization at the community level and the policies of the centralized state (or colonial) government have ruled out any other type of relationship between communities, except where the state itself intervenes. We might conclude, then, that where water resources are privately owned (by individuals or particular communities), any potential differences in control of the water resource which are inherent in its nature will become realized in the relationships between individuals and communities. While contemporary laws prevent individuals from attaining control over the access to water resources by other individuals, so far they have not prevented individual communities from controlling the access of other communities to those resources.

THE VILLAGE AND THE STATE

Just as social relationships at the community level can be divided into two different spheres, the public and the private, so can intercommunity relationships be divided into two spheres, one involving dyadic private relations, and the other involving relationships mediated through a public institution—the state. The state is now in the process of replacing such private relationships between communities with public ones by placing water control under its own jurisdiction wherever the water is used by two or more different communities. When it does so, the relationships between such communities over the shared resource become more consistent with those of the public sphere of community social organization.

The state's role in the relationship between communities, although superficially parallel to that of municipal offices vis-à-vis individual community members, is really quite different. State officials are specialists; community officials are not. While state officials are members of the larger community they govern, their offices are not rotated among all the members of the larger community. The community government operates mainly by cooperation and consensus; the state can operate, for the most part, without either. The state government, because it has a much larger body of constituents than the community, has a much larger pool from which to draw its financial and physical support.

Finally, and perhaps most importantly, the state has its own full-time paid labor force—a body of policemen, such professional experts as engineers and bureaucrats, and even workmen—who owe allegiance to and are dependent for their livelihood upon the state government itself, no matter from which particular communities they come. The state relies on this special labor force to carry out its decisions and projects without assent from the population at large. The community, in contrast, can only operate through the willful cooperation of its members. Because of this advantage the state operates more independently of its constituents than the community government, and more efficiently. Independence means greater power, and greater power permits greater effectiveness in carrying out projects. Furthermore, because the state has such a tremendous work force to draw upon, it may divide up the labor. The population at large continues to work in order to contribute materials and funds to support the state government's staff, while the staff are completing state projects. Again, the division of labor contributes to the greater effectiveness of the state government's operation.

CHANGE IN WATER CONTROL ORGANIZATION AND THE STATE

The government's program for agricultural development through the modernization of hydraulic technology has been one—not the only or even necessarily the most important—source of change at the community level. A number of different branches and agencies of the government are involved in this program, directly and indirectly, but one particularly relevant in the valley today is a subsection of the Secretaría de Agricultura y Ganadería (SAG). Since the late 1950's, this agency has been constructing small reservoir dams in various communities in the valley; two of the communities, Tomaltepec and Teotitlán del Valle, have been mentioned in previous chapters.

The SAG is authorized by federal law (passed between 1930 and 1940) to construct new hydraulic works in rural communities and to establish new forms of water control within these communities. In particular, the federal laws specify that water control be administered by a group of individual canal users called a junta de aguas. The laws specify the duties of this group (basically, to obtain permission from the government to use government-owned water resources, to construct new hydraulic works, and to obtain funds for such construction and the necessary property and facilities for the constructions), the qualifications for its members, the manner of selection of members, their rights and obligations, and the form of the group's organization and operation. The junta de aguas acts as an agent of the executive branch of the government, in conjunction with the SAG, and must be authorized by the SAG. The SAG may at any time inspect the junta de aguas and may remove its officers or nullify its decisions if the SAG considers them to be illegal, inappropriate, ineffective, or otherwise unsatisfactory. Whenever the SAG contributes to the construction of a new hydraulic work, a junta de aguas is established, so that the users may receive the new construction legally through an authorized representative body.

The junta de aguas, therefore, is the only legitimate and authorized water control organization in communities in which government dams are constructed. In order to receive government aid in the construction of new hydraulic works, a community of canal users or potential canal users must accept the organization specified by the government and must submit itself subsequently to the control, supervision, and constant surveillance of a government agency. The community proper, the village, is not mentioned in the specifications for organization; the only units mentioned are the canal users, the junta, the SAG, and the executive branch of the government. The local community as a unit is completely ignored, bypassed by the federal laws relating to water control.

Bypassing the community as a unit of organization in this way had important ramifications in community organization for two reasons. First, the community itself had always considered itself owner of the water resource, and its executive body had complete jurisdiction over water control within the community. Second, no executive officers had previously existed who were not responsible to the community as a whole, and none had ever been directly responsible to, or supervised by, a specific agency of the federal or state government (except in the most general sense). Furthermore, control of water for irrigation had never fallen to one particular public official, nor was it ever required that the official responsible for supervising water resources, facilities, and use be a user himself. But the new laws now declare that a particular interest group within the community be self-governing with respect to its common interest in canal irrigation and that its authority derive from the government agency, not the community.

In certain ways, this special interest group resembles an ejido, which also has its own property—land rather than water—and its own governing body. But the land allotted to ejidos was almost invariably formerly owned by haciendas, not by the communities themselves; the water resources in question, on the other hand, were generally owned, at least in the eyes of the community, by the community itself. The government therefore appropriated not private property but what was considered to be communal village property for the use of a special interest group. If this group is smaller than the whole community, the introduction of a distinction based on inequality will undermine the ideal through which the community is integrated—its public and communal activities, resources, and officials.

The formation of juntas de aguas may not appear to be much of a change at the community level. The types of management which prevailed in the older system are still performed by the new; officials have to see to it that water is distributed equitably, that users take turns in an orderly fashion, that the facilities are kept in good condition. The water control officials are still elected, though it is specified that they be elected annually (unlike the ayuntamiento, which is elected every three years) and that they be canal users, not just members of the community; and the official positions are still rotated among the individuals who are subject to their control. And yet, there is a difference. Once the junta is formed, water control is set apart from the ordinary administrative duties of community officials and becomes a function of an arm of the state and federal government; water control officials are set apart from other public officials in the community because they are delegates of the state and federal government agencies. Although junta de aguas officials are neither full-time specialists nor paid employees of the state, they do become part of the government-controlled executive arm of the larger society with access to, and support from, the independent and extraordinary power of that government.

In the past, the local community was almost entirely independent of the state government in the administration of almost all internal affairs. To be sure, the government has specified some forms of administrative organization, some duties of certain officials, some of their qualifications, and their manner of selection; and its authorization is necessary to legitimize some of them. But for the most part, these specifications remained general. Apart from the requirement of direct public elections and literacy as a qualification, nobody seemed to care much how closely all the specifications were adhered to, and there was considerable leeway for local modifications in organization, as we have seen.

What is perhaps the most important difference between government intervention in the form of local community government, on the one hand, and local water control, on the other, is that for the former, the government merely proclaims laws and expects the communities to carry them out; while in the latter, the government institutes organizational changes in direct connection with its installation of hydraulic works which affect the means of production. The community becomes eligible to receive the benefits of the special powers of the state by changing its organization and conforming to state specifications. Conversely, if it does not receive these benefits, there is neither the necessity nor the motivation to change.[1]

The distinction between change associated with technological innovations and brought about by state level decisions and change brought about through community level decisions becomes important in understanding long-term development. States can cause organizational change at the community level, directly or indirectly, without the accompaniment of technological change. But when the organization applies to the use of technological facilities which are unchanged, and for which the community already has an organization, it may be difficult to bring about change without either threats of punishment for nonconformity or promises of considerable rewards. The reallocation of land was brought about by both—severe punishment for those who continued to hold too much and rewards for those who took their lands away. But although the government also required that all private property be registered and taxed, today hundreds of peasants avoid both registration and taxation. The threat of being caught seems to be small, and the reward for registration and paying taxes even smaller.

---

[1] An illustration of the lack of motivation on the part of the community to conform to state government specifications of local organization is the matter of municipio size. While the state specifies a minimum population of 5,000 for a municipio, over 25 percent of the municipios in Oaxaca actually have fewer than 2,000 inhabitants.

When the state institutes changes in connection with state-supported technological development, the rewards are immediate and material—they are part of the change. In the eyes of the SAG, for example, modernization and increased efficiency of the use of water depend not only upon the construction of the new hydraulic works but upon closely supervised administration in a form which will maximize the effectiveness of the new works in production. A community which accepts aid from the SAG for a new hydraulic facility gets a package deal. Organizational change is seen as merely an aspect of technological change, not a result or prerequisite.

It is possible for a community to institute technological change without the help or influence of the government and without organizational change. The type and scale of the innovations, however, are subject to restrictions at this level which pose no problems to the state. It is not just that the state can build bigger, better, more complex, more expensive dams, more quickly than can local communities; for some hydraulic projects, communities have neither the money, labor, time, technical know-how, nor materials to carry them out by themselves. But if the state subsidizes such projects, and its agents feel that the most effective use of these projects requires a certain type of organization, then the community which profits from the new works is obliged also to increase its profits by submitting to the specified changes in organization.

SUMMARY AND CONCLUSIONS

Organizational change can occur without technological innovation. This has happened, as we will see, even with regard to water control. But such changes do not necessarily bring about more effective use of water for productive purposes. Communities may also bring about technological change without organizational change, but their capacity to do so is relatively limited. State governments have a far greater capacity to increase the effectiveness of the use of water for productive purposes through both organizational and technological change. Once the local community becomes dependent upon the state for technological change, however, it becomes highly vulnerable to organizational change as specified by the state government—particularly if more effective use of the technological innovations to maintain higher productive levels is at stake.

Since the inception of canal irrigation techniques in the Valley of Oaxaca more than 2000 years ago, the state seems to have displayed only limited interest in developing the hydraulic technology to increase agricultural production until about two decades ago. In recent times, the state government has seen the construction of new hydraulic works and concomitant organizational change as a way of raising the effectiveness of water use, the level of production, and the standard of living of the population at large. Few other aspects of production permit such significant participation and such tight control on the part of the state. Ejidos have tended to be small and not much different from nonejido communities. So far, the government has not had many ways to influence farmers in their methods of cultivation or irrigation. By installing new hydraulic facilities and requiring that their use be organized in the manner the state considers most effective, it has been able to influence the means and levels of production. So far, however, this influence has been rather restricted. In the near future, it seems likely that it will become more widespread.

V

THE ROLE OF WATER CONTROL IN OAXACA'S HISTORY

INTRODUCTION

In the Valley of Oaxaca, canal irrigation seems to have developed simultaneously with the emergence of the state. The first part of this chapter will present the evidence for their simultaneous development and the implications of the discussions in previous chapters for interpreting this evidence. And because the true importance of canal irrigation to political organization in the Valley of Oaxaca can best be seen in the context of change, particularly in the changing relationship of the state to the local community, this chapter will also detail historical change throughout the known period of canal irrigation in the valley.

Furthermore, there are various ways of organizing canal use and its administration; the selection of a particular alternative at a particular time is a function of the larger social setting. The consequences of various types of social settings for the organization of water control and the effectiveness of water use may be quite different, as we have already seen in regard to current changes in irrigation technology through government intervention. The fact that certain types of organization may be more effective for water use than others has important implications for our understanding of cultural evolution in this area, as we shall see.

ORIGINS

During the Early and Middle Formative periods (roughly 1500-500 B.C.), a number of permanent, nucleated agricultural communities were established on low piedmont spurs near water courses on the flat alluvial floor of the valley. These communities participated in a widespread network of long distance trade in exotic goods and raw materials with other parts of Mesoamerica (Flannery, 1968b). In addition to interconnection through trade, these areas also shared similarities of style, settlement pattern, subsistence activities, and possibly social organization. Although not much is yet known about burial patterns and grave goods in the Valley of Oaxaca (and the interpretation of what we know about mortuary practices elsewhere is still subject to controversy), differences in Middle Formative burial offerings in Oaxaca and elsewhere in Mexico suggest slight inherited differences in social status, perhaps even a system of ranking (Flannery, 1968b). Differences in residence types in Oaxaca in the Middle Formative also appear to lend support to this interpretation. Though we still know little about the ways of life and social organizations of Early and Middle Formative Valley of Oaxaca communities, we know that they were argiculturalists; that they exploited a wide variety of environmental zones; and that they probably had a social organization resembling that of tribes or perhaps certain types of chiefdoms found elsewhere in the primitive world. While resources from zones above the valley floor and piedmont were exploited, there is little evidence that these zones were permanently used for cultivation or settlement. Similarly, there is only limited evidence that canal irrigation was used here or elsewhere in Mesoamerica during the Early and Middle

Formative, though the discovery of wells and apparently associated water-drawing vessels does suggest that well irrigation on the valley floor was extant (Orlandini, 1967; Flannery, personal communication, 1969).

Some time after 500 B.C. a number of striking changes occurred. Both the number and size of settlements increased, suggesting a considerable rise in the total population. Many new settlements appeared off the valley floor in the piedmont, near tributary streams. A few sites which appear to have had a special function— perhaps ceremonial, administrative, or defensive—were built on hilltops. Many of these had special types of construction—again, perhaps with ceremonial functions—at the very top (Plate 8d). One of these sites, Monte Albán, was later enlarged to become one of the most spectacular Classic sites in all of Mesoamerica. Social status differentiation appears to have become considerably more pronounced during this period, marked especially by greater and more distinct differences in graves (Chadwick, 1966) and residences. Monumental architecture, calendrics, and a form of writing also appeared. Many of the objects previously used in long distance trade, which had begun to diminish in importance in the previous period, now seemed to disappear entirely (Flannery, 1968b).

In this period, the Late Formative (known in the Valley of Oaxaca as the Monte Albán I period), appears the earliest archaeological evidence for local canal irrigation (Neely, 1967). A series of irrigated terraces, associated with Monte Albán I type pottery, was found at a site called Hierve el Agua, which is located in the mountains just east of the valley proper (Plate 8a). The canals on these terraces were preserved in excellent condition by heavy travertine deposits from the water they carried. The water source is a group of still-active springs just above the terraces. Radiocarbon dates of 420 B.C. and 310 B.C. are available from Monte Albán I levels in the terraces at the site of Hierve el Agua (Flannery, personal communication, 1969). If the early canal irrigation facilities in the valley resembled in form the fossilized system from this period at Hierve el Agua, then it must have been very much like that in use today: very simple, with no large stone or earthen dams, only a series of small trenches and tiny aqueducts whose construction and maintenance required a minimum of labor.

Within the valley proper, the irrigation water is usually travertine-free, making ancient canals far more difficult to discover. So far no ancient canals have been detected from surface exploration of Late Formative sites, except for Monte Albán itself (Neely, personal communication) though it is likely that excavation of certain other sites will turn up traces of Late Formative canals. On the other hand, the location of many of the Monte Albán I sites in relation to permanent tributary streams indicates that villages were located with regard to possibilities for canal irrigation (Plate 8b,c). Furthermore, the sites are located not in the lower piedmont where more flat land is available, but in the upper piedmont where water can be diverted more easily into canals and controlled over longer distances. Finally, it seems likely, from the location of the Early and Middle Formative sites, that agricultural production in the preceding period depended upon a year-round water supply. Since the piedmont soils are extremely dry during most of the year and the water table is so deep that it is not feasible to use well irrigation, if the earliest residents in the piedmont sites were to support themselves as well as their counterparts on the valley floor did, they would probably have had to use canal irrigation (see Map 8).

Further evidence of the existence of canal irrigation in the Middle or Late Formative has been found in other parts of Mesoamerica. At the site of Amalucan in Puebla, Fowler (1969) discovered filled-in earthen canals of this age; a Formative period masonry dam is known from Tehuacán, Puebla (Brunet, 1967).

The period from 300 B.C. to A.D. 800 witnessed the growth and development of a complex urban civilization throughout the Mesoamerican highlands. So far, we know little about the political organization of this period beyond the fact that there seem to have been territorially distinct areas such as those centered about the Valley of Teotihuacán and the Valley of Oaxaca.

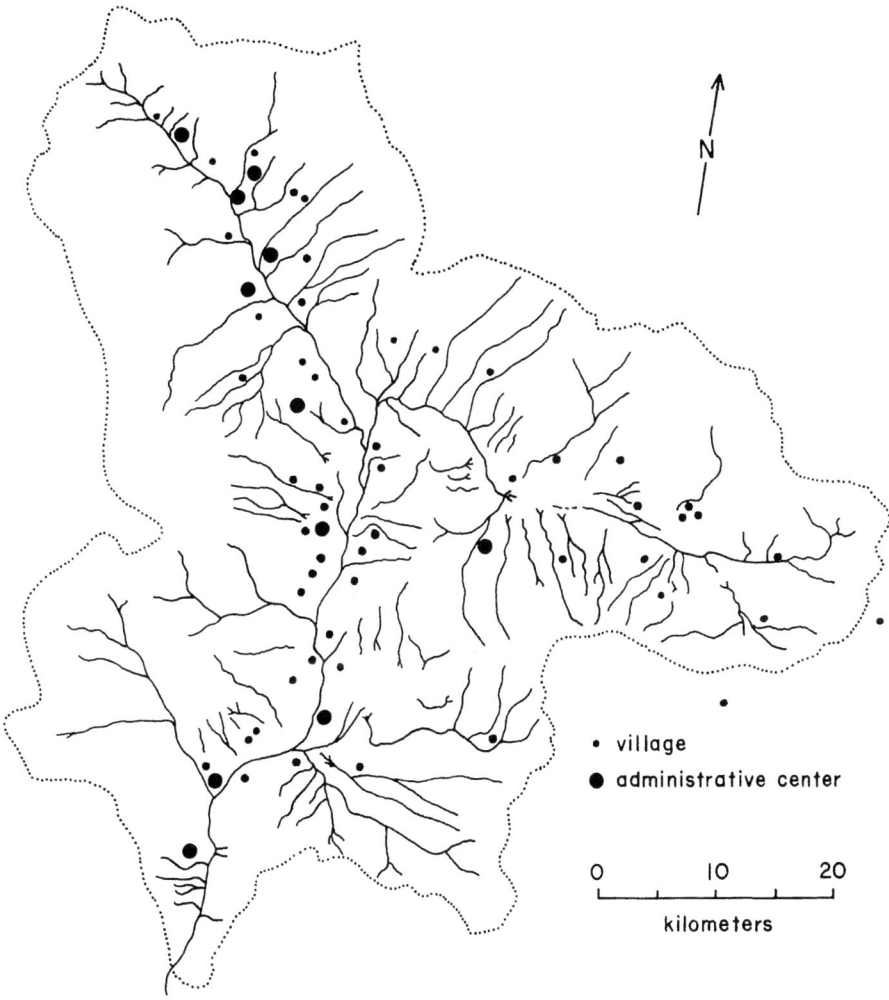

Map 8. Monte Albán I period sites in the Valley of Oaxaca as of 1969.

We also know that within these areas there were particular centers with special political (and perhaps also religious) functions and significance, such as the city of Teotihuacán and the site of Monte Albán, and that these areas appear to have been based upon a system of social stratification with several distinct classes. By this period, then, there are likely to have been a large supporting population of peasant commoners and a smaller group of full-time governing specialists.

The role of canal irrigation in this development remains subject to considerable controversy. Many Mesoamericanists, such as Palerm and Sanders, believe there is sufficient evidence to show that it was undoubtedly important (Palerm, 1955; Sanders and Price, 1968); but aside from its being a basis for higher productivity and sharp differentiation between types of land, there is little evidence to show how canal irrigation might have influenced either political structure or social organization in general.

Indications of the importance of the role of canal irrigation in the development of political or administrative specialization and centralized government in the Valley of Oaxaca during the Late Formative and Classic periods are provided by the settlement pattern. In early Monte Albán I, we find some of the first permanent sites on the upper piedmont tributary streams. Sites at

Map 9. Early Monte Albán I: Santo Domingo Tomaltepec.

Tomaltepec (see Map 9) and Santa Marta Etla (Map 10 and Pl. 8c) provide good examples of the early type of site. They are small, covering areas of approximately two or three hectares. The sites are situated within about 150 meters of the streams. Present-day canals pass between the sites and the streams, and ancient canals were probably constructed in approximately the same places.

In the center of the Tomaltepec site are two relatively large mounds. Plastered floors indicate that residences were constructed on top of these mounds. Smaller, less elaborate residences probably surrounded these mounds. We might tentatively suggest that the residences in the central mound groups were occupied by highly ranked individuals of some sort, perhaps members of a "chiefly" lineage, while the less impressive residences surrounding the mounds were occupied by their subordinates, perhaps lesser kinsmen.

By late Monte Albán I there are already several distinctly different sorts of sites. Many of the older Monte Albán I sites continue to be occupied, and new ones (apparently ordinary residential areas) continue to be established among the tributary streams (see Map 10). Other new sites, also in the piedmont zone but slightly

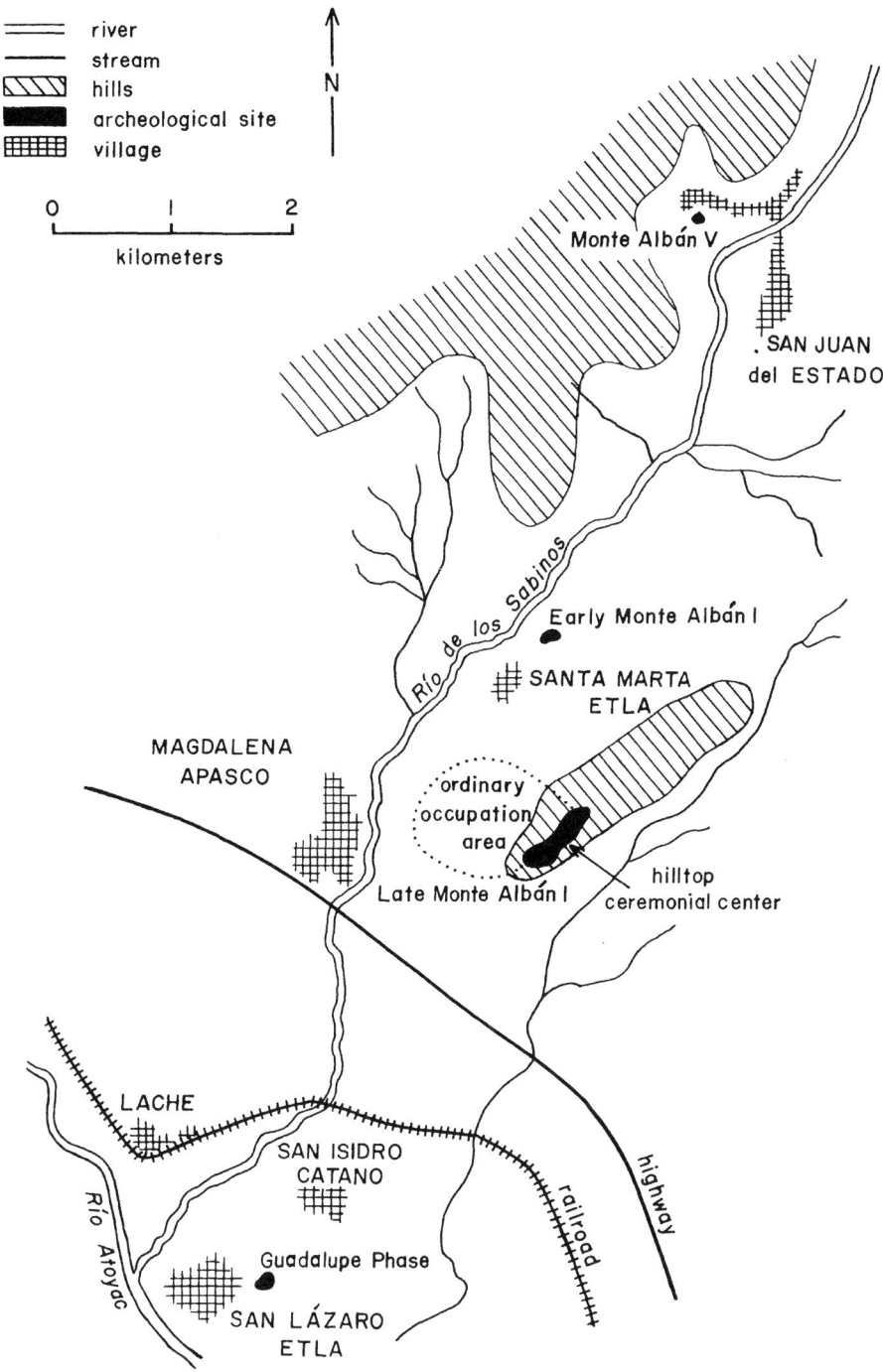

Map 10. Sites on a piedmont tributary stream.

removed from the residential areas, appear on hilltops overlooking the tributary streams. The architecture of these new sites, which are considerably larger than the older ones, is monumental in scale and style. Mounds in the center are generally arranged in groups of four around a square patio—an arrangement which continues into the Classic period. There may be several distinctive categories among these sites. Probably the largest, most spectacular, and most important is Monte Albán itself. But the sites near Huitzo, Magdalena Apasco (Pl. 8d), and Ayoquesco, among others, are impressively large. Unfortunately, since these sites were almost invariably enlarged during Monte Albán II and III, it is difficult to map their form and extent during the Late Formative without some excavation. Smaller hilltop centers were also constructed during this period in a number of areas, including San Gabriel Etla, San Agustín Etla, San Luis Beltrán, and a number of others.

The suggestion is that political specialization in the early Monte Albán I period developed and grew in connection with expansion of settlement on the piedmont tributary streams. The location of many of these specialized hilltop sites, overlooking habitation areas in the upper piedmont zone, suggests that their function had to do at least in part with the administration of the use of water in these streams. The occupants of these sites might, for example, have played a role similar to that of the state today: intervening in intercommunity disputes over the sharing of a single water source, regulating the allocation of water among such communities, and so forth. Or, it may be that the occupants of the sites claimed ownership or special jurisdiction over the water sources and extracted tariffs and labor from canal users in exchange for access to water, using this reserve to build and maintain their palatial residences.

Unfortunately, this is only speculation. We are a long way from reconstructing the actual form of political integration of the sites during the Late Formative and Classic periods. While expansion was occurring in the piedmont zone, new sites were also springing up along the valley floor, older sites were expanding, and both were using the new monumental architecture. We have yet to relate the piedmont sites to the valley floor sites, or to relate either to Monte Albán.

There has been considerable speculation about the nature of political organization during the Classic in Mesoamerica, in the lowlands as well as the highlands (Wolf, 1959:102-29). In Oaxaca, we have evidence that its growth and development were somehow related to expansion in settlement and population size and to technological change. We should, however, be extremely cautious in interpreting the administrative role of the hilltop communities during the Late Formative and Classic periods using settlement pattern alone. If, as I hope to show, the organization of canal use and the respective administrative roles of the state and local governments have varied very greatly in the past 500 years, we would need much more information to make such judgments. Did the occupants of these hilltop centers resemble in political function and economic power the caciques of the Post-Classic period, the hacendados of the late Colonial period, the government bureaucrats and engineers of today, or something quite different? Certainly a great deal more research is required before we draw any conclusions on that point.

If we cannot say more about the details of the relationship of the new political structure to the use of canal water, we can surely say that the organization of water control must have been consistent with the organization of the society as a whole. Thus it is likely that by the Classic period, differences in control of water use were associated in one way or another with differences among members of the society based upon social class or status. But the fact that canal irrigation and centralized organization apparently had their origins at roughly the same time, at least according to our evidence in the Valley of Oaxaca, leads us to an even more difficult problem of interpretation. What, if anything, did canal irrigation at its inception have to do with the change in social organization which led to the growth and development of a class stratified society?

While our understanding of contemporary water control systems in the Valley of Oaxaca cannot provide us with evidence for the character of water control organization in earlier periods, certain aspects of the social change we observe at present may provide us with useful models for the processes of change in the past. We have observed, for example, that in contemporary Oaxaca, there are at least two types of organization which may be applied to water control—one at the community level and the other at the state level. These two types are different not only in scale, but in form and operation. While either alternative may be applied to the resources themselves, the organization of the state level provides what appears to be a more effective way of using the resources for productive purposes than does that of the community level. This is not simply a matter of greater technological resources and capabilities, but of tighter organizational controls directly applied toward increasing productivity through the most effective use of water. The organization of water control at the community level has as its main goal keeping the peace among community members. The state level organization clearly is capable of achieving both the peace-keeping goal and the goal of higher productivity through greater effectiveness of water use.

It is likely that during the Late Formative, when both irrigation and social class stratification were first being established in the Valley of Oaxaca, at least two, if not more, alternative organizations were in existence. One was likely to have been smaller, more localized, perhaps less stratified and generally less powerful; the other probably tended to have the opposite characteristics, as well as a different structure and mode of operation. We might speculate, for example, that one was based upon kinship, and the other upon some type of social differential which set apart classes of people according to hierarchical levels. If organization of the second type—which is likely to have been the newer type—were applied to water control, it may have increased the effectiveness of the use of water, with the result of increasing productivity. Repeated local applications of this form of organization, its continual replacement of other forms of organization in the regulation of social interaction, and its greater effectiveness in terms of productivity would have strengthened the new form of organization in the society, perhaps at the expense of the older.

But even if we accept as likely the fact that the new type of organization was more effective in increasing productivity through water control, and that its application toward this end strengthened its position in the society in general, it is also clear that the new type of organization was applied to, and affected by, various other sorts of economic and social factors. We might ask, then, whether or not canal irrigation was different in some way from these other factors, or whether its relationship with the new form of organization was somehow special and distinctive. In the Valley of Oaxaca, where all documented types of pre-Hispanic water control features were extremely simple to construct and maintain, it appears that we might rule out any special capacity of the new organization for mobilizing labor and materials or having special technological know-how as being the important or distinctive element in this relationship. It seems more probable that control over the allocation of water was its central focus.

Three factors about the general situation during this period seem to be relevant. First, canal irrigation probably played a part in the growth of the population and in a change in its settlement pattern. A rise in population and change in settlement pattern might well present special conditions of stress for an older form of social organization, and provide conditions for developing a new form. Second, canal irrigation seems to have been a technological innovation. Its use required some sort of social organization, and since it was new, it might have been more open to new forms of organization than other, older technological aspects of production, the organization of whose use was already established. Third, the use of flowing water for canal irrigation may imply certain inherent potential differences in control of the resource. This is perhaps true of no other resource in the means of production which were available in the valley at that time. Since differences in political control among members of the population in general would have been characteristic of the newer form of organization (at least to a higher degree than in the older), canal irrigation seems to be a likely focal point for the replacement of the old by the new. Or, to put it another way, if changes were imminent, those which involved social differentiation in control would be selected for by the new canal system and supported by success in its application. This last factor is evident in the contemporary replacement of local community controls by state controls over water. Although the character of the particular forms of organization involved at present is clearly different from that of the ancient forms, the relationship between the two at each period is certainly parallel.

This model for the relationship between canal irrigation and political structure during the initial establishment of canal irrigation assumes that the elements of a certain type of political structure are already in existence. The model does not propose that canal irrigation causes a social form to emerge, nor does it necessitate any particular form. However, while it assumes that there are various alternative types of organization which may be applied to canal irrigation, it also assumes that some types are more effective in increasing productivity through water use than others. If change is to come about, and if the new type of organization is more effective in the use of water for productive purposes, then water control provides an important locus for the selection of the new type over the old. In this way, a change in the society as a whole could come about through the selective advantages of certain forms of organization with regard to water control. If significant changes are occurring in the technology of canal irrigation and in social or political organization at the same time, it seems very likely that the newer social or political forms receive support, in the form of selective advantage, from their direct application to the new techniques of water control. In terms of significant technological change, the Valley of Oaxaca seems to have undergone its most radical change during the period when canal irrigation was first introduced. Between 500 B.C. and the present, there seem to have been periods of growth and expansion, as well as some decline in the technology of water control, but these changes are neither so well documented nor, apparently, so significant. Another significant, if less radical, change is occurring at present.

POST-CLASSIC HISTORY

By the time of the Spanish conquest, in the early sixteenth century, certain aspects of social and political organization which had evolved during the Classic period had either disappeared or been seriously modified, while others had continued and developed. The most obvious—some would say, the *only* obvious—indication of such change was the rather sudden abandonment of the hilltop site at Monte Albán. This abandonment is paralleled in many other parts of Mesoamerica (Wolf, 1959; Cowgill, 1964). The causes and significance of these abandonments, whether common to all or particular to specific areas, remain unknown or disputed. No matter what the degree or precise nature of the change, the organization among the Zapotecs encountered by the Spanish colonists was almost certainly not identical to that of the Classic period. For this reason, we cannot directly infer what conditions might have existed more than four centuries previously from what the Spanish chroniclers wrote about Post-Classic Zapotec social and political organization.

What the Spaniards did find was a society divided in at least two different ways (Whitecotton, 1968): it was stratified, with classes of peasants, noblemen, and "lords," or, as the Spaniards called them, caciques; and, although in some respects the Zapotecs were a unified nation ruled by an emperor, or king, or supreme lord, the population was divided into a number of frequently warring, competitive, often hostile, independent lordships or *cacicazgos*. Each of these lordships was ruled by a single lord and consisted of (1) a head community where the lord resided (sometimes), which the Spaniards called a cabecera, and (2) other smaller communities or sujetos ranging in number from one to a dozen or more. It appears that except for mobilized warfare against an outside enemy and payment of tribute to outsiders, there were few occasions or activities in which these various lordships ever came together as a single unit. Certainly there was interaction among the various lorships, both through feuds and warfare and through intermarriage of noble families. To a greater or lesser degree, all recognized and paid homage to the supreme lord and his capital at Zaachila (a site continuously occupied since at least 1300 B.C.). In certain respects the religious organization of the society was centralized, with the highest priest and the entry to the Zapotec underworld (where the souls of all Zapotec dead reside) localized at Mitla (a site continuously occupied since at least 500 B.C.). But with the exception of certain special contexts, the society was for the most part decentralized. In many respects, its organization resembled what has elsewhere been called a "feudal" society.

The earliest well-organized, detailed, descriptive documents for the area are the *Relaciones* of 1580 (Paso y Troncoso, 1905). While these documents provide interesting and useful descriptions of many aspects of Zapotec social and political organization, economy, and agricultural resources and activities, they provide almost no information at all about water control. Canal irrigation is said to have been practiced in Etla, Huitzo and its dependencies, Cuilapan, Tlalixtac, Teotitlán del Valle, and Teitipac, but not at Zimatlán, Zaachila, Santa Ana Tlapacoyan, Macuilxóchitl, or Mitla, among a large number of places. For most places where its existence was noted, canal irrigation was described as being on a small scale, sometimes only seasonal. For many places where irrigation was said not to have been practiced, it was observed that a water source was available but not used for this purpose. No mention is made of organizations for maintenance, nor of systems of water allocation. Unfortunately, there is almost no description at all of the central part of the Etla arm, where canal irrigation was known in some periods to have been far more important than elsewhere in the valley.

In addition to problems of omission, these documents pose a number of problems for evaluation and interpretation. For one thing, they were written more than half a century after the conquest. The conquest resulted in certain very important changes in social and political organization, not to mention drastic population decreases through disease. While the *Relaciones* were being written, the population was in a state of crisis, decimated by epidemics, and disoriented by the undermining of old institutions which were only partially replaced by new ones. Few remained who could remember or describe the pre-conquest situation, and the priests and bureaucrats who wrote the documents seemed to have difficulty understanding and interpreting what little information these people could provide. Many of the reported details are at best subject to suspicion, and at worst, completely unreliable. For example, it hardly seems possible that the commoners in some towns ate no maize, but only wild fruits and grasses, as the documents repeatedly claim.

The ethnohistorical documents, then, have extremely limited usefulness for our understanding of the role of water control in the immediate pre-conquest and early colonial periods. They tell us that canal irrigation was practiced in a few, but not all, of the areas they describe and on a small scale. They tell us nearly nothing about the areas where we suspect it to have been most important. In these documented areas, we might assume that the organization of water control was not striking enough in form or performance to draw the special attention of the chroniclers at the time they wrote. While this omission is suggestive, we cannot say how much it reflects on the character of the observers, or to what degree it may be attributed to the observed phenomena.

COLONIAL PERIOD

Descriptive information for various aspects of social and political organization during the later Colonial period is far more abundant and reliable. Unfortunately, it still tells us little about water control and is far from complete for the different areas in which canal irrigation was practiced. Taylor's paper (1969) on colonial land distribution in the Valley of Oaxaca provides a very useful summary of the available information about problems and techniques of water control and of where canal irrigation was practiced during this period, as well as a description of the history of changes in political organization subsequent to the conquest.

If it is true that in pre-conquest and immediate post-conquest times canal irrigation was practiced on an extremely small and limited scale, during the colonial period (and particularly in the Etla arm) it was expanded and developed extensively to become the basis for the outstanding productivity in Etla. By that time, the most important canal-irrigated crop by far was wheat. In the southern arm of the valley, which had begun to specialize in sugar cane production, only Cuilapan was noted for extensive use of canal irrigation. In the eastern arm, canal irrigation was important in Tlalixtac, San Juan Guelavía, and San Juan Teitipac. New waterworks were constructed in a number of areas:

Major water-diverting projects for household and agricultural use were undertaken in at least two cases. The Jalatlaco River was banked and channeled directly into Antequera (Oaxaca City) from San Felipe del Agua in the early eighteenth century and an irrigation canal one and one half leagues in length was under construction near Zimatlán in 1719 (Taylor, 1969:4).

Aside from canal irrigation, water control measures were also taken in response to the threat of serious flooding and the damages it caused, by such things as heavy deposition of river sand. As early as the mid-sixteenth century, protection and provision for the city of Oaxaca became an important factor in water control: "Corvee labor was used to divert the Atoyac River near the city to lessen the danger of floods" (Taylor, 1969:3).

Various aspects of colonial policy with regard to the native population resulted in a gradual and relatively peaceful transition from the pre-conquest form of social organization to the new forms which characterized the labor colonial years. The colonial administration recognized and protected the native administrative elite during the early period by perpetuating rules of inheritance, inalienability, and organization of native cacicazgos; by granting the native nobility special rights and privileges, and the authority to govern their former subjects; and by generally allowing the nobility to mediate between the colonial administration itself and the peasant population. On the other hand, the colonial administration promulgated laws granting and protecting lands for the peasant communities, and it established a representative, elective political structure consisting of sets of offices which were rotated among community members at the community level for internal administration. Though at first the nobility kept the right to vote and to hold office among themselves, eventually the commoners also began to demand and receive such rights. During this period, private land ownership was gradually established and accepted by the population. Thus, in addition to old cacicazgo lands, there were both communal village lands and privately owned tracts.

As time went on, the nobility and caciques gradually lost prestige and political power in direct proportion to the commoners' increasing assertion of rights for themselves and rejection of the authority of the native elite. And as their authority and influence declined, the nobility began to lose not only their hold upon political offices but also their lands, while commoners began to rise in wealth, land ownership, and political power. In fact, Taylor points out, caciques could best insure continuing protection of their lands and a favorable position in the community by avoiding the formal political hierarchy altogether and accepting a less formal role in influencing community affairs. Eventually control over land, resources, and people became associated not with the social class or the rights of the elite, but rather with private property ownership rights, wealth, and the new democratic form of political organization at the community level. Along with these changes came the gradual fragmentation of former lordships into smaller and smaller groupings, so that independent political units increased in number while they decreased in size.

The fact that water resources could become private property, combined with the fact that such resources might be used by a number of different individuals or communities which did not themsleves have a share in resource ownership, and with the further fact that different communities tended to be competitive, hostile, or uncooperative with one another, resulted in special problems of water allocation. To illustrate the form these problems took and the various solutions found, I quote at length from Taylor.

Prior to 1686, the canyon which supplied water to one of the Villa de Etla mills was sold by the cacique of Etla to a private party who first diverted the stream, completely shutting off Etla's water supply, and later agreed to "rent" water to Etla for its mill at the exorbitant rate of 6 pesos per day. The San Agustín mill was forced to cease operations in the mid 17th century when the owner of the Molinos de Lazo closed off the stream which supplied the mill. By 1686, an agreement was reached similar to that of the Etla case: San Agustín agreed to pay the Molinos de Lazo six pesos daily for four months of the year, and three pesos during the remaining eight months (Taylor, 1969:163).

Water for irrigating Indian wheat and corn fields in the Valley of Etla was equally uncertain. Towns located on the alluvial plain, far from the headwaters of the mountain streams were most likely to lose their water supply. Eight Etla towns have been identified as relying upon other communities for their source of water for irrigation. In several cases, their water was completely cut off; but in most, a rental or distribution agreement was worked out with the party closest to the source of the stream. The towns of Soledad Etla and San Juan Guelache obtained water for irrigation from tomas de agua belonging to the cacique of Etla to whom they paid an annual rent. Guelache's water supply was temporarily cut off in 1669 when the cacique rented the toma de agua to Juan de Santaella, owner of a nearby mill. Guelache found a satisfactory solution to its water problem in 1695 when it purchased Santaella's mills. Three towns, the Villa de Etla, Santo Domingo Etla, and San Agustín Etla, were obliged to pay as much as 6 pesos per day to Spanish and creole landowners who controlled the source of their water supply. Rental records for Santo Domingo Etla run from 1634 when the community rented from the Dominican monastery of Etla and the Molinos de Lazo, to 1799 when a renter of the Molinos de Lazo arbitrarily blocked off the stream from Santo Domingo's fields and refused to renew the rental. In another instance, water from a stream originating on the lands of the Molinos de Lazo was rented by San Agustín as early as the 1630's (Taylor, 1969:164-165).

When two or more Indian towns using the same source of irrigation disagreed over the right to its use, the royal guideline of "reparto de aguas por dias como le paresce" was applied. In the case of a disputed toma de agua belonging to Soledad Etla which diverted water from the Atoyac River to irrigate fields of Soledad, Nazareno, and Guadalupe Etla on the west bank of the river, the judge apportioned 14 days of irrigation to Soledad because it owned lands nearest to the toma, 9 days to Guadalupe, and 7 days to Nazareno. A 1631 dispute between Reyes and Nativitas Etla over use of the Río Magdalena was resolved in favor of Nativitas because this stream was the town's only source of water while Reyes was said to irrigate from other sources (Taylor, 1969:165).

Irrigation from the Río Salado was a mixed blessing to Guelavia since irrigation brought with it internal wranglings over the distribution of the water. In 1807 jealous citizens with small holdings shut off the canal which supplied water to other Indians, destroying their crops (Taylor, 1969:183).

The extremely bitter land disputes between Mitla and Hacienda de Xaaga began in the mid-16th century when an estancia which later became part of the hacienda contained one of Mitla's two principal sources of water (Taylor, 1969:184).

Where water resources were controlled through private property rights, the power of the upstream owner over the downstream user was not only asserted and used to the advantage of the upstream owner, but was not even subject to intervention or mediation on the part of the state. However, private upstream owners could only exploit their advantageous position in regard to downstream users by charging money for access to the resources; it does not appear that their position in regard to water allowed them to have any other sort of control over the downstream irrigators. When the upstream owner was a whole community and the downstream user was also a whole community, the state apparently could intervene and mediate. When it did intervene, it did not necessarily favor the upstream owner or distribute the water equitably, but apparently tended to reach a compromise which would suit the situation at hand. When the state did not intervene—that is, when there was no grounds for disputing ownership rights—downstream communities were liable to suffer considerable disadvantages. Unfortunately, we are given no details about either internal community water control or inter-community control, aside from the sale of water by individuals to communities and the distribution mediated by the state. If many of the arrangements found during this period carried over after independence from Spain was established, some additional information may be provided by descriptions from later times.

But before turning to the subsequent period, we might consider the relationship between the form of water control as described so far and the political and economic organization of the later colonial period. During this period in the valley, two important subcomplexes of organization emerged: one concerned private property ownership on a large scale, exploiting not only the natural resources but the needs of the peasant population, and the other concerned the internal arrangements of the so-called "closed corporate community." By this time, the colonial government was sanctioning both of these developments although it did not directly participate in the use of resources or the processes of production to control (much less increase) the effectiveness of their organization. When it came to the control of water, the colonial administration appeared to show interest only where the city of Oaxaca was concerned; it did not attempt to replace either private or community control over water. It intervened to keep the peace and to protect the welfare of its Spanish colonial subjects but not, apparently, to increase the productivity of the population at large. While initially it had directed great attention to the exploitation of certain mineral resources such as silver and gold and certain exotic raw materials such as cochineal dye, it never showed a parallel interest in agricultural resources and development.

With the help of the colonial administration (or perhaps, despite it), certain private landholders were able to amass great wealth. Some of these individuals were descendants of the old caciques, through whom they had inherited their land and fortunes. Others were Spaniards who had received or inherited grants from the crown. Still others were relative newcomers, entrepreneurs who had managed to purchase great estates. These private landowners had the initiative—and the power, whose source was their own private wealth—to undertake the construction of new water control devices such as dams, canals, and reservoirs, which they could use to increase their own private profits. The organization which determined who controlled the water in these cases was based upon a system of inequality in the distribution of wealth through private property ownership. The entrepreneurs who undertook the construction of hydraulic devices were able to acquire and direct the services of others simply by paying them; these individuals offered their services because they needed or wanted the money which the entrepreneur had and they lacked. Entrepreneurs were able to control the water and (to some degree) its use by others because they owned land and water upstream, and there was no power which had greater jurisdiction over their resources than they themselves.

Because they were wealthy and others were poor, these private landowners were able to command the full-time services of as many laborers as they could afford to pay. Peasant communities, on the other hand, having to rely upon the cooperative efforts of their own members, frequently could not mobilize enough funds or labor at one time to construct devices as elaborate as those built by private entrepreneurs. It appears that most of the innovations and many of the new constructions were the product of private efforts rather than public ones. Perhaps the one outstanding exception in this period was the church, which played a role similar in many ways to that of the private entrepreneurs. Unfortunately, I have not been able to discover anything about the role of the church in water control during colonial times in the valley.

POSTCOLONIAL, PREREVOLUTIONARY HISTORY

Though many changes in the formal political structure (particularly at the higher levels of government) were brought about when Mexico gained independence from Spain, the character of economic organization, the roles of the private entrepreneur and the peasant community, and the relationship between the peasant community and the state and national government were not radically altered until after the revolution and the reforms which followed in the 1920s and 1930s. During the 19th century—the period of prerevolutionary independence—the strength and domination of the wealthy private landowners grew, perhaps receiving extra impetus near the close of the era when the powers of the church were severely curtailed. Detailed published accounts of water control are difficult to find for this period, but it ended so recently that there are still some people who recall the situation before the modern reforms were carried out.

The region just south of Etla in the northern arm of the valley was one of the most, if not the most, productive areas of the valley. Most of the good arable land on the eastern side of the valley was owned by about half a dozen haciendas; the most wealthy and powerful of the landowners were two brothers, Don Francisco and Don Rafael de la Cojiga. The major water sources for canal irrigation originated at San Juan Bautista Guelache and San Agustín Etla. These sources were at that time owned by the two villages respectively, and the hacendados were required to pay the villages annual rental fees for the use of the water. My informants, older men from Guadalupe Etla, estimated the fees at about 200 pesos per year, which they considered to be an extremely high sum. (They told me that their wages for working for the haciendas ranged between 35 and 50 centavos per day.) When villagers sharecropped hacienda land, the hacendado paid for the water they used to irrigate the land. It is interesting that this case is a reversal of the situation described by Taylor for the colonial period, when certain hacendados sold water to villages. I gather that ownership and rental could work both ways in this and the previous period, the owner and renter being either hacendados or villages. As Taylor pointed out, villages in the valley of Oaxaca managed to hold on to a fair proportion of the land and fend off encroachments by the haciendas to a greater extent that elsewhere in Mexico.

In the late 1920s and early 1930s, Elsie Clews Parsons visited Mitla. She observed:

Even if Mitleyeños wanted to irrigate more extensively they would find that their water supply had been monopolized by Don Luís at the head of the valley, by Victor and Amador for fields and palenquera on the south side of town, and by Victor again and the Quero family through an aqueduct which takes off from the river below the bridge. The ranches of Don Pedrillo and of Tanivé are also irrigated, but I do not know whether they exhaust any of the water the town should claim. It is plain that irrigation is of foreign introduction; there is no communal regulation whatsoever, or any appreciation that water rights may be even more valuable than land rights. Comparing the dry and neglected fields of Mitla with the irrigated and well-tended fields of Tlacolula or Matatlán, Mitleyeños on the whole appear but indifferent farmers (Parsons, 1936:53).

Although new evidence has now made it clear that irrigation had been practiced in the region, if not in the village itself, long before the arrival of the Spaniards, Parsons' observation on the lack of communal regulation is provocative. In villages which owned water resources and villages which, as a unit, purchased water from hacendados, it is likely that there was some form of communal regulation; yet in Mitla, certain individuals appropriated water for themselves. It turns out that these individuals were wealthy landowners, not ordinary villagers, and were of Spanish ancestry. It seemes to me somewhat unlikely that the value of water rights was not appreciated by the villagers. However, the dominance of these landowners prevented the assertion by the community of its presumed rights. The fact that the individual named Victor in the quotation above was very active in community politics and had served an unprecedented two consecutive terms of office as presidente just about the time of Parsons' visits leads us to further suspect that the domination of these landowners played a major part in the lack of assertion of the community rights over water. (Don Luís was also active in state and national politics.)

As political leader of the community, Victor Olivera would certainly not be likely to influence the community in such a way as to limit his own personal power as a private landowner. If the fields of the villagers were dry and neglected, at least partial responsibility must rest with the wealthy landowners who could profit not only by monopolizing the water resources, but by the comparative poverty of the villagers which was partly the result of their water deprivation. For if the lands of the villagers were dry, and the villagers themselves were consequently poor, many of them would be forced to turn to the wealthy landowners for work. And if the villagers were poor while these landowners were wealthy, the landowners would have greater power, prestige, and influence, and thus greater capacity to control community affairs. Finally, their capacity to control community affairs could be used for their own protection and enrichment—as it would, for example, when they neglected to lead the community to assert its rights to control its water resources.

Though this case might not be typical, it illustrates a phenomenon characteristic of the period which followed independence from Spain. The colonial administration had attempted to limit the strength and independence of the colonists by interceding on the behalf of the Indian communities, defending them from encroachments on their rights by the colonists. Such restraints on the Spanish landowners were lifted when Mexico gained her independence. Of course, villagers might still litigate against the landowners, but it did not appear that the new national policy placed special emphasis upon protecting their rights in general or upon restraining the landowners (with the exception of a few short periods) as had been the case with the colonial administration.

The only reference I could find to the role of the church in water control after independence occurs in a case study of Soledad Etla (Iszaevich Fajerstein, 1969). In the 19th century the church controlled the distribution of water here, requiring, in return for access, that irrigators pay a regular fee and also the standard tithes. I presume, then, that the church could exert pressure upon villagers to pay tithes by the threat of denial of access to water. Apparently the church had control over the water because its source was on church-owned land. But unlike the private hacienda, the church could demand more than just payment for the use of water from the downstream irrigators. Although it could use other sanctions to enforce payment of tithes, withholding of water was one additional alternative which was made available if it owned upstream water resources. Unfortunately, I have so little information about church-controlled water distribution that further comments or conclusions would be unjustified. However, since this case suggests that the role of the church in relation to the peasant community in terms of water control was different from the relationship between the community and the hacienda or the state government, the difference might bear further looking into when more information is available.

To continue with the Soledad case, when the power of the church was overthrown, the properties of the church passed into the hands of the haciendados. The water which it formerly controlled was shared by a number of haciendas and peasant communities. One source was a canal from San Andrés Zautla, which passed through the hacienda of Catano, the villages of Nazareno and Soledad, and the hacienda of Guadalupe before emptying into the Atoyac. Another was an enormous tank (reservoir), reported to be several hectares in size, situated on the hacienda of Alemán, which also was filled by water from the Río Zautla. Unfortunately, no details were given about how this water was allocated or controlled, but it appears that control was in the hands of the hacendados, not the villages.

SINCE THE REVOLUTION

When the land of Hacienda de Alemán was redistributed about 1921, the hacienda administrator had the tank destroyed. It was filled in and is now used as ordinary cultivated land. Since it was never reconstructed or replaced, the land which was once irrigated in this area no longer gets water.

As an interesting aside, I might note here that the large stone dam and canals built by Victor Olivera on his land to irrigate his extensive properties to the west of the town of Mitla were also abandoned after the redistribution of hacienda lands. Whether this was because the water resources themselves had diminished so greatly that the water works could not be used or for some other reasons, I never found out. Victor Olivera's grandson—and namesake—still lives in Mitla and is comparatively well-to-do and influential in local politics. In fact, in 1969 he was elected presidente of Mitla; but his position is not nearly as powerful as that of his grandfather, years ago. It may be that a change in the policy of the community concerning water rights, along with the redistribution of land and restraints on the power of the former wealthy landowning families, had something to do with the abandonment of the dam. The lands in this area which were once the property of the Olivera family now look just like the rest—dry and neglected.

I encountered numerous abandoned ruins of hydraulic constructions in other parts of the valley, mostly small dams and mills which had been built, and were once owned and operated, by hacendados and other private entrepreneurs. Villagers often accounted for this abandonment in terms of the decrease in the water supply. It is true that such a decrease existed, but it seems curious that the decrease occurred so suddenly and simultaneously with the evacuation of the hacendados. The revolution caused the hacendados to leave, or at least abandon their properties, but it did not cause the water supply to run out. Rather, it seems that the reorganization of control and rights to land and water may have been accompanied by a decrease in the effectiveness of their use for productive purposes. This decrease may have been only temporary, and is certainly now being counteracted by a further reorganization of control, in which the state is replacing the community, just as the community earlier replaced the hacienda. But while these shifts were taking place, there really has been a gradual decrease in the water supply. Since the changes in technology and control of hydraulic works have not been correlated in a one-to-one relationship with the decrease in supply (nor, apparently, are they in direct response to the decrease), it has been difficult to compare and evaluate the effectiveness of each type of control organization. I have only been able to do so on a very impressionistic and speculative basis, with considerable reservations. But I will return to this point in a later chapter.

To return once more to the Soledad Etla case, it seems that when the hacendados departed from the scene, the villages themselves were left to make arrangements for the distribution of the remaining water resource, namely the canal from Zautla. Some of the hacienda lands which were redistributed and converted into ejidos were to be shared between the villages of Soledad and Nazareno, which also shared the water which flowed in the canal. At first, the two villages signed an agreement by which each of them would receive water from the canal for 15 days of every month, one alternating with the other. But when the lands were actually redistributed and Nazareno got only one-fifth as much of it as Soledad, Nazareno felt that it had been treated unfairly. Therefore Nazareno, being the upstream member of the two villages, prevented the water in the canal from flowing toward Soledad, but offered to allow it to flow once again if Soledad would give some of the redistributed land back to Nazareno. The two villages argued for some time; but their arguments ended abruptly when Zautla, still further upstream, decided to use all the water in the canal for itself. At that point, neither Nazareno nor Soledad had access to any water from the canal at all. By 1942, because of the decrease in supply, water had stopped flowing in the canal altogether.

This was the only case I found in which two separate communities attempted to share water on an equal basis, without dominance of one community or state intervention. The attempt failed immediately when Nazareno tried to use its upstream position to advantage to force Soledad to give it some land. Land shortage is a considerable problem in this area; in fact, throughout the recorded history of the valley, competition for land has been the major source of conflict between communities. Communities generally have resorted to either litigation or violence to settle such conflicts. But this was a case in which one of the communities had a strong bargaining position, due to its advantageous location with regard to a water source. The attempt by a community to use this sort of advantage to gain benefits for itself at the expense of a downstream community has been documented for other societies. But the claims of the upstream communities must be justified in terms of the rules of the society. In this case, Nazareno could justify its claim because the land in question had been redistributed somewhat arbitrarily—not according to the rules as Nazareno understood them. In other words, the basis for Nazareno's claim had nothing to do with its position on the water course; this was an extraneous factor. On the other hand, there were no rules which required that Nazareno, or any upstream community, share water equitably with a downstream community. Since there was no basis—legal, moral, or practical—for the sharing of water between the two communities, their initial agreement was on shaky grounds to begin with. Soledad, then, had no justification at all for its demands for an equitable share of the water. The attempt by Nazareno to use its advantage in this conflict was never brought to a satisfactory conclusion because its bargaining position disappeared when the water source disappeared. Nazareno had no more claim on the water that Zautla took than Soledad had on the water that Nazareno took. By that time, the water shortage had become more pressing than the land shortage—so even Zautla had no bargaining position.

Soledad today is one of the wealthiest, most progressive, and most productive villages in the entire Valley of Oaxaca. Its land is, and always has been, among the most fertile on the valley floor. And yet, its inhabitants say that they are in need—specifically of water. If there had been enough water in the Río Zautla, and if it had been allowed to flow to Soledad, Soledad farmers would, in effect, lack for nothing. I emphasize this point because it has bearing on our understanding of the relationships between the environmental zones, the villages situated in these different zones, and perhaps the history of their relationships. In the Etla arm, even the wealthiest, most productive, best situated villages on the valley floor could use, even consider themselves to need, water from piedmont tributary streams. As long as such water could be made available, and as long as there were other villages situated upstream, the welfare of downstream villages depended upon the cooperation of the upstream villages to allow them access to this water. We may speculate, then, that throughout the history of canal irrigation in the valley, as long as there was sufficient water in the streams, the relationship between upstream and downstream communities included some provisions for achieving cooperation between them over the use of water, even when the downstream communities were situated on the valley floor.

I have recounted the story of the conflict between Nazareno and Soledad in this chapter, rather than in the section on conflict in Chapter II, because direct arrangements between villages over the allotment of water are becoming a thing of the past. The current laws regarding government policy on water control and the hydraulic development programs were only initiated in the 1930s and did not begin to really take effect in Oaxaca until nearly three decades later. If water had continued to flow from Zautla to Soledad and Nazareno, the government would probably by now have intervened, and would have established itself as the sole authority over intercommunity allocation. While the prerevolutionary administration was content to completely ignore water control in this area, the current administration is deeply concerned and highly committed to playing an active, leading role in the development in hydraulic technology and reorganization of control. As a result of its efforts, the administration hopes to have an increased productivity and increased effectiveness of land and water use on the one hand, and direct integration of control organization at the community level with that of the state on the other hand.

SUMMARY AND CONCLUSIONS

We do not know if water control was an important issue in village-state relations before the conquest. As I have suggested, it might have been so in earlier times, perhaps before the post-Classic reorganization of the society. But during the period of recorded history in the valley, we have seen that the role of water control in politics and in social and economic change has varied considerably. Its relative importance at any one time to any one element of organization has depended upon the nature of the social organization, the manner in which power and property were distributed among the population, and the role of the state government in relation to local communities, individual activity, and economic development. The role of water control, then, has varied even when the resources have remained more or less the same, their importance for production has remained the same, the general scale of hydraulic devices has remained the same, and the general techniques of irrigation have remained the same. In fact, in one sense even the nature of social and political organization has varied little since the time of the conquest; there has always been a centralized state in this area, and the peasant population has been organized in the same sort of closed corporate communities. There was no major transition such as would occur in the case of a transformation from tribalism to statehood. But slight variations, particularly the ones that marked the difference between the prerevolutionary and postrevolutionary periods, had important consequences for the role of water control in social change and economic development. Thus, we cannot judge the importance of the historical role of canal irrigation only on the basis of its scale or changes in its form. Nor can we assume that because the resources were small and dispersed, because water was scarce, and because the techniques and devices of irrigation were simple, the relationship between the state and water control took one particular form or another. The type of resources and small scale irrigation technology available in the Valley of Oaxaca today may become just as important to the central government as large-scale water resources and technology were elsewhere. This is not to say that all the alternative types of organization of water control are equal, that the selection of one over another has nothing to do with the technology or scale of waterworks themselves. Some types of organization have greater potential, can use the resources more effectively for production, than others. The hacendado organization, for example, was more effective than the village organization; but effectiveness in the use of water resources is not the sole factor in selection, nor necessarily the predominant one at any one time. At present, it appears that this factor is predominant; it seems likely that this explains why the state is replacing the community in the control of water. And this replacement has other consequences for social change at both the village and the state levels of the society. In the colonial period, both the state and water control had different roles. During the 2,000 years before the conquest, their roles might have been different in still other ways.

VI

OAXACAN IRRIGATION COMPARED WITH OTHER REGIONS

INTRODUCTION

The role of water control in the evolution and structure of social organization became a central and controversial issue in anthropological theory when, in 1938, Karl Wittfogel published his theory of oriental society. Four significant points he emphasizes in his theory are:

1) Water, as an agricultural resource, has certain properties which make special demands upon the social organization of the people who use it. Wittfogel stressed the factor of cooperative labor in construction and maintenance of waterworks, which requires coercive power to command cooperation and administrative bureaucracy to direct it.

2) Water-control institutions may have far-reaching consequences or effects upon other institutions of the society such as property laws, science, religion, politics, and class structure.

3) The effects of water-control systems on other institutions vary with the scale and type of facilities and with environment.

4) A certain type of society can be explained or accounted for in terms of its special adaptation to irrigation and water control (Wittfogel referred specifically to political despotism in the Orient.)

It seems to me that while the theory of oriental despotism started out as a way of accounting for institutionalized despotism (particularly in the Far East), it soon became something else as other anthropologists began using it, criticizing it, or applying it broadly. First of all, it was interpreted as a kind of environmental-technological determinism. That is, it was interpreted to mean that given the use of water for irrigation, certain forms of social organization were bound to follow—namely centralization of control and coercion of communal labor. And to extend this logic further, centralization and coercion always had their source or origin in water control.

Second, centralization and coercion and other institutions such as writing, science, bureaucracy, class structure, and the like were connected to, and even considered consequences of, large-scale water control, and at the same time these were characteristics of statehood and civilization. Consequently, the theory was interpreted to mean that the two—large-scale water control and statehood (civilization)—were causally connected. That is, it was theorized that the origin of early states (civilizations) lay in the demands made by water control upon the society; given large-scale water control, statehood (civilization) would follow.

In 1955 Julian Steward called a conference on the subject of the origins of states. Contributions were in the form of archaeological descriptions of all the major early civilizations known in the world; the purpose was to compare them and find general similarities. In all cases (with the possible exception of Mesoamerica), the existence of waterworks from early periods in the development of these civilizations was documented. Even in Mesoamerica they were thought likely to have existed, though documentation was yet to come. Putting together these facts, Steward found considerable support in all cases but one (Mesoamerica) for the broader interpretation of Wittfogel's theory.

But the controversy had just begun. Archaeologists and ethnologists alike brought forth evidence and arguments to controvert the theory as they understood it. By this time, however, since many of Wittfogel's arguments were apparently misinterpreted, and since the controversy had taken on its own momentum, the actual statements he had made earlier had become more or less irrelevant. We may thus turn away from Wittfogel's problems and interests to the actual ones which emerged in the controversy which followed. This controversy centered on the two points mentioned above: whether or not social organization necessarily had to be adapted in a certain way to water control, and whether or not irrigation—or large-scale irrigation—was the primary cause of the origin and development of civilizations and states.

In reference to the second point, the problem of what to do with Mesoamerica was one area of controversy. Many archaeologists accepted the negative evidence and presumed that the "hydraulic theory" was so undermined by this exception that it could not be a general law. If Mesoamerica could develop a civilization without irrigation, there must be other causal factors, and the same causal factors could well have been operating in other areas. So irrigation was not necessarily the primary cause, even in those areas which did have irrigation.

Palerm, on the other hand, was one of those who believed that although there was no direct evidence of irrigation in Mesoamerica, the importance of water control was already sufficiently proven to support the hydraulic theory even there (Palerm, 1955); and that in any case, negative evidence is inconclusive and so cannot be used to controvert the theory. His evidence for the importance of water control was drawn from highland Mesoamerica. There remained the problem of whether civilization began there or in the lowlands and the further problem of how the two were connected. Later excavations by MacNeish (Brunet, 1967) Woodbury (1966), Neely (1967), and Fowler (1969) supported Palerm's contention that irrigation works existed in the early periods, but the highlands/lowlands controversy has not yet been resolved. Further, there remained the question of scale; so far it seems clear that the Mesoamerican waterworks did not approach the scale of those of China, the Near East, India (Dales, 1962), or Peru.

Other problems of archaeological nature were also brought up. Some involved the relative dating of waterworks of large scale and evidence of civilization or statehood. Adams (1966), for example, suggests from his evidence that small-scale works existed in Mesopotamia long before statehood or civilization, while large-scale works were not constructed until considerably later. Adams and others also argue logically against the hydraulic theory, pointing out that single and simple causes are not enough to account for civilization, and emphasizing other factors like trade and warfare as equally (or more) important influences.

Evidence from areas outside the great early civilizations was also brought to bear upon the controversy. Relatively large-scale waterworks existed in some areas, such as the American Southwest among the Hohokam (Woodbury, 1961), where there was no evidence of statehood or despotism. And in addition to Mesoamerica, there are other areas where civilization and statehood arose—albeit later and perhaps influenced by earlier civilizations—in the absence of large-scale waterworks, in Africa and Europe for example.

In addition to archaeological evidence, but not always apart from the archaeological controversy, there was ethnographic evidence. Millon, one of the outstanding figures in the controversy, attacked the generalizations of the hydraulic theory through a comparison of seven different societies in which irrigation was used (Millon, Hall, and Diaz, 1962). In the conclusions they emphasized the diversity among the societies in their responses to water control and the element of conflict as a consequence of irrigation, which was frequently ignored by previous authors. Leach, using Ceylon for his illustrations, pointed out alternatives in social structure for building waterworks and allocating water (Leach, 1959; 1961).

The controversy and the evidence brought to bear upon it have yielded several important points. First, we have learned that societies which use irrigation vary widely in complexity and form of social organization, and that they vary just as widely in the manner in which they handle water control. Second, it is also apparent that water control may present some special problems to a society, depending on the nature and form of the resource and technology of irrigation, which must be dealt with by the institutions at hand. Whether or not water becomes an important or decisive factor in these institutions depends very much on the social structure itself. The problems of water control may indeed account for a great deal of what goes on. Whether (and to what extent) water control influences the social organization must be determined for each case separately. Third, as we might have expected, along with the wide diversity there are certain similarities among systems of water control in different societies. Further examination of these similarities might be useful in telling us more about the nature of water control in particular societies, and about the societies themselves.

It is not the intent of this monograph to make such a wide comparison. Most of the literature on the subject does not lend itself easily to comparison, and a brief comparison would demand that I take each example out of the larger context in which it was found, so that their presentation would be shallow and probably misleading. On the other hand, I believe it would be valuable and interesting to show how Oaxacan irrigation systems compare with a few others, and to see how comparison with others can shed light on the historical changes which possibly occurred in Oaxaca. Therefore, I have chosen only a few examples from the vast literature in order to bring out specific points. (Perhaps most obvious is the omission of examples from the Near East. After some consideration, I decided that the context there was so different that it would not be very helpful to bring them into the comparison.)

The topics I have selected for cross-cultural comparison are similarly limited. Only six are discussed here: social change, variation according to resource type, cooperative labor, water distribution, disputes, and village-state relations.

Though many other aspects of water control and social organization could perhaps have been discussed, these seemed to have the most direct bearing upon the issues raised in this study.

SOCIAL CHANGE

Hackenberg (1962) provides an example of social change associated with irrigation which suggests some possible, though not necessary, consequences of the use of a particular kind of water source. The example comes from his case study of the Pima and Papago Indians of the southwestern United States. The point he makes is that starting from the same social origins, and given the same stimulus to change, the Pima and Papago diverged in social structure. The one major difference between their situations was that the former had a water source which could be shared among different communities, while the latter had multiple, separate water sources among the communities. The implication is that the difference in water supply forms was responsible for the divergence in social structure, and that the specific characteristics of the Pima structure (including a supravillage government, centralization of control, and even social differentiation) were consequences of their having had a multivillage water source.

The canal irrigation water sources in the Valley of Oaxaca could be looked at in two ways. On the one hand they are multiple and separate, but on the other hand, a few of the sources are shared by a number of villages, which would perhaps make them parallel to the Pima case. We do not know how water-sharing villages were integrated internally or with other groups of villages in the early periods of cultural development of the valley. It is clear from contemporary Oaxaca that the simple fact that two or more villages may share water does not mean that they will cooperate on sharing or any other matter. If they did cooperate, perhaps at some other period of time, then their cooperation might have led—as in the Pima case—to new forms of social organization. On the other hand, we see no archaeological evidence that there has ever been a valley-wide cooperative effort linked to water control. Valley-wide cooperation, which might have existed in the preconquest period and almost certainly existed in the Classic could not have been the result of valley-wide water sharing; the sources are too small. Moreover, the instability of valley-wide integration, as indicated by the fragmentation of village groupings like the municipio or the former cacicazgo, and the constant warfare of the post-Classic period, might be attributable in part to the lack of a common resource. Perhaps a comparison with the Valley of Teotihuacán during similar time periods would be interesting, for there a large number of villages are involved in sharing the single main water source. Millon et al. observed a great deal of conflict and competition in contemporary times; but during the Classic, another form of integration may have existed, at least partially helped along by the cooperative efforts of using one water resource. In any case, the evidence from Oaxaca suggests that the sharing of a single water source does not inevitably lead to cooperation and the formation of supracommunity control systems, nor need such supracommunity systems of integration be linked directly to shared water resources.

VARIATION ACCORDING TO RESOURCE TYPE

The Pima-Papago case illustrates another point: different types of water resources may be accorded different responses in a single society (or, as in this case, in two societies with originally similar structures). A second illustration is provided by Sahlins (1962) in his study of Moala in Fiji. He points out (1962:286) that the treatment of allocation rights to water from "stream" sources is different from that of rights to "spring" sources. The former is associated with the hierarchical seniority structure of the kinship organization, while the latter is quite informal, associated with no such hierarchical arrangement. He relates this difference to differences in the nature of the sources and their use.

A third illustration comes from Japan, from a study by Beardsley, Hall, and Ward:

The resources for irrigation include small ponds owned and managed by individuals, ponds managed by communities, canals owned and managed by irrigation cooperatives, and rivers in the public domain (1959:128).

These illustrations bring out two points. First, the fact that the social form of response to water control problems varies even within a society due to variations in the nature or size of the source. This suggests that, to at least some degree, the problems are determined by the nature of the source; hence the solutions are indirectly affected by the nature of the source. In Oaxaca there are also different sorts of water sources, aside from the streams used for canal irrigation; there is well irrigation, using the subsurface water table, and floodwater irrigation, using rainfall run-off, each of which has a different sort of social organization from that of canal irrigation management. The second point brought out is that control over water within or between communities entails at least the possibility of inequitable distribution from a single source. Certain types of sources do not lend themselves to this inequity, while others do, and it is to these sources that we should look for evidence of inequality. In Oaxaca we have also found that social control by the community is applied only to the type of source that implies differential access, not to other types of resources such as the subsurface water table (Flannery, et al., 1967:453).

COOPERATIVE LABOR

The next matter I will consider is variety in cooperative labor for maintenance of waterworks. In Oaxaca, as we have seen, this cooperation is generally carried out through the institution of tequio, which is also used for cooperative labor in other situations.

In the Japanese case mentioned above, cooperative efforts on the part of the whole community were required to drain and clean ponds every three or four years. This became a festive occasion for the entire neighborhood. Otherwise, minor maintenance operations were carried out by individuals (and by some persons who were paid a token fee for their work from village taxes).

Somewhat more complex organization was described for northern Thailand (de Young, 1966):

> In the north the need to maintain the elaborate irrigation systems has resulted in a rather formally organized communal task: villages in a given area are assigned responsibility for their part of the feeder canals and the smaller ditches in their section; in addition, each village must from time to time send a labor force to work on the main irrigation system. In San Pang and two neighboring villages—a 'section' that embraces some 2,000 *rai* (800 acres) of paddy fields—two chiefs are elected to supervise the irrigation work of the section; it is the duty of these chiefs to see that the water is kept flowing and is properly regulated at the main feeder branches, and they have the authority to order communal labor for any necessary repairs. During the growing season this involves a considerable amount of work, for the chiefs must continually inspect the many branches as well as the main irrigation ditch; therefore, the villages pay them a fixed amount of rice for their work (de Young, 1966:80).

Despite differences in detail, northern Thailand, Japan, and Oaxaca share a basic similarity in the manner in which cooperative labor is obtained for work on irrigation facilities. This similarity has to do with the scale, formality, and relative degree of coercion of cooperative labor in these societies. All three societies have achieved the level of statehood, though cooperative labor is instituted and organized on the local community level, without the intervention of higher state officials. But the fact that such a degree of coercion—or cooperation—is achieved without direct action on the part of the higher authorities does not mean that the larger structure is irrelevant to the ability of the peasant communities to organize themselves. The importance of the larger structure can be more easily seen when we compare cooperative efforts in these societies with similar efforts in less highly advanced societies.

Moala lies somewhere between chiefdom and inclusion in a state. Since European contact, it has been somewhat integrated into a larger state system, but it has retained to a considerable degree the basic structure of its indigenous chiefly organization. The power of the "government chief" is, as the name implies, backed by the government, whose extra support has probably altered the relationship between chief and subject. In Moala, collective labor is a generalized institution (somewhat like tequio) applied to many projects aside from irrigation such as clearing new plots, building houses, and so forth; these collective activities are supervised by the government chief. In only one village was it stated that collective labor was ever called out for canal building and maintenance; at the time of the study, only 15 men were available to do the work. This labor was applied to a source of the stream variety; the spring variety did not require collective labor for maintenance. Apparently, however, the control of the chief over collective labor as applied to canal or dam maintenance is inadequate to maintain as many dams as would be possible under other circumstances.

> While irrigation has declined in importance throughout the island in recent years, it does not appear that the theoretical potential of this productive mode was ever fulfilled. With suitable technology...and an appropriate social organization, many of the valleys evidently would have been more effectively exploited (Sahlins, 1962:55).

Sahlins cites as an example one case where a part of the valley remains uncultivated because it is not irrigated; it cannot be irrigated because of failure in repeated attempts to maintain a dam of only about 10 feet in width. It is suggested that the ability of this society to coerce collective labor for such work is limited by its social organization, and that this limitation results in a limitation on the effectiveness of water use.

Aboriginal Hawaii, perhaps even more than Moala, was intermediate between the tribal and state-like organization; but in Hawaii the approach of the organization to statehood was the result of internal development, rather than European contact as in Moala. In Hawaii, communal labor was also a regular, generalized institution, but with certain modifications with regard to water:

> The quantity of water, measured by the time permitted for flooding, was proportional to the time spent by the cultivator and his family in building and maintaining the ditch and dam furnishing the water. In other words, water rights were regulated not by the area of land cultivated but by the amount of work done to promote

and maintain the water supply. The labor expended on the ditches by a planter was of course governed by the amount of land he wanted to irrigate. The building and maintenance of dams and ditches and the periodic cleaning of the ditches to keep the flow unobstructed, were communal activities directed by the land supervisors (Handy, 1940:36).

This situation is reminiscent of the arrangement used in certain villages in Oaxaca by which "voluntary" contributions are made by irrigators to the village treasury in proportion to the amount of water desired by the contributors. In the Hawaiian case the coercion to labor is derived from the need of the irrigator for water, not from direct application of force, though the presence of some authority capable of denying access to those who refuse to cooperate can be assumed.

But there is another characteristic associated with cooperative labor in Hawaii which suggests even more "statelike" organization:

The high chiefs and local leaders of intermediate status initiated large enterprises such as ditch construction and repair, and cleaning of ditches....The local stewards, as supervisors of construction and maintenance of irrigation works, formed a 'primitive bureaucracy' (Sahlins, 1958:16).

The contrast between Moala and Hawaii brings out more clearly two points made above. First, the organization of the local community, the level at which cooperative effort is carried out, reflects higher level organization. Moala is organized on a more tribal basis than Hawaii; it has not really incorporated the structure of the state, whose effect is apparently still peripheral. Moalans are not "peasants." Hawaii approaches statehood much more closely, and this more advanced structure is reflected throughout, on the local as well as the regional level. The organization of labor here resembles that of peasants in Oaxaca, Japan, and northern Thailand more closely than does that of Moala. Second, the ability of the society to obtain cooperative efforts is greater in societies with a state-like structure than in societies with tribal structures. Hawaii was able to utilize its water resources more effectively than Moala because it was able to organize cooperative labor more effectively. In neither case was it a matter of applied force, and in neither case did the highest levels of government intervene.

It was difficult to find comparable descriptions of cooperative labor on irrigation facilities in more primitive societies. However, my final example, the Kalinga, a well-known case of extensive and elaborate irrigation in a Philippine Island tribal society, provides a good illustration (Barton, 1949).

Neighbors and relatives pool their labor to build irrigation ditches, but it appears that there is no name for such an association of owners (Barton, 1949:103).

Sometimes a man is granted permission simply in order that the owners may have another helper in cleaning the canal or on his promise, with his relatives, to clean the canal once or twice (Barton, 1949:104-105).

Here cooperative efforts are quite limited. There is no resort to the community for a cooperative labor pool, and cooperation even among individuals is often difficult to achieve. Barton cites a legal case in which a man was physically assaulted by another who shared the same canal because he did not contribute adequately (in his attacker's opinion) to the maintenance of the canal.

In peasant or near-peasant societies, the village was the normal unit in which cooperative labor was called out to work on maintenance. In tribal societies, it was more often an individual matter or a cooperative effort by the family and friends of users of the same canal; those whose personal interests were at stake. The scale of cooperative efforts and the degree to which they could be enforced differed and reflected upon the scale of the works themselves. Where cooperation was weakly enforced, considerable quantities of land sometimes went uncultivated and unirrigated, not for lack of water, but for lack of labor to maintain waterworks.

WATER DISTRIBUTION

The next, and perhaps most interesting, subject for comparison is the organization of water distribution. It was on this topic that I found the widest range of variation among different societies. The basic problem in allocation has to do with the nature of the flowing resource: downstream irrigators cannot use the resource when upstream irrigators are using it. The solution to this problem must provide rules or ways of making decisions about who takes the water first, how irrigators are to alternate or take turns, and the length of a turn. In some societies, the advantage of the upstream irrigator is recognized and incorporated into the system. In others, it is denied and obviated by the rules of allocation. In Oaxaca the latter was true, but the manner in which this was done was only one of a large variety of possible ways to achieve the same end. I have chosen only six examples out of the many available in the literature to illustrate the extent of variation.

The Kalinga

The population is distributed in numerous small villages and hamlets. Water sources are small streams, which may be used by more than one village, or one village may have more than one stream. In addition to irrigated land, there is hill land which is cultivated by slash-and-burn techniques and used only a few years at a time. Land is privately owned by individuals and may be bought and sold. There are no social classes, no chiefs, no kings or ranked kin groups. A group of influential men persuade, advise, and help to make peace among villagers, but they are not elected or formally invested with any power. Conflicts between villages, as between individuals, are frequently settled by violence. The most important relationships in the society are those of kinship. Water rights in the society are organized as follows (Barton, 1949):

> He who builds the first rice field irrigated by a spring owns the spring, whether it gurgle up inside the field or not. A man who builds a field just below his must pay him for the water that passes from his field, the usual price being one pig, although it might be that he would not exact this payment if the second builder was a kinsman...In like manner, the second builder might demand from a third the payment of a small pig or chicken. Having received this payment, or having waived it by silence, or owner may divert the water from his field to another field; for example, he must not pipe it away in a conduit, but must permit it to flow its natural course....
>
> The lands of the owners along an irrigation canal are divided into groupings...The grouping is such that the fields in each group or section lie in an ascending-descending relationship. Each group receives water in proportion to its area. [They take turns, each getting water for a part or more of a 24-hour day.] This arrangement is to protect the lower fields, for if the ditch were allowed to run into all the fields, the water would be insufficient to reach the lower fields....
>
> Now, suppose an outsider wants to build a field and draw water from the canal. He may not build a field on the same level as that of any owner. He may build a field below their lowest fields if he secures permission. And he will probably secure that permission in this way: he will give a bribe to the most influential of the canal owners, and when this man puts in a word for him with the other owners, 'everybody will follow— what else can they do?'....
>
> An owner of the canal is in the same position as an outsider when it comes to building a new field on land acquired after beginning the project. A canal owner may make fields only on land owned and declared before the building of the canal began....
>
> Flowage rights exist among Kalinga users of water. The first users of water from a stream have the right to prohibit any diversion of water upstream from them. Enforcement within the bounds of a single town is accomplished without trouble. It is said that much of the land above the town of Lubwagan could be irrigated without endangering, except in periods of drought, the supply to present fields lower down, but that the owners of these fields prohibit more fields. Flowage rights often cause great troubles and perpetual feuds between towns (Barton, 1949:103-05).

Sonjo

In this east African tribal society, "Control of water for irrigation is vested in a council of village elders...who hold their positions as members by hereditary right" (Gray, 1963). These individuals are responsible for planning and directing the whole irrigation system of the entire community. They have special inherited rights to water, which they are privileged to take first, when they wish, and as much as they wish. The other members of the community fall into various categories with lesser rights to use water. Those who have not inherited water rights by patrilineal primogeniture must be satisfied to take what is left when the "officials" of the council of elders have finished. To obtain water, either they must ask permission of a close relative who has such rights, or obtain permission by paying council members for the water. But those members of the council of elders who have rights and authority do not have it as individuals; they have it only as a corporate group.

Moala

Here irrigated land and irrigation facilities are the private property of named kin groups and not part of the public domain. Thus the village chief, in his chiefly capacity, does not have control over the distribution of water or disputes concerning water; this was the responsibility of the kin groups.

Some villages have multiple water resources, and many or all of the kin groups residing in them own irrigable land. In others, such as Nuku, there is only one major water source, and only one kin group holds the title. They are called the "owners of the water."

The ranking of a family in this society finds expression in its relative physical position in the irrigation complex:

> In the Nuku stream complex a number of local kin groups (*tokatoka*) are represented, and each is located in a separate portion of the system, each controlling a given diversion point. In traditional custom, each family, furthermore, has a definite position within its local kin group area. The familial disposition is determined by its seniority, with the higher ranking house closer to the main water source and diversion point. Continuity of this social organization of use would be effected by the older son planting with or near his father and succeeding the latter, while younger sons are allotted plots further below the source (Sahlins, 1962:133).

The "owners of the water" themselves "occupy the uppermost plots and thereby control the key diversion." However, they do not try to gain any special advantage from their position as titled owners or from their upstream position. Rather,

> The 'owners of the water' will freely allow access to a major irrigation complex to all other kin groups of its home community and also to people of related groups of nearby villages...Relatives of the 'owners of the water' thus obtain indefinitely extended usufructory privileges (Sahlins, 1962:283).

In villages with only one major irrigation source, the owners of the water who controlled allocation from the highest diversion point were responsible for "maintaining equitable flow for the groups below" and for settling disputes over water from their source. But their control extended only to the upper most diversion point and not to the lower diversion points controlled by other kin groups.

Hawaii

This example provides a very clear illustration of the extent to which the organization of distribution is incorporated into the larger social structure. As in Oaxaca and among the Sonjo, but unlike the Kalinga or Moalans, physical position on the canals was apparently quite irrelevant to control over distribution. However, social status, as in the Sonjo case, was directly connected to the degree of control. Unlike the Sonjo who had only two levels of status, "elders" and others, the Hawaiians had several levels, and the degree of control was related to the relative status of the controller. Hawaii does resemble the Kalinga case, to a limited extent, in that access to water was associated with labor contributions to maintenance. However, in Hawaii this association was much more formal and explicit and involved coercion through the threat of deprivation.

> The system of access to water used in irrigation was the same as that of access to land. The high chiefs and the local stewards supervised the allocation. The water allocated was proportional to the amount of labor supplied by any land manager in constructing the ditch, and to the acreage planted. Thus, the amount of water controlled by status levels was proportional to the amount of land controlled, and to the corresponding number of subordinate relatives. During the dry seasons, the high chiefs and men of local importance could adjust prearranged allotments. Any commoner who refused to contribute labor to the maintenance of ditches and dams could be deprived of water rights or lands (Sahlins, 1958:15).

Pul Eliya

This is a small peasant community in Ceylon (Leach, 1961). Since ancient times, there have been two types of irrigation works, small village tanks associated with individual communities and central reservoirs and feeder canals associated with larger regions. The central government now, as formerly, controls the larger variety of irrigation works, while the local community controls the smaller village tanks—a situation similar to Oaxaca. Pul Eliya has only a village tank; it is not connected with any large regional irrigation works, nor has it ever been.

Even so, the central government has had considerable effect upon local water-control organization. Although the regulation of water use is an internal village matter in Pul Eliya, the central government can determine how much land is to be irrigated by placing an upper limit on this amount. It can also control how much is irrigated by restricting the amount of nonirrigated land that can be cultivated by slash-and-burn techniques.

In Pul Eliya today there are two irrigated areas, an "Old Field" and a "New Field," the latter having recently been opened up for cultivation due to government intervention. There are distinct differences between the central systems of the Old Field and the New Field. The organization of control in the Old Field is so complex that it would be difficult to explain in brief, but it was summarized by Leach as follows:

In the Old Field, land is subdivided so as to minimize, as far as possible, the consequences of unavoidable inequalities in the distribution of water (Leach, 1961:157).

The intricate system for the allocation of water to the Old Field is strongly traditionalized and is not tampered with; the complexity of the allocation system is such as to make it almost impossible to change it anyway (Leach, 1961:157).

...[it is] effectively decentralized, and no single individual or group of individuals exercised any real authority over its operation... (Leach, 1961:64).

Each landholder in the Old Field owned rights to certain lengths of irrigation ditches and water; each owner maintained that part of the ditch which passed through his plot. But in the New Field, a new situation arose:

To feed these new lands, several new main irrigation ditches have had to be constructed, but these ditches are private property. They belong to those particular individuals whose land the channel serves. These private rights in irrigation ditches are jealously guarded and are becoming of very special significance in the developing policy of the village (Leach, 1961:95).

When the New Field was opened up, authority over the land and water was delegated to the "irrigation headman," who is, "in theory, elected by the villagers themselves" (Leach, 1961:28). The ultimate result of the opening of these new lands to which the old rules did not apply was to enable the "irrigation headman" to provide "himself and his friends with a dominating economic position in the village."

The old system was constructed so as to prevent any individual's gaining either special advantage from physical location or control over the whole irrigation network. But once the restraints of that system were lifted, differential control and access immediately appeared. The old system was embedded in the complex social organization of the community; the new system was initiated by outside intervention and ran counter to the old system in many ways. The consequences of the change in water control had an impact beyond irrigation practices themselves. They influenced the whole economic organization of the community.

The potential for change in water control at the village level through government interference has been discussed for Oaxaca; this case provides perhaps a more radical example. I shall return to this point below. It is interesting to note here that although this case illustrates the fact that social structure may counter the potential for differential control inherent in canal irrigation by providing restraints of its own, it also shows that once these restraints are lifted, that potential may be rapidly realized.

Bali

I mention this last example mainly to show that in a peasant society the village is not necessarily the only kind of minimal unit for local water control. In Bali, irrigated land is subdivided into a large number of irrigation cooperatives; each controls water from a single source with a single dam and canal (Geertz, 1959). Each is an independent corporate group, self-regulating, with its own rules and purposes. It may include just a few individuals or several hundred. The members of this type of group come from different hamlets, and a single hamlet may contain members of a number of such different groups. The smaller groups are joined together into larger, looser groups, which are grouped again into still larger groups which are coordinated by central government officials.

> The result is a series of highly complex but markedly decentralized systems for the allocation of irrigation water, operating on a traditional basis in a complex society with a population of more than 1,000,000 (Millon et al., 1962:68).

Summary

The differences in organization of water distribution among the six societies I have mentioned are so great that it would be foolish to attempt to classify them or devise a typology at this point. I have purposely chosen two societies organized on a tribal basis, the Kalinga and the Sonjo; two chiefdoms, Moala and Hawaii; and two peasant societies, Ceylon (Pul Eliya) and Bali to emphasize the point that even at similar levels of complexity, different types of solutions to the problem of water distribution are found.

In only two of the societies mentioned was the special position of the upstream irrigator recognized and incorporated into the system. Among the Kalinga the special rights of the upstream irrigator were protected even at the cost of decreased effectiveness of water use, since upstream irrigators were able to prevent the expansion of land cultivation by asserting their special rights. In Moala, the upstream irrigators were formally charged with responsibility for equitable water distribution. Furthermore, the ranking of families in the system was expressed in the physical positions of the families within the canal complex; highest ranking families occupy the uppermost positions. In other societies, as in Oaxaca, relative position on the canals appeared to have little or nothing to do with water control or access. In Hawaii, where there was ranking of social status in the larger organization, differential control over water followed the same lines as the differential ranking of chiefs and subordinates. Among the Sonjo, as in Hawaii, differential control was part of an inherited social position. In Pul Eliya's traditional system, differential control and access were prevented from emerging by a complex system of land division and inheritance. In the new system, however, differences have arisen, partly because of the creation of a particular office, "irrigation headman," by the central government. In Bali, it appears that local level control resembles the traditional system of Pul Eliya, though not on a village-unit basis, while higher level controls, as in Hawaii, follow the levels provided by the larger social system.

But we have known all along that societies vary widely in the types of water control organization they use; this has been brought out in the literature, particularly in reference to the small-scale types of irrigation systems mentioned here. It was suggested earlier in this chapter that the types of problems posed by particular types of water resources and facilities may evoke social responses which are different from those associated with other types of water resources and facilities, but even within these limits, the variations seem to be infinite. Before going on to make further conclusions about this variation, let us consider two more topics for comparison: disputes and the relation of the local community to the state in reference to water control.

DISPUTES

Disputes over irrigation water are cited frequently in the literature. The study by Millon et al. (Millon, Hall, and Diaz, 1961-62) of the Teotihuacán irrigation system focuses primarily upon this, and the problem of disputes is emphasized in their seven-society cross-cultural comparison. I will briefly mention a few examples, two of which were not covered by their study.

Kalinga

Here, as in Oaxaca, disputes between villages are more likely to become serious than disputes within communities. Barton cites a litigation in which a village cut off the water from a canal flowing through its territory, so that a second village, with whom the first had been feuding, could not use it. The second village was forced (by the demand of the first) not only to make payments but also to build a new canal for the first, before the first would open up the canal which supplied the second with water. The water and the canal which supplied the water in this case were owned by neither village.

Here competition over water was not the main issue; the two villages were fighting over another matter entirely. However, the upstream village was able to use an advantage—its control over the water supply of the downstream village—not only to win the fight but also to gain an additional prize, the service of the downstream community in providing it with a new canal. This situation is reminiscent of a similar one which occurred in Oaxaca, cited in an earlier chapter, involving the villages of Nazareno and Soledad Etla.

Moala

Here, as I noted above, the "owners of the water" are supposed to settle any disputes over water from their stream.

> Instances of abuse are rare...[In] perhaps the most common type of settlement...the injured party goes secretly to the diversion that has lessened his water supply and breaks it open. This avoids the embarrassment of having to confront a relative with a charge so heinous as deprivation of water. At the same time, it does not prevent repetition of the offense (Sahlins, 1962:84-85).

Moala provides a good illustration of why internal disputes in the community are rare. Ties of kinship and the desire to live peacefully with one's close neighbors are so strong that individuals are highly reluctant to wrong their closest associates by breaking the rules. But when they do, the same ties, the same desire, are likely to prevent serious accusations or violent retaliations.

There are often other factors beside kinship and neighborhood ties which tend to deter internal disputes.

> It would be possible for a village chief to intervene in a water dispute if the controversy develops into a fight in the village. Then the chief would attempt to settle the dispute not because he is 'owner of the water' or somehow its highest custodian, but because the peace of the village *is* his domain (Sahlins, 1962:285).

In Oaxaca, the situation is quite similar. It is at the intervillage level, where such peace-keeping factors as the village chief's surveillance do not exist, that disputes are most likely to occur. In Oaxaca, the keeping of the peace at that level is the responsibility of the state. But the state is so remote that such a situation is called to its attention only when the dispute has become prolonged and serious, involving, for example, outbreaks of violence.

Japan

In Japan, irrigation works are far more complex and extensive than in Oaxaca, Moala, or among the Kalinga. With the greater number of individuals, communities, and facilities involved, one might expect an increased potential for, if not frequency of, conflict:

> ...some fields are disadvantaged by conditions that are ideal for others. Each unit of a canal organization is in a sense a separate sovereignty treating with others for a satisfactory working compromise. This uneasy confederation is more apt to follow historical precedent than laboratory theories of hydraulic engineering. Although cooperation is mandatory, it is not achieved without a certain amount of hard feeling or even open conflict. Serious tensions prevail at every level of the rather complex organization (Bearsdley, Hall, and Ward, 1959:134).

> ....a source of friction is the tradition of unequal water rights. In time of drought the villages on reclaimed land in Kojima Bay get shortchanged, according to their view. Their claim to this water goes back only a century, at most, and they are at the tail end of the canal. Hence, older villages upstream claim prior right to the water. In any case they have first access to it, and it is their own people who decide, as water guards, how much to let through. Frictions, thus, are inevitable. (Beardsley, Hall, and Ward, 1959:136)

Such friction occurs at every organizational level down to the *oaza* (village) and, in some cases, among individual farmers within the *oaza*. (Beardsley, Hall, and Ward, 1959:136)

Summary

The reasons for dispute have to do with the basic allocation problem: the potential for differential access between upstream and downstream irrigators. The elaborate, complex, decentralized network of control in Japan has not been able to eradicate the problem—at least not without considerable strain. It is difficult to tell whether or not the frictions in this system are detrimental to the effective use of the water resources, or whether they might be eased by a different type of organization. We might leave these as open possibilities which could be better understood when more research has been done. On a much smaller scale (as in the case of Oaxaca), it does appear that such frictions are detrimental to effective water use, and that centralized organization may not only decrease conflicts but may increase the effectiveness of water use as well.

VILLAGE/STATE RELATIONS AND WATER CONTROL

The relationship of village to state in reference to water control was a subject of some importance in my description of Oaxaca. I have already mentioned several instances of village/state relations in the preceding examples. The case of Pul Eliya was particularly relevant because it showed how state intervention could not only alter the regulation of water but also, through this type of intervention, alter the entire social and economic structure of the community.

The case of Japan brings out a different aspect of village/state relations which also applies, though perhaps to a lesser degree, to Oaxaca:

Irrigation...involves the prefectural and the central governments; national measures for river control, dam building, and land reclamation have direct impact on the *buraku*. But, in contrast to many phases of life which the central government absorbs completely once it touches them, irrigation problems are too complex and variant to permit higher government to take over and mold the situation at will...Higher levels of government...must rest content with sharing this responsibility with local units of government (Beardsley, Hall, and Ward, 1959:127).

The figures for irrigation facilities suggest the complexity of irrigation development in the prefecture as a whole: there are 10,000 irrigation ponds and somewhat more than 5,700 inlets from streams. Despite this, drought and flood are perpetual threats (Beardsley, Hall, and Ward, 1959:127).

Land reclamation and water management tend to lie beyond control by the individual farmer and rest with the community, the landlord, or feudal lord. In Japan, as with other Asian countries with similar economic features, political power has been closely related to the control of land and water (Beardsley, Hall, and Ward, 1959:116).

As in Oaxaca, the diversity and large number of water resources force the central government to delegate authority over the lower levels of division and maintenance to local community governments or associations. This is the reason why, for example, the SAG creates local juntas de aguas which are supposed to run themselves. But the forms of the juntas de aguas can be somewhat more standard and more closely supervised because the resources and facilities themselves are more standard and simpler than those of the Japanese irrigation systems, not to mention far fewer in number.

The above-mentioned relationship between political power and water control was found, but to a far more limited extent, in Oaxaca. That is, the great power of the Spanish colonists, both before and after independence from Spain, was realized in their control over water. And since water was a source of wealth, and wealth a source of power, water often indirectly provided a source of power. The example offered by the Mitla case was an illustration of the form the relationship took in Oaxaca. A different form is suggested in the Pul Eliya case, where the relationship between water and political power was more direct. In contemporary Oaxaca, as the state becomes more involved in hydraulic development, connections between political power and control over water may emerge more strongly. But in view of the rules established in connection with water control, it appears that the power will not be personal, but institutional.

SUMMARY AND CONCLUSIONS

In this chapter I have compared a number of different societies which use small-scale irrigation works. I took up a number of different issues for comparison: structural change through regional cooperation, variations within societies according to types of water sources, cooperative labor, variations in water distribution, disputes over water, and village/state relations in respect to water control. On each subject, different points were made by the comparison, though two points were repeatedly emphasized: the range of variations is extremely wide, and the source of variation lies in the fact that the organization of water control in each case is embedded in the larger social setting. However apparent this emphasis upon the differences found among irrigating societies, it was not the main purpose of this chapter. Rather, the differences were underlined in order to make clear areas in which we might search for similarities, and areas in which we should forego generalizations.

Now that we have made the comparisons, we may turn to consideration of some interesting and relevant points concerning peasant societies in general. These were brought out or implied by certain similarities among the responses of these societies to the problems of water control. Hopefully these points will be useful both in interpreting the role of irrigation in Oaxaca itself, and in the more general framework of the development of early civilizations, the subject of the controversy mentioned at the beginning of this chapter.

First, as I pointed out, peasant societies in general appear to have stronger coercive means of enforcing collective labor than do tribal societies. The strength of these means may be reflected in the more productive use of land, water, and relatively primitive technology. It is important to note that these coercive means are frequently not centered in the state apparatus itself—its bureaucracy, its army or police force, or its specialized upper classes. Rather, they are local and perpetuated within the community structure, not necessarily enforced from without.

Second, however, these coercive means, like peasant society in general, are not entirely independent of the state apparatus or structure. Peasant society, by definition, exists only in the context of statehood; of necessity, there must be some structural connection between the two. So even though coercive means at the local level may operate apart from the state, their existence is dependent upon the existence of the state.

Third, local peasant organizations, like tribal organizations, are in fact more limited in their capacity both to organize collective labor and to keep the peace than is the state. While disputes are generally kept minimal at the local level by the local institutions, these institutions lose force at the intercommunity level. Neither tribal structures nor local peasant community structures provide adequate institutions for intercommunity relations. The state, on the other hand, provides exactly such institutions. To a far greater extent, then, states are able to keep the peace, avoiding or settling disputes at the intercommunity level, as well as to organize and coerce collective labor on a scale beyond the capacity of the local organizations. Therefore, they are more capable of making productive use of land, water, and technology through their organizations. In addition, they are capable of using a technology which includes such complex labor and peace-keeping requirements that local structures cannot handle them.

Fourth, the means of the state to organize productive activities are limited, on the other hand, by the complexity of these activities—water control in particular—at the local level. Japan provided an illustration of what is perhaps the extreme case; Bali provided another. We must conclude, then, that some of the characteristics which enable states to operate more effectively at the supralocal level handicap their effective operation at the local level (e.g., they are centralized). Since local-level activities are basic to the subsistence of the society as a whole, states clearly must rely upon local organizations for the management of certain essential processes of production—namely, those which are too complex in detail for the state to handle.

Finally, this interdependence of state and peasant organizations is important to understand when we consider the origins of statehood. Most theoretical discussions on the origins of statehood stress structure at the top of the hierarchy. But not all direction and management come from the top. This fact is most important for relating changes or influences in the processes of production to the origins of statehood. This is not to say that the upper levels are not important, nor that the evolution of states does not involve a radical change in local-level organization. Both local and supralocal levels are involved in the change to statehood. But generally, so much attention is paid to the supralocal organization and to its productive advantages, that the nature and importance of local organizational change is ignored. Perhaps it is too often assumed that the local organization is simply a branch of the state. This is often not so, as we have seen in the cases of Oaxaca and Ceylon (Pul Eliya) and many other societies. It would certainly increase our understanding of the origins and development of statehood if we paid greater attention to the interdependence, the interaction, and the different roles (and potentially different structures) of the supralocal and local levels of state societies, in the realms of both production and social structure.

To return, finally, to the controversial issue of the role of irrigation in the origins of statehood and in the structure of social systems in general, we may conclude the following:

1) There is no fixed social response to canal irrigation. How a society deals with canal irrigation depends upon the framework of existing institutions within which the society must work.

2) Nevertheless, the problems posed by differential access and the need for cooperative labor are general, and vary according to the type of the source, its size, the technology of water control, and its scale. The fact that such differences do affect social response is certainly suggested, if not demonstrated, by the fact that within the same society, irrigation facilities of different types and sizes are accorded different treatment. Certain types of responses on the part of a social structure permit more efficient or more effective utilization of water resources and hydraulic works than do others. In other words, though societies may handle canal irrigation in an enormous number of alternative ways, some ways are more effective than others, no matter what the society, because of their relevance to the problem itself. The effectiveness of production depends not on the adaptation of the system of control to the social setting, but on its effectiveness with regard to the specific problems of irrigation. One could even measure the sacrifice (or gain) in productive capacity made by a society using one system of water control, as opposed to another system, by estimating how much more (or less) land could be irrigated if the alternate system were used.

3) While certain characteristics of states do in fact permit more effective utilization of certain resources and technology than those of tribal organizations, this increased effectiveness does not arise entirely from the upper levels of state organization. Part of this effectiveness lies in characteristics of peasant society at the local level of organization. We may see the upper stratum and the lower stratum of state societies as two distinct but interdependent systems, which may deal with separate areas of water control, different types of resources, or different levels of integration. The effectiveness of one stratum depends at least in part upon the effectiveness of the other; yet the reasons for their effectiveness in each case might be different.

4) While water control does not necessarily *cause* any particular social system to arise, it may serve as an important vehicle for social change, particularly where statehood or its characteristics are involved. We have considered examples of such change in water control systems in Ceylon and Oaxaca. If increased productivity through more effective water control is possible and desirable in a given social context, statehood will have a selective advantage, since states do offer the means of increasing effectiveness of water control on either higher or lower levels.

5) The fact that canal irrigation can provide a

context in which state-like organization has a selective advantage, added to the fact that all the major early states first arose in regions in which irrigation was perhaps the primary means of increasing agricultural production, suggests that canal irrigation may very well have played a unique historical role in the evolution of certain forms of political and economic structure. Perhaps the focus upon certain characteristics of social structure in past discussions of the differences and similarities among early states has led to a mistaken conclusion about the relationship between the development of states and irrigation. For example, though it may be true that states must have centralized structures at the upper levels of the government hierarchy, it may not be necessary for states to exercise centralized control at all levels of organization of canal irrigation systems, in order for the latter organization to have critically influenced the structure of the state. In fact, the existence of statehood—in terms of a supralocal and powerful centralized authority—may be a prerequisite for the successful functioning of decentralized local-level organizations of water control. This may, for instance, be the case in Japan and Bali. For all that irrigation may have played a critical role in the evolution of a state, the state itself need not have directly controlled the irrigation. We should consider the relationship between local and supralocal organization in state societies and the role of irrigation in local organization as elements of this emerging state/irrigation relationship.

If small-scale irrigation systems can be organized in a variety of ways, from simple kinship through state-like structures, we cannot assume that the discovery of small-scale works in certain archaeological time periods is automatically indicative of the absence of state influence. Other sorts of evidence must be used in order to support such an assumption. Nor must it be assumed that the primary role of the higher levels of state organization in regard to irrigation is to build bigger and better hydraulic works; it may play an entirely different, though equally important, role. In relating irrigation to statehood, we should consider:

1) the relationship of irrigation to agricultural production itself.

2) internal relationships between local community members in reference to water control and to other elements in the processes of production.

3) relationships between communities in reference to water control.

4) the role of the state in intercommunity relationships.

5) the relationship between the state structure and the internal relationships between local community members.

Using these guidepost considerations, we might better understand how complicated the organization of a society really is and how irrigation fits into this organization.

The early states may or may not have been similar in the relationship of their upper levels of the administrative hierarchy to the construction and control of hydraulic works. If they were, it is of course not so difficult to explain why, in terms of adaptation to the requirements of irrigation. But it is also possible that they were not similar in this way. They may, on the other hand, have been similar in the way in which the control of water at the local level was related to community organization and, in turn, the way in which community organization was related to the higher levels of the administrative hierarchy. If we were to find similarities in the latter types of relationships, but not in the former, we might have a rather different view of the processes by which states—and statehood—evolved. In fact, we might have a different understanding of the nature of statehood itself.

VII

GENERAL CONCLUSIONS

For a number of important reasons, water has been singled out by many anthropologists as a natural environmental resource with special sociopolitical significance. One reason is that the earliest civilizations arose in areas where water scarcity was a major agricultural problem. Another is that some anthropologists believe that the nature of water as an agricultural resource implies certain specific sociopolitical problems and responses. Wittfogel, perhaps the most outstanding proponent of this belief, explained the inherent implications of the use of this resource as follows:

No operational necessity compels [man] to manipulate either soil or plants in cooperation with many others. But the bulkiness of all except the smallest sources of water supply creates a *technical task* which is solved by *mass labor* or not at all [italics my own] (Wittfogel, 1957:15).

A second reason to consider water as having special implications for sociopolitical organization was suggested in this paper. When it is used for canal irrigation, water must flow in a limited channel from a high place to a lower place. This means that full access to the resource cannot be had by upstream and downstream irrigators at the same time. The potential difference in access and control inherent in the physical nature of the flowing resource may have important implications for differential political or economic control, since the actions of upstream irrigators will directly affect the productive capacity of downstream irrigators, but not the reverse. In other words, canal irrigation provides a potential source of power differences which may be expressed in the political and economic organization of the society or inhibited by special sociopolitical devices.

Both cooperative labor on a large scale and differential political power through differential economic access and control are characteristic of statehood or civilization. The question of whether or not the rise of these characteristics in early civilizations was even partially due to the effects of dependence upon hydraulic resources and technology remains controversial. Similarly controversial is the question of the manner and degree to which the inherent qualities of water as a natural resource do, *in themselves,* imply such characteristics of cooperative labor and differential power in any society which uses canal irrigation.

The problems of cooperation, for labor on the one hand and for allocation on the other, are distinct and analytically separable. Mass labor is associated only with larger-scale hydraulic facilities. It may, however, be applied to various types of hydraulic problems—flood control as well as irrigation—and various types of work—both construction and maintenance. In fact, it is also applicable to other sorts of problems and facilities, including transportation and road building, architecture, and some types of land reclamation, to name a few. The problems of allocation, by contrast, are specific to canal irrigation and apply to it on every scale. Consequently, the roles and relative importance of either of these factors in a society may vary and be considered independently of one another, though their mutual effects upon one another should also be taken into consideration.

It is necessary to emphasize this point because either factor may gain or lose importance when viewed in different perspectives. In the short run, for example, collective labor may appear to have little or no importance in either the way society is organized or the way the irrigation works are regulated; in the long run, however, it may turn out to have a great deal of importance. Or, to take another example, the allocation of water may be dealt with in one way on the local community level and in another way, with different consequences, at the intercommunity level. In a given society, we may find greater variation in response to the problem of allocation than to the problem of collective labor or the reverse.

Because there is so much room for variation, so much complexity in the way in which societies may respond to the problems mentioned above, we cannot gather any significant conclusions about the ways in which they affect the response without examining each one in detail. If we can generalize, it will not be about the responses themselves, but about the relationship between the problems and the responses. Before discussing this statement further, however, let us review our findings about the manner and degree to which the problems of canal irrigation affect and are affected by the political organization of a single society: the rural community in the Valley of Oaxaca.

OAXACA AS A CASE STUDY

Environment

In its general aridity, the Valley of Oaxaca resembles the other areas of the world where early civilizations arose. During the summer months, it rains irregularly; during the rest of the year, it rains not at all. Its high water table zone with moist soil is extremely limited in extent, and the rate of evaporation is high. Its main rivers have now ceased to flow continuously throughout the year, and water scarcity is increasing.

Tributary streams, rather than the main rivers, provide the main sources of canal irrigation. Thus, there is no single, centralized irrigation system for the valley as a whole. The number of villages sharing the same irrigation source has generally been small, rarely exceeding three or four at the most. With the current decrease in water supply, this number has been diminishing further; most often there is only one village to a source.

Canal irrigation from tributary streams is only one of several irrigation techniques used in the valley. Floodwater farming (which sometimes also uses canals but is far more restricted in seasonal use and shared participation) and well irrigation are also important techniques, though they are not generally publicly controlled like canal irrigation. Canal irrigation is not only not the sole type of water control; it is also very restricted in extent. Probably fewer than half of the villages in the valley use this technique today.

Technology

Valley of Oaxaca canal irrigation, then, is practiced on a small scale, with small and simple devices. Large masonry and cement dams are rare and new; brush dams and earthen canals constitute the traditional repertoire of canal-irrigation devices. Only in recent times has construction become a difficult or exacting task, through installation of new devices which generally lie beyond the capacity of the local community.

Neither erosion nor silting present any substantial problems for the aboriginal Oaxacan form of canal irrigation. Terraces are sometimes used, but apparently are not difficult to build or to maintain. Thus, collective labor for maintenance is needed infrequently and can be provided adequately by the local community.

Allocation

Since the first quarter of this century, water has become a public resource. Before then, villages themselves treated water as a public resource, but private individuals outside the village (hacendados) could own water sources and require payment for their use. Even now, upstream villages may require payment from downstream irrigators who are not members of the village. But the state has intervened between communities in many cases, preventing upstream villages from exploiting downstream villages in this way and taking charge of allocation itself.

Within the village, allocation of water is consistent with the general traditional patterns of participation in public affairs. The officials in charge of allocation are selected in the same way as other officials and have similar powers and responsibilities. All official positions are rotated among the members of the community at large. The titles, numbers, and divisions of labor among the water control officials in canal-irrigating villages are variable, but this variability apparently has no special significance.

Access to water by village members is open to all who request it. Sometimes fees are required, but not invariably. The actual basis for determining who gets water and how much, is private property ownership. Almost all irrigated land is privately owned, and the community has no control over how much land is owned by an individual. There are often sharp differences among community members in the amounts of irrigated land they hold. Those who hold no irrigable land do not generally request access to water. In sum, differences in access to water are based upon differences in private property ownership, not upon relative physical position in the canal system.

Thus, the potential for differences inherent in the physical nature of the system is not realized in the political or economic organization. While upstream-downstream differences are obliterated by a rule of equal access, actual differences in access are caused by the existence of differences in private land ownership. In other words, such differences have nothing explicitly to do with physical location and everything to do with the socioeconomic structure which provides for private property ownership. Similarly, control over water has nothing explicitly to do with physical position on the canals; responsibility for this control is rotated among village members regardless of how much land they hold or where.

Social Change, the State, and Water Control

Oaxaca is a particularly interesting case for study because there is evidence here that canal irrigation and statehood emerged during roughly the same period. Exactly what the relationship between the two may have been at that time remains a subject of speculation. However, we may be almost certain that they were connected to one another in some of the ways considered below. Subsequent changes in water control and sociopolitical organization suggest possible aspects of this relationship at the time of its origin.

For a number of historical reasons, the rural community in the Valley of Oaxaca has remained more or less isolated and self-sufficient politically, socially, and economically for several centuries. This relative isolation and independence is being gradually undermined at present by the policies of the national government in the area of economic and social development. The most successful facets of government penetration at the community level have had to do with the provision, by the government, of special services and facilities which the community itself cannot provide. And one of the most important of these has been the development of modern hydraulic facilities, particularly large dams, reservoirs, and cement canals. When the government installs such facilities in a community, it may influence the form of control over maintenance and allocation at the community level. By bringing about changes in one aspect of public affairs, it can and does bring about other changes indirectly.

The technology of water control has been an important locus for change in Oaxaca because it is perhaps the most important single factor influencing the productivity of agriculture. Thus its importance is underlain by environmental factors, on the one hand, and by the manner in which social change is so often brought about (through the provision of special technological services by the government) on the other. If the state played a similar role in relation to the local community in the past, then canal irrigation might have provided a similarly important locus for social change from the time of its inception over 2300 years ago.

MASS LABOR AND ALLOCATION IN OAXACA

Mass Labor

Because the scale of irrigation works in the Valley of Oaxaca has traditionally been small and because the sources of water are multiple and dispersed, opportunities and needs for mass labor upon irrigation facilities have been comparatively rare. Even on this scale, it was possible to find differences in the effectiveness of different types of organization of cooperative labor. Historical data indicate that hacendados were somewhat more effective in the deployment of labor and materials in the construction of irrigation facilities than are present-day communities. However, present-day communities are effective enough in their ability to organize and "coerce" cooperative labor efforts to provide what is needed in the way of construction and maintenance upon their own irrigation facilities. It is a decrease in the availability of water in the environment, rather than a lack of cooperative labor, that limits the extent of land irrigated by the traditional devices.

The type of organization of labor which is necessary to construct the newer types of irrigation facilities which are now being installed in some communities by the state government is, in fact, beyond the capacity of the rural community as it now stands. Implicit in this type of organization is not so much large numbers of cooperating individuals, but rather a division of labor which entails full-time specialization in certain skills (engineering) and production (materials and machinery). Although large numbers of individuals are needed to maintain such an organization—not only engineers, industrialists, and skilled and unskilled laborers but also bureaucrats—it is their *specialization,* their division of labor, which enables them to advance beyond the individual community in capacity to provide such services as the construction of the new irrigation facilities, rather than simply their numbers.

It would be useful, then, to note that the relative effectiveness of "mass labor" depends not only upon large numbers of cooperating individuals, but also upon a type of cooperation that involves specialization in both labor and management. Although the construction of modern irrigation facilities in any one community in the valley may involve only one or two hundred individuals directly, it is predicated upon the cooperation of several thousand individuals who are less directly involved. These other individuals are the ones who develop the technical know-how, produce the materials and machinery, do the paper work, and so forth. And these individuals, in turn, depend upon the cooperation of the entire nation in order to specialize in the way that they do. In sum, the need for mass labor on irrigation facilities depends not only upon the scale of the facilities but also upon the technological type of facilities. The newer facilities in the Valley of Oaxaca, though still on a relatively small scale, are of such a type that they require a complex division of labor and larger numbers of cooperating individuals.

Collective labor to maintain the traditional canal irrigation facilities is needed only on a small scale. Truly large-scale cooperation is needed only to improve, modernize, and expand facilities, and only if the new facilities are of a certain type. The requirement for such large scale cooperation is not determined environmentally—that is, by the nature of the resources—but rather technologically and by the economic policies of the state, which currently involve expansion and modernization. The same may not be true of other types of water resources in other areas of the world. But in this case, it does apply. The implication is that in cases where water resources are small and dispersed, there is little relationship between the nature of the resource and mass labor. Mass labor and specialization may or may not be applied, depending upon the nature of the technology and the policies of the society in question.

Cooperation on a smaller scale, involving only a few hundred individuals, is not a negligible factor, however. We have seen that differences in types of organization on this scale in the Valley of Oaxaca have resulted in differences in productive capacity and in effectiveness of exploitation of water resources. Although the present-day type of organization appears to be somewhat less effective than that of the last century, it is certainly more effective than many other sorts of organization. Cross-cultural comparison has permitted us to consider other types of organization of cooperative labor in relation to that of rural communities in Oaxaca. Oaxacan communities fall into a larger category of types of organization that we may call "peasant types." As we have seen, peasants appear to have more effective means of organizing and coercing collective labor than tribal types.

In the Valley of Oaxaca, the manner in which collective labor is organized and coerced is not specific to canal irrigation, nor is there any indication that cooperation in canal construction and maintenance is the basis for cooperation in other endeavors involving collective labor. Rather, it is achieved through a generalized institution, tequio, which is characteristic of the organization of traditional communities in the Valley of Oaxaca whether or not they use canal irrigation. It is clear that collective labor is necessary in order to maintain canal irrigation facilities, but it is not necessary to have such facilities in order to have either a need for collective labor or a means of organizing it.

Collective labor not based on kin or friendship ties, whether on a mass scale or a smaller, community scale, is a characteristic of states and peasant societies. It may be applied to irrigation facilities, but also to other endeavors. It is brought about through generalized institutions which are not in themselves direct responses to the technical problems of canal irrigation or water control in general. Rather, the institutions are characteristics of this type of society. As for the evolutionary role of needs and responses to the technical problems of water control, we shall return to them below.

Allocation

The underlying problem of allocation, as stated above, is how to organize access to water in the face of potential inequalities in access between upstream and downstream irrigators. The responses to this problem must make explicit the basis upon which water is to be allocated among those who have access to the resource and the manner in which allocation is to be controlled.

In the Valley of Oaxaca, the response to this problem at the community level is different from that at the intercommunity level. Within the community, unequal access and control based upon physical position in the canal system is denied. Access is based upon landholding and community membership alone, regardless of physical position. Control rests not with individuals, but with the community at large. Though the state government has recently intervened in the manner of organization of control in some communities, it has not significantly altered the process of allocation itself.

Between communities, there are two possible alternative responses. According to one alternative, the relative physical positions of the irrigators are taken into account. The upstream communities have first and greatest access, control the timing and quantity of water made available to downstream communities, and require payment from downstream irrigators for access to the resource. This is a special arrangement which applies to water resources in particular, and not to any other social, political, or economic interaction between the communities.

According to the other alternative, the state government intervenes between communities in much the same way that the community intervenes between individuals. Rights to access are determined by proportions of irrigable land held by the communities (and, in some cases, by the need for water for other purposes, such as domestic consumption in the city). And control rests with the state rather than with any community or group of communities.

Responses to the problem of allocation, then, may or may not take into account inequalities in access based upon physical position. When they do—in this case, at the intercommunity level—they do not necessarily have any further political implications. Inequalities in access and control apply only to the water resource, and not to any other aspect of the economy or other political or social interaction. But when they override physical inequalities, they do so on the basis of inequalities in power and control which also apply to other aspects of sociopolitical organization. These are not inequalities between *persons* or *communities,* but between *levels of organization.* At the community level, inequalities between the individual or household and the community at large are expressed in the organization of control over the allocation of water: the community at large has primary rights and power over control. At the intercommunity level, inequalities between the community and the state are expressed. The rights and powers of the community are subordinate to those of the state in the allocation of water.

The existence of two somewhat opposed alternatives for intercommunity regulation of water allocation appears, as such, only in the synchronic view. Regarded diachronically, the two alternatives have a different significance in that one—the government-controlled alternative— is steadily replacing the other. This replacement is part of a larger program in which resources are being nationalized as part of the policy of modernization. This program includes increasing the effectiveness of resource use and the productivity of agriculture in general through government control and guidance and the breakdown of rural community isolation. In other words, it is part of a trend to increase the mutual participation of the state and the community in one another's affairs which is a part, not simply a by-product, of national development and growth. As this mutual participation increases, the authority of the higher level of organization—the state government—becomes increasingly important and apparent in the management of individual and community affairs. Its increasing control of allocation of water at the intercommunity level is only one aspect of the larger process.

In the problem of allocation, we may contrast two poles of response. At one extreme is the type of response which favors particular individuals (or individual communities) and is based upon physical advantages in differential placement in a canal system. At the other extreme is the type of response which replaces individual differences in control by organizational hierarchies of control; the power differential which was once accorded to individuals on the basis of physical position, becomes accorded to structures in the larger organization on the basis of levels of inclusiveness. That is, control differentials are not expressed between otherwise equal individuals, but between otherwise unequal levels of organization. Thus special inequalities are relegated to the domain of generalized inequalities.

In the case of Moala, mentioned in the last chapter, generalized inequalities and specific advantages due to placement in the canal system were, to a very limited extent, superimposed. Here there was a ranking of families within kin groups, and the higher-ranking families (if the rules were followed) were placed in higher positions along that canal system than lower-ranking families, thus gaining greater control over the allocation of water. In Oaxaca, there is no such formal ranking of individuals, families, or communities. There is no physical location which corresponds to a level in the hierarchy of the organization of control. Even so, the hierarchy occasionally does become expressed in physical terms. For example, when several communities share a water source, as was the case in San Agustin, the state government had control over the uppermost diversion point which controlled the amount of water allocated to each village, while the communities had control over each of the downstream diversion points which divided the water among the several canals of each community.

Differences in control, whether they are individual or hierarchical, are implicit in the use of canal irrigation systems where water is scarce and more than one individual or community uses the canal. Communities may go to great lengths to prevent accumulations of power or control by individuals through the physical advantage in the canal system (as was the case in traditional Pul Eliya) while they assert communal authority. Or such differences in control and position may coincide with one another, as they did in Moala and among the Kalinga. In Moala, however, differences in control were part of a generalized rank as well as part of a physical position. Among the Kalinga (as was sometimes the case in intercommunity regulation in Oaxaca) such differences were, when they were expressed, specific to water resources and had no further implications. But in no case—with the possible exception of the Pima according to Hackenberg's historical interpretation—did individual differences lead to the establishment of generalized hierarchical levels of control. Rather, such hierarchical levels, when they existed, tended to replace individual physical differences or, in one case at least, to coincide with them.

If power differentials inherent in canal irrigation resources do not necessarily lead to the establishment of generalized institutions of hierarchical control, then we may ask if the nature of the resource has any influence whatsoever over social response. The fact that different responses are accorded to different types of water resources within a single society, as illustrated by Moala and Oaxaca, for example, indicates a qualified positive answer. The problems presented to a society by a single, flowing, shared resource are different from those presented by multiple, stationary resources. It is only to be expected that responses to different problems will be different. But the extent to which responses to similar problems must be similar is quite limited. Apparently, responses to the problems of allocation from shared canal irrigation resources are cross-culturally similar only in that they incorporate some established power or control differential. This differential need not become a generalized institution, nor need it be associated with physical advantages in location on the canal network. The existence of this power differential is peculiar to the shared use of canal irrigation resources, as opposed to other types of resources; though application to canal irrigation resources is not distinctive to generalized institutions which incorporate power differentials.

ENVIRONMENT, TECHNOLOGY, ADAPTATION, AND EVOLUTION

If certain characteristics in the nature of water as an agricultural resource neither require nor produce specific and regular social responses in and of themselves, should we disregard these characteristics entirely when we consider the role of water resources in social organization and cultural evolution? Is the latitude for variation so great that we can discover no relationship between the nature of the resource and social response? Although the discussion of the past few pages may seem to have indicated that this is true, we have reason to suspect that it is not. Let us review, then, the evidence and arguments to the contrary presented so far in this study.

Variation in Response and the Nature of the Resource

The fact that societies do not always respond to similar problems in exactly the same way is obvious; we would not find the degree of cross-cultural variation that exists today, if this were not true. But although there is room for a great deal of variation, and although a large number of responses will be adequate to meet a society's needs, it is also true that some responses are more effective in meeting certain needs than others. Societies do not always respond to problems of resource exploitation in such a way as to maximize productive capacity; in fact, it can be argued that they never do. But some societies clearly are more effective in exploitation and production than others. Furthermore, these societies are more effective at some times in the course of their history than at others. Their effectiveness in this area depends largely upon the combined factors of organization and technology, and these vary widely in type, scale, and detail from society to society and historical period to historical period.

It is a basic tenet of evolutionary theory that societies (like organisms and populations) which respond more effectively to environmental problems will, in the long run, expand at the expense of those which respond less effectively. If this is so, clearly the more effective responses made by some societies are the basis for their expansion and growth. Or, to phrase it differently, if a society is to expand and grow, it must find more effective ways of responding to its environmental problems, exploiting resources and increasing production.

The effectiveness of a response is determined not only by its sociocultural context, but by the nature of the problem itself. For example, although small-scale cooperative labor may be adequate to build and maintain canal irrigation facilities which will supply limited quantities of water to a limited amount of land, mass labor applied to facilities on a large scale or to more complex types, may result in the provision of water from the same source for much more land and many more people. And if the society depends upon canal irrigation to intensify and increase production, its ability to expand depends upon its means of organizing labor on a mass scale for application to canal irrigation facilities.

But water is a type of resource to which the application of organized labor will produce greater effectiveness in exploitation; this is not necessarily true of other resources. To return to Wittfogel's statement quoted at the beginning of this chapter, let us modify it as follows: the nature of the resource (water) is such that effectiveness in its exploitation can be increased only by the application of cooperative labor on a mass scale. In the absence of mass cooperation, growth and expansion are difficult, if not impossible, to achieve. Furthermore, the society which can organize mass labor for application to facilities for exploitation of water resources will be more successful. It will grow faster than, and possibly at the expense of, the society which cannot so organize, if both are dependent upon such facilities and resources for production. In other words, if the problem combines both water control and expansion, then the most successful solution will be mass labor. The fact that mass labor will produce more effective results is determined by the nature of water, a resource which does not lend itself well to noncooperative efforts.

Although societies have responded to the problems of exploiting water resources in a great variety of ways, those which were in the process of rapid expansion and development (and were at the same time dependent upon the exploitation of these resources for intensification of production) had much less latitude for response. Because of the nature of the resources, they had to increase cooperation on a mass scale and to devise means of organizing such cooperation through specialization of bureaucrats and laborers. The similarities between such societies in their response to the problem of water resource exploitation had to do with both the nature of the resource and with the fact that they were expanding. The nature of the resource determines what sort of response will be most effective, and the situation of the society—whether or not it is expanding and dependent upon water control—determines whether or not it is required or able to respond more effectively this way.

Millon and his associates pointed out that certain types of responses to the problems of canal irrigation, those involving centralization of authority, were "exceptional." Though we are not speaking of that particular characteristic, the same statement applies to responses involving mass labor on a very large scale. But the exceptionality of these cases derives not from the relationship of the response to the nature of the resource, but rather (at least in part) from the exceptionality of successful, rapidly expanding, irrigation-dependent societies.

Wide cross-cultural variation in response to the problems of water control in general does not imply that the nature of water resources has no relation to the response. Rather, it signifies only that societies can "get along" without maximizing effectiveness in resource exploitation. The fact that the range of variation in the more effective responses is far narrower indicates that the nature of the resource does effect the response; it determines, at least in part, which responses are more effective than others. Which

Environment and Technology

The nature of the environmental resources—water resources in particular—determines to some extent the types of problems to which a society must respond and the types of responses which will be most effective. Cooperation in labor for construction and maintenance provides more effective ways to exploit water resources, to solve the problem of conveying water from one place on the ground to another. The degree to which such cooperation is necessary, on the one hand, and the degree to which it will provide the basis for expansion through more effective exploitation, on the other, are determined by still other aspects of the environment and technology.

To focus first upon technology, we have discussed mass labor and specialization in relation to the new technological devices now being installed in the Valley of Oaxaca. Mass labor on this scale was not necessary, or even possible, before certain technological innovations were made. Once they had been made, of course, mass labor was needed to utilize them. Before they were made, there was no dependence upon a similar scale of mass labor to construct and maintain irrigation facilities in the Valley of Oaxaca. But once they existed and became an essential part of the modernization and development program, comparatively effective use of irrigation resources did depend upon mass labor.

The new technology of irrigation devices in the Valley of Oaxaca both produces and depends upon change in social organization. It requires change in the organization of mass labor such that sufficient numbers of individuals will be free to be trained as specialists and to devote their full-time attention to the maintenance and application of this technology. It produces change in that those communities which receive new installations are dependent upon mass labor (and the organization this implies) in order to exploit their water resources effectively. In other words, once this special technology is applied and associated labor force and organization are developed, certain other segments of the society become dependent upon this particular segment for a part of their means of subsistence.

The extent to which a community "needs" the installation of one of the newer facilities depends in part upon social, as opposed to environmental variables. The fact that any community needs a new facility results from the government modernization program. In this sense, all the communities will eventually "need," and thus become dependent upon, the mass labor organization behind the new technology. If the ends of the modernization program are realized, the society as a whole will depend upon it. This is just one example of a type of change brought about by the development of a new technology which involves specialization. Specialization on this scale can and must be provided by levels of organization higher than the individual community; thus communities which partake of the new technology become dependent upon such higher levels for provision of special technological services. In other words, this is an example of the creation of a dependent tie between the community and the state through the development and provision of complex technological services.

But, as I indicated, the extent of need in a community for improvement of technological devices for water resource exploitation is partly dependent upon environmental factors. Here, the question is not "does the community need such-and-such devices" but, "among the many areas in which technological innovation is possible, which is the most important, which will result in the most change, which is likely to receive the most interest and cooperation on the part of both the community and the state?" This is not as easy a question to answer as it may seem at first, though our initial response may perhaps be correct. It does seem likely that in arid areas where access to water is the single most important variable affecting production improvements in water-control devices would be the most sought after and applied innovations. Certainly any program which attempts to increase productive capacity in the rural community by technological modernization would have to place great stress upon improvement in water control technology. But there is no one-to-one correlation between aridity and the installation of modern irrigation facilities. Furthermore, it seems that schools, electricity, and motorized vehicles are far more widespread in the Valley of Oaxaca than are new irrigation facilities. Even so, improvement and modernization in such facilities is an essential part of the government's program. In the long run, sustained modernization and development will clearly depend upon the ability of this society to expand its effective use of water resources. The relative importance of development in this particular area, of course, is directly related to the general aridity of the environment and to the degree to which effective use of water increases productive capacity—which, in this case, is considerable.

ORIGINS OF STATEHOOD

Once I attempt to draw conclusions about social response to water resources and irrigation technology to interpreting the role of this response in the origins and development of statehood, I am treading on dangerous ground. Therefore, I will be brief and will caution the reader that the following are merely suggested relationships.

(1) I have emphasized the point that organization on the community level in peasant or state societies may be different and separate from that of higher levels of organization. Similarly, the organization of labor and allocation may be different on the local level from that of the higher level. Local level organization may be quite important in the management of water control, particularly in societies with small-scale resources and facilities.

As Millon and his associates pointed out, the range of possibilities and of actual variation in response to problems of water control organization at the local level is enormous in societies with small-scale resources and facilities. Because of this, we may not be able to determine archaeologically what the response was at a given period. In view of this fact, it is perhaps more interesting and more rewarding to seek generalizations about the relationship of communities to higher levels of organization in reference to water control.

(2) I have pointed out the manner in which new technology may require—and result in—new types of social organization. In fact, new technology applied to irrigation facilities themselves was found to have this effect. The change which was required by this technological innovation had to do with specialization of labor; the change which resulted had to do with the creation of a dependent tie between the community and the state through provision of special services and facilities.

The fact that water control facilities were an important locus of change had to do with the aridity of the climate and the need to increase production through more effective water resource exploitation. But the fact that such changes involved a new organization of cooperative labor on a mass scale was at least partly due to the effectiveness of such an organization as a response to the problem of maintaining water resources.

It is suggested that technological changes in irrigation and other water-control devices in ancient civilizations had consequences similar to the modern ones. That is, they involved specialization and relatively extensive cooperation in labor as well as increased dependence by local communities upon higher levels of organization for the provision of services considered essential to their livelihood. Although other matters might also have involved similar responses, the importance of water-control facilities in this regard appears to be stressed by the fact that the early civilizations or states were situated in arid environments.

What is perhaps particularly important about the use of "mass labor" or specialized large-scale labor organizations for water control devices is that it is by this means that the local community organization is changed and made dependent upon that of the higher levels of the state. This dependency of relation—organic integration in Durkheim's terms—is a distinguishing characteristic of states, as opposed to tribal societies.

This is a complicated point and deserves more attention than we have space to give it here; I mention it only because it seems to offer a fruitful line for further discussion.

(3) Though there are many possibilities for social response to the problem of allocation, all involve some power differential. Some alternatives organize the power differential inherent in the nature of a flowing resource in a non-localized hierarchy of control. This denies the right of upstream irrigators to have greater control merely on the basis of advantageous physical position. One way for higher levels of organization to assert their authority is for them to intervene in the allocation of water between communities in such a way that upstream irrigators retain no special advantage.

Internal relations in communities are highly influenced (though not completely structured) by ties of kinship, friendship, and so forth, and these relations are generally sufficient to maintain the peace and reduce disputes. Such relations do not, however, generally obtain on any scale in intercommunity relations. It is one of the functions of the state to keep the peace between its component communities. It is particularly in its capacity as peace-keeper that the state is effective in allocation; by keeping the peace and ensuring equitable distribution, the state enables the society to exploit water resources more effectively than it otherwise could.

The existence of shared canal irrigation resources creates a special role for the state in intercommunity relations. When the state takes this role, the resources are more effectively exploited. At the same time, the state strengthens its authority in regard to the communities. To put it another way, more effective exploitation of the water resources depends upon—and results in—the assertion of the authority of a higher level of integration, the state, in intercommunity relations. This relationship is similar to the relationships among mass labor or specialization in labor, new technology, and community dependence on the state.

(4) The use of water resources for canal irrigation provides a context in which the following social responses are likely to increase effectiveness in production: (*a*) mass or specialized labor on a large scale; (*b*) changes in community organization through state-level provision of services and facilities; (*c*) dependence of communities upon higher levels (or organic integration); (*d*) hierarchical controls of allocation and access; and (*e*) assertion of authority by higher or state-level organization. In other words, it is a context in which selection for these responses is likely to take place. This is even more likely in societies situated in arid environments which rely heavily upon canal irrigation and other sorts of water control involving collective use or labor for purposes of production. In conjunction with many other features, these responses characterize the organization of states as such.

Therefore, it should be no surprise that some of the earliest states arose in environments in which the process of selection heavily favored those characteristics of statehood which are also effective responses to problems of canal irrigation and other forms of water control. In fact, it would be very surprising for states to have evolved in these areas if effectiveness of responses to water-control problems were *not* a major factor in selection.

But we cannot argue that water control played an important role in the emergence of statehood simply because early states evolved in arid environments. Why did they evolve in this particular type of environment? Here we may suggest that certain characteristics of statehood were being selected for to a greater extent in these environments, due to the context provided by the use of certain types of water resources. If the nature of the resource indirectly determines the effectiveness of the response, then the nature of the water resources has indirectly determined where statehood was most likely to arise.

APPENDIX

RESUMEN EN ESPAÑOL

(por David J. Wilson)

Introducción. La irrigación con canales es una técnica de agricultura muy antigua y esparcida, y su origen y naturaleza son temas muy debatidos. La mayor parte de los argumentos se enfocan en si los requisitos burocráticos de la irrigación con canales de mayor escala es un factor causal en el desarrollo del Estado. Esto es un problema especialmente interesante en el Valle de Oaxaca donde la irrigación con canales aparece por primera vez en el período del Formativo Tardío, durante el cual conjeturamos que el estado zapoteca Clásico estaba en el proceso de formarse. En este volumen el propósito de la doctora Susan Lees es estudiar los aspectos sociopolíticos de la irrigación con canales en el valle de Oaxaca, siempre teniendo en cuenta esta controversia. Una cantidad considerable de información preparativa que trata acerca de los aspectos geomorfológicos, hidrológicos y cultural-geográficos de la irrigación con canales se ha proveído por Anne Kirkby (Vol. 1 de esta misma serie). Los problemas que se incluyen en el presente volumen son: ¿cómo se regulan los recursos del agua de los canales en las aldeas oaxaqueñas? ¿podría ser esta regulación un factor en el desarrollo del estado?

El trabajo está basado en el reconocimiento de unas 24 aldeas ubicadas en las tres regiones del Valle de Oaxaca (Etla, Tlacolula y Zimatlán). Una desventaja del método de reconocimiento fue que no se pudo estudiar ninguna aldea intensivamente. En cambio, una ventaja fue que este método permitió a la investigadora obtener una idea mucho más amplia de la variación que le hubiera dado el estudio de una sola comunidad.

Por ejemplo: si la investigación se hubiera basado sólo en Tlalixtac de Cabrera en la región de Tlacolula, se hubiera concluido que el agua de riego, que allí se le encarga el presidente, era una fuente de poder político. Por otro lado, si hubiera estudiado sólo San Juan del Estado en la región de Etla, es posible que concluyera que el agua de riego no era una fuente de poder político sino sólo de trabajo tedioso, ya que allí se administra por un comité de cinco oficiales públicos de bajo rango. En realidad, en la muestra de 24 aldeas hubo virtualmente 24 soluciones al problema del agua. Por tanto la Dra. Lees concluyó que la forma del uso del agua se origina en la estructura social de la sociedad en la cual se encuentra; como quiera que una aldea dada tienda a solucionar los asuntos de la comunidad, también manejará del mismo modo los problemas de la asignación y distribución del agua.

Organización de la comunidad. La autora da un repaso sobre la organización socio-política de las aldeas del Valle de Oaxaca tal como se especifica en la constitución de México. Discute tales puestos como presidente, síndico, regidor, suplente, alcalde, agente y topil; y tales instituciones sociales como mayordomía y el sistema de cargo. También discute dos instituciones—guelaguetza y tequio—que se suponen ser precolombinas en origen y, por eso, tienen implicaciones tanto arqueológicas como etnológicas.

La guelaguetza es una institución que se caracteriza por labor comunal voluntaria, o más bien, el retardado intercambio recíproco de bienes o servicios equivalentes, muchas veces en un contexto ceremonial. El tequio es una forma de labor comunal y obligatoria que se practica actualmente en muchas aldeas zapotecas, para el cual todavía se llama a los trabajadores por medio de una trompeta de concha.

Problemas del control del agua y sus soluciones. En este capítulo la autora describe las 24 aldeas que ella estudió de las cuales unas 22 practicaban la irrigación con canales, otra practicaba el riego a brazo y la última practicaba sólo la agricultura de secano (temporal); estas dos últimas se estudiaron para tener un "control."

En general, los canales tradicionales en el Valle de Oaxaca son pequeños y se originan en unas desviaciones que se llaman "tomas." Estas son sencillas presas hechas de ramas que se colocan de un lado al otro del río. Pero el uso de estas técnicas antiguas (presumiblemente) esta disminuyéndo rápidamente a causa de la disminución de los recursos del agua debido a (1) las bombas de agua de río arriba que sacan el agua de los pozos y reducen así el nivel del agua freática, y a (2) las necesidades extensas de agua en la ciudad moderna de Oaxaca. La mayoría de las facilidades nuevas en la época presente se construyen por la Secretaría de Recursos Hidráulicos, que a veces hace subcontratos para ellas con la Secretaría de Agricultura y Ganadería. Unas cuantas aldeas emprendedoras, como San Juan del Estado, construyen sus propias facilidades modernas, utilizando el sistema de tequio para la construcción y mantenemiento de ellas. El gobierno federal nunca interviene en los problemas de irrigación local excepto en los casos de facilidades que el mismo gobierno construye.

La autora examinó también la relación entre las aldeas de "río arriba" y las de "río abajo" utilizando el mismo río a lo largo de los afluentes de Mixtepec, San Agustín y Guelache-San Gabriel Etla. En sólo un caso (San Gabriel Etla y San Miguel Etla) encontró que dos de estas aldeas habían colaborado en la labor de tequio, con trabajadores de ambas comunidades mejorando las facilidades de irrigación. No encontró en ningún caso evidencia del "despotismo" por parte de la aldea de río arriba, aunque algunas comunidades de río arriba desviaron el agua para venderla a otras aldeas. La mayor parte de las aldeas que compartían el mismo río habían solucionado el problema por medio de turnos. Cada una de estas aldeas podía desviar el agua en un día fijado o en cierta hora fijada. Los casos de conflicto sobre el agua eran muy pocos; esto se puso en contraste notable con los conflictos sobre los terrenos, que son muy comunes en el Valle de Oaxaca, y han ocurrido al menos desde los tiempos coloniales.

Dentro de las aldeas, la asignación del agua entre individuos variaba. Unas diez y ocho aldeas tenían sistemas para decidir el orden por el cual los individuos en la comunidad usaban el agua de los canales. Dos aldeas no tenían de ningún modo tal control interno; dos otras no tenían control interno, pero sí tenían control externo sobre el uso del agua por las aldeas contiguas. El orden de uso no se determinó en ningún caso por la ubicación geográfica del individuo en el canal; más bien se determinó por las autoridades encargadas de la distribución del agua. Muchas aldeas hacían uso de asignaciones calculadas llamadas "tareas."

En 9 de las aldeas, no se requería que los individuous pagaran el agua que se usaba. En otras 9 se utilizaba una forma de pago llamada "cuota" en cuanto a (a) la duración del uso o (b) la cantidad de terreno regado. En otras 4, la cantidad de agua permitida se relacionaba con la ayuda financiera pagada a la comunidad por el consumidor individual. En algunas comunidades, la asignación de agua se dirigía por un juez de aguas o repartidor, o bien un consejo llamado "la junta de aguas;" tales puestos especializados muchas veces se justifican en que impiden los conflictos. Y en otras comunidades, la asignación del agua se lleva a cabo por los regidores, suplentes, o aun los topiles que tienen poca autoridad verdadera. La conclusión de este capítulo es que el control del agua en Oaxaca es una faena administrativa común y corriente que se asigna a la estructura directiva de la comunidad, que es una serie de puestos que se alternan entre los miembros de la aldea por medio del sistema de cargo; de esta manera la asignación injusta del agua es casi imposible.

El control político y el acceso al agua. Lees examinó detalladamente tres aldeas (San Agustín Etla, Tlalixtac de Cabrera y San Juan del Estado) para contestar las preguntas siguientes:

1. ¿Existen diferencias verdaderas entre los individuos en cuanto al acceso al agua y al control de su distribución que se esconden bajo el "ideal" de igualdad de oportunidad que las aldeas profesan? Respuesta: Sí, existen tales diferencias.
2. Si existen tales diferencias, ¿se relacionan con la geographía?, es decir, ¿tienen los de *río arriba* una ventaja en comparación con los de *río abajo?* Respuesta: No, tales desigualdades no se relacionan con la geografía; el sistema de cargo hace alternar a las autoridades de manera que los de río arriba que riegan no tienen ninguna ventaja.
3. Si existen tales desigualdades, ¿se relacionan con la jerarquía cívico-política?, es decir, ¿reciben más agua los que son más importantes en la política y las ceremonias de la aldea? Además de eso, ¿consiguen estos hombres más poder político debido al acceso desigual al agua, o vice versa? Respuesta: No, las desigualdades no se relacionan con la jerarquía cívico-política. El puesto de director del agua no es uno de poder sino un cargo de trabajo difícil, y de todos modos se alterna. Nadie logra controlar el poder por medio del agua o vice versa.
4. Si la geografía y el poder socio-político no controlan el acceso desigual al agua, ¿qué es lo que sí lo controla? Respuesta: Lo que sí controla la cantidad de agua que se recibe es la cantidad de terreno que se tiene. Las personas con más terreno *necesitan* más agua, pero éstas son muy pocas veces las que distribuyen el agua. Sin embargo, muchas veces la gente con más terreno es tan rica que puede adelantarse más en la jerarquía cívico-religiosa.

De manera que: La división decisiva en las aldeas es entre el poder público y el poder privado. El tener un puesto público no es una fuente del poder ya que los cargos se alternan y se espera la conformidad. El poder personal viene de la riqueza, que se relaciona con la cantidad de terrenos, no con el agua—la gente que tiene más terreno recibe más agua, pero la irrigación con canales por sí mismo no conduce a la desigualdad.

Los papeles de la aldea y del Estado en el control del agua. Dentro de la comunidad rural, el control del agua se alterna por medio del sistema de cargo, pero entre las aldeas no funciona este sistema. La aldea de río arriba tiene la ventaja sobre la de río abajo pero, en realidad, los pleitos apenas ocurren. Puede que haya una relación de comprador/vendedor o patrocinador/cliente entre las dos aldeas; esto es mayormente una característica del sector privado de interacción. En algunos casos la aldea de río arriba ha sido anteriomente un barrio de la de río arriba; es posible que todas se hayan originado en esta manera.

El Estado tiene sus propios especialistas, junto con ingenieros y arquitectos, quienes no existen en la aldea. Por eso el Estado puede ofrecer facilidades nuevas y más poderosas–pero el precio de éstas es la pérdida del control de la asignación del agua, o sea que esto es el resultado. El Estado es capaz de operar más "independiente de los constituyentes" que las autoridades de una aldea, ya que tiene sus propios policías y expertos. La Secretaría de Recursos Hidráulicos está en el proceso de desarrollar las estratagemas del control del agua más allá de la capacidad de la aldea, pero dejan tales estratagemas en manos de los agentes de la SAG-SRH cuya responsibilidad no es a la aldea sino al gobierno federal. Hay muchas maneras por las cuales la organización tradicional de la aldea está exenta de la intervención estatal, pero la irrigación con canales no se incluye entre ellas; es un aspecto de la cual puede encargarse un sistema de más alto rango. La nueva Junta de Aguas funciona como un agente de la rama executiva del gobierno federal y es responsable a ella, no a la aldea. Por eso la aldea pierde cierta parte de su autonomía, y el agua se administra por las leyes federales. Por ejemplo, en vez de alternarse como un cargo, las autoridades del control del agua (1) tienen que ser eligidos (ca. cada tres años), (2) tienen que ser personas que utilizan los canales, o sea que no es suficiente ser miembro de la comunidad y (3) tienen que ser alfabetos (tradicionalmente esto no era importante en los puestos de cargo).

El papel de control del agua en la historia de Oaxaca. Lees discute los cambios durante el período del Formativo Tardío (Monte Albán I): la irrigación con canales era un sistema muy esparcido; se aumentaban las poblaciones; se abrió el somontano para habitación; se colocaron centros administrativos en los cerros. El estado zapoteca se desarrolló durante este período de muchos poblados basados en la irrigación con canales (500 - 0 a.C.). Algunos sitios (v.gr. Santo Domingo Tomaltepec, que se probó por Lees junto con H. T. Wright en 1969) parecen tener "palacios" de estuco habitados por una nobleza, mientras que otros aldeanos vivían en jacales. Las tumbas de este período demuestran estratificación social, especialmente en Monte Albán.

Durante el período Clásico (300 - 600 d.C.) hay un desarrollo evidente del estado, pero no existe todavía una demostración desde Oaxaca de grandes proyectos de agua tal como la presa de Purrón en el Valle de Tehuacán. Algunas áreas (v.gr. cerca de San Agustín Etla) se desarrollaron en sumo grado, pero quizá hubiera sólo "tomas" tradicionales.

El libro reciente de William Taylor describe la irrigación colonial en el Valle de Oaxaca. Los españoles emprendieron aumentos mayores en los canales, especialmente en el Valle de Etla, y también en Cuilapan, Tlalixtac y otros lugares. En áreas como San Agustín Etla se desvió el agua para los molinos. Los caciques que eran dueños de los recursos hidráulicos cobraban el uso del agua. Las haciendas del siglo XIX fueron los mayores explotadoras de los canales, pero durante la Revolución de 1910 aquéllas se destruyeron y abandonaron sus canales y presas.

La irrigación oaxaqueña comparada con otros regiones. Lees comienza por resumir cuatro puntos hechos por Wittfogel.
1. El agua, como un recurso agrícola, tiene ciertas características que hacen ciertas exigencias en la organización social de la gente que la utiliza.
2. Las instituciones del control del agua pueden tener consecuencias de largo alcance o efectos en otras instituciones de la sociedad tales como leyes de propriedad, ciencias, religión, política y estructura de clase.
3. Los efectos de los sistemas del control del agua en otras instituciones varían según la medida y el tipo de facilidades, y con variables ambientales.
4. Un tipo de sociedad, caracterizado por el despotismo político, tiene su origen en un compromiso total al control del agua.

Lees discute estos puntos con respecto a los datos de Oaxaca; los Pima y Pápago del sudoeste de EE.UU.; Fidji; Japón; Bali y Ceilán. Sus conclusiones son que mientras las sociedades campesinas (tales como Oaxaca, Ceilán y Bali) tienen medios de coerción más fuertes para exigir la labor colectiva que las sociedades "tribales" (como los Pima y Pápago), estos medios no son independientes del aparato o de la estructura del Estado. Los campesinos locales son mucho más limitados que el estado no sólo (a) al organizar la labor colectiva sino también (b) al mantener la paz. Por otro lado, la habilidad del Estado de organizar actividades productivas puede ser limitada por la complejidad o la diversidad en el nivel local, como son las diferentes clases de irrigación que se utilizan en Oaxaca o Japón. Debemos fijarnos mucho más en las comunidades locales que organizan actividades demasiado variadas para una administración eficiente del Estado.

Además, no hay una respuesta social fijada en cuanto a la irrigación con canales. Las sociedades la manejan con las instituciones que tienen, cualesquieras que sean. Pero las diferentes clases de recursos hidráulicos se manejan en distintas maneras–los canales en una forma distinta de los pozos, por ejemplo. Y algunas clases de recursos se manejan mejor por los de la región a causa de su complejidad.

Otras clases de control del agua—especialmente los canales—pueden responder a la intervención del estado, y al hacer esto llegan a ser vehículos importantes para el cambio social, ya que el Estado cambia la administración de este recurso y puede demandar nuevas reglas en la comunidad tales como las que se han introducido por la SRH en Oaxaca. La irrigación no es la causa del Estado, pero la irrigación con canales provee un contexto en el cual una organización como el Estado tiene una ventaja selectiva, no sólo para aumentar la producción sino también para cambiar el sistema sociopolítico local (en una forma que otros tipos de agricultura no pueden realizar).

Para encontrar los orígenes del Estado debemos aprender primero cómo se originó la burocracia. Esto *no* se explica por la irrigación, ya que toda la evidencia que tenemos demuestra que para hacer frente a la irrigación *no* hay necesidad que se desarrollen huevas instituciones sociales. Lo que demuestra Lees es que el uso de la irrigación con canales puede hacer que la aldea sea vulnerable a la intervención del Estado, que últimamente llega a mayor centralización y al cambio social rápido.

REFERENCES

Adams, Robert M.
    1966 The Evolution of Urban Society: Early Mesopotamia and Prehispanic Mexico. Aldine Publishing Co. Chicago.

Barton, R. F.
    1949 The Kalingas: Their Institutions and Custom Laws. University of Chicago Press. Chicago.

Beals, Ralph L.
    1967 The Structure of the Oaxaca Market System. Revista Mexicana de Estudios Antropológicos Tomo xx:333-42.

Beardsley, R. K., J. W. Hall, and R. E. Ward
    1959 Village Japan. University of Chicago Press. Chicago.

Bowerman, James
    1967 Ethnographic Sketch: Santiago Ixtaltepec. Unpublished m.s., Stanford University. Stanford, California.

Brunet, Jean
    n.d. Geologic Studies. *In:* The Prehistory of the Tehuacán Valley Vol. I, Figs. 49, 50 and 51. University of Texas Press. Austin.

Cancian, Frank
    1967 Political and Religious Organizations. *In:* Handbook of Mesoamerican Indians. Wauchope, ed. Ch. 14:283-98.

Chadwick, Robert
    1966 The Tombs of Monte Albán I Style at Yagul. *In:* Ancient Oaxaca. John Paddock, ed. Stanford University Press. Stanford, California.

Cook, Scott
    1965 The Metateros of Teitipac: An Ethnography of a Zapotec Peasant-Artisan Group. Unpublished m.s. Stanford University. Stanford, California.
    1969 Price and Output Variability in a Peasant-Artisan Stoneworking Industry in Oaxaca, Mexico: An Analytical Essay in Economic Anthropology. Unpublished ms.

Cowgill, George L.
    1964 The End of Classic Maya Culture: A Review of Recent Evidence. Southwestern Journal of Anthropology Vol. 20:145-159.

Dales, George F.
    1962 The Role of Natural Forces in the Ancient Indus Valley and Baluchistan. *In:* Civilizations in Desert Lands. Woodbury, ed. University of Utah Anthropological Papers No. 62.

de Young, John E.
    1966 Life in Modern Thailand. University of California Press. Berkeley and Los Angeles.

Fjellman, Stephen L.
    1966 General Ethnography, Santa Ana del Valle. Unpublished ms. Stanford University. Stanford, California.

Flannery, Kent V.
    1968a Archeological Systems Theory and Early Mesoamerica. *In:* Meggers, ed. Anthropoligical Archeology in the Americas. The Anthropological Society of Washington. Washington, D.C.
    1968b The Olmec and the Valley of Oaxaca: A Model for Inter-Regional Interaction in Formative Times. *In:* Benson, ed. Dumbarton Oaks Conference on the Olmec. Trustees for Harvard University. Washington, D.C.

Flannery, Kent V., Anne V. T. Kirkby, Michael J. Kirkby, and Aubrey W. Williams, Jr.
    1967 Farming Systems and Political Growth in Ancient Oaxaca. Science Vol. 158, No. 3800:445-54.

Fowler, Melvin L.
    1969 A Preclassic Water Distribution System in Amalucan, Mexico. Archeology Vol. 22, No. 3:208-15.

Geertz, Clifford
    1959 Form and Variation in Balinese Villages. American Anthropologist 61:991-1011.

Gray, Robert F.
    1963 The Sonjo of Tanganyika: An Anthropological Study of an Irrigation-Based Society. Oxford University Press. London.

Hackenberg, Robert A.
    1962 Economic Alternatives in Arid Lands: A Case Study of the Pima and Papago Indians. Ethnology I:186-95.

Handy, G. S. Craighill
    1940 The Hawaiian Planter, I. Bernice P. Bishop Museum Bulletin 161. Honolulu.

Iszaevich Fajerstein, Abraham
    1969 Soledad Etla, Estudio de un Proceso de Modernización. Tesis Profesional (M.A.), Escuela Nacional de Anthropología e Historia. Mexico, D.F.

Kirkby, Anne V. T.
    1973 The Use of Land and Water Resources in the Past and Present Valley of Oaxaca, Mexico. Memoirs of the Museum of Anthropology, No. 5. Ann Arbor, Michigan.

Klug, Linda M.
    1965 General Ethnography, San Miguel del Valle. Unpublished ms. Stanford University. Stanford, California.

Leach, E. R.
    1959 Hydraulic Society in Ceylon. Past and Present No. 15:2-26.
    1961 Pul Eliya. Cambridge University Press. Cambridge.

Lewis, Oscar
    1964 Pedro Martínez. Random House (Vintage Books). New York.

Malinowski, B. and J. de la Fuente
    1957 La Economica de un Systema de Mercados en Mexico. Acta Anthropológica Ser. 2, Vol. 1 and 2. Mexico.

Millon, Rene, Clara Hall, and May Diaz
    1961- Conflict in the Modern Teotihuacán Irrigation System. Comparative Studies in Society and History
    1962 Vol. 4.

    1962 Variations in Social Responses to the Practice of Irrigation Agriculture. *In:* Civilization in Arid Lands. Woodbury, ed. University of Utah Anthropological Papers No. 62.

Neely, James A.
    1967 Organización Hidráulica y Sistemas de Irrigación Prehistóricos en el Valle de Oaxaca. Boletín del Instituto Nacional de Antropología e Historia, Mexico, No. 27.

Orlandini, Richard J.
    1967 A Formative Well from the Valley of Oaxaca. Paper presented at the 32nd Annual Meeting of the Society for American Archaeology. Ann Arbor, Michigan.

Paddock, John
    1966 Mixtec Ethnohistory and Monte Albán V. *In:* Ancient Oaxaca. John Paddock, ed. Stanford University Press. Stanford, California.

Palerm, Angel
    1955 The Agricultural Basis of Urban Civilization in Mesoamerica. *In:* Irrigation Civilizations: A Comparative Study. Pan American Union Social Science Monograph I. Washington, D.C.

Palerm, A. and E. R. Wolf
    1957 Ecological Potential and Cultural Development in Mesoamerica. Pan American Social Science Monograph 3. Washington, D.C.

Parsons, Elsie Clews
    1936 Mitla, Town of the Souls. University of Chicago Press. Chicago and London.

Paso y Troncoso, Francisco Del
    1905 Papeles de Nueva España. Segunda serie: Geografía y Estadística. Madrid, Establecimiento tip. Sucesores de Rivadenyra.

Pérez Jiménez, Gustavo
    1968 La Institución del Municipio Libre. Costa-Amic, Mexico.

REFERENCES

Reichman, F. R.
    1964 Ethnography of Tlacochahuaya de Morelos. Unpublished ms. Stanford University. Stanford, California.

Sahlins, Marshall D.
    1958 Social Stratification in Polynesia. University of Washington Press. Seattle.
    1962 Moala. The University of Michigan Press. Ann Arbor.

Sanders, William T.
    1968 Hydraulic Agriculture, Economic Symbiosis and the Evolution of States in Central Mexico. *In:* Meggers, ed. Anthropological Archeology in the Americas. The Anthropological Society of Washington, D.C.

Sanders, William T. and Barbara J. Price
    1968 Mesoamerica. Random House. New York.

Secretaria de Agricultura y Ganaderia
    1968-1969 Boletín Informativo de la Dirección General de Ingeniera Agrícola. Nos. 12,3,. Mexico.

Steward, Julian H. (ed.)
    1955 Some Implications of the Symposium. Irrigation Civilizations: A Comparative Study. Pan American Union, Social Science Monograph 1. Washington, D.C.

Taylor, William B.
    1969[1] The Valley of Oaxaca: A Study of Colonial Land Distribution. Unpublished Ph.D. Dissertation. The University of Michigan. Ann Arbor.

Welte, Cecil R.
    1966 Index of Populated Places in the Valley of Oaxaca Listed in the Census of 1960 and Shown on the 'Map de los Localidades del Valle de Oaxaca.' Oficina de Estudios de Humanidad del Valle de Oaxaca. Oaxaca de Juárez.

Whitecotton, Joseph W.
    1968 The Valley of Oaxaca at Spanish Contact: An Ethnohistorical Study Unpublished Ph.D. Thesis. The University of Illinois. Urbana.

Wittfogel, Karl A.
    1938 Die Theorie der Orientalischen Gesellschaft. Zeitschrift fur Sozialforschung VII:90-122.
    1957 Oriental Despotism. Yale University Press. New Haven.

Wolf, Eric R.
    1955 Types of Latin American Peasantry: A Preliminary Discussion. American Anthropologist No. 57:452-70.
    1959 Sons of the Shaking Earth. University of Chicago Press. Chicago.
    1966 Peasants. Foundations of Modern Anthropology Series. Prentice-Hall. Englewood Cliffs.

Woodbury, Richard
    1961 A Reappraisal of Hohokam Irrigation. American Anthropologist Vol. 63, No. 3:550-60.

Woodbury, Richard, and James Neely
    1965 Report on Irrigation in Tehuacán Valley. *In:* Current Research: Western Mesoamerica. Paddock, ed. XXXI, 1:133-36.

---

[1] The Taylor dissertation has since been published as *Landlord and Peasant in Colonial Oaxaca*, Stanford University Press, Stanford.

Plate 2. Canal-irrigating villages in the Valley of Oaxaca: *a* Tlalixtac de Cabrera seen from the south, strung out along the left bank of the Río de los Molinos (see Map 5); *b* Fabrica San José at San Agustín Etla (see Map 7) seen from the north. On the Hill in the center lie the archaeological remains of a probable Middle and Late Formative irrigating community.

Plate 3. Irrigation facilities at Tlalixtac de Cabrera: *a* division point for canals going to the *barrios* of San Miguel (left) and La Trinidad (right; see Map 5); *b* the *derivadora* or sluice at the dam above town; *c* a small boulder diversion dam along one canal; *d* a canal bridge crossing a dry arroyo.

Plate 4. Irrigation facilities at San Juan del Estado: *a, b* views of the main *tanque* or reservoir above town (see Map 6); *c* the *derivadora* or sluice; *d* a canal flowing through town.

Plate 5. Irrigation facilities at San Agustín Etla: *a* the main village *tanque*, or reservoir, above town; *b* the main canal leading into town from four kilometers up in the mountains; *c* the lock on a major canal; *d* the government *caseta de distribución* for intervillage water division (see Map 7).

Plate 6. Irrigation in other parts of the village: *a* dry canal winding through the village of Guadalupe Etla; *b* a small canal leading from the main atoyac River at Guadalupe Etla; *c* aerial view of the lower Mixtepec River (foreground) as it flows toward the Atoyac River (background) near Santa Ana Tlapacoyan. All flat land shown in the photograph is canal irrigated.

Plate 7. Ancient and modern irrigation sites at Santo Domingo Tomaltepec: *a* aerial view of the Canyon northeast of Tomaltepec, from which its water comes. Arrow indicates the modern dam reservoir. Circle indicates archaeological site B-176 (see Map 9), a probable Late Formative canal-irrigating village excavated by Wright and Lees in 1969; *b* the new Tomaltepec dam (left foreground) and reservoir built by the Federal government in the 1960s.

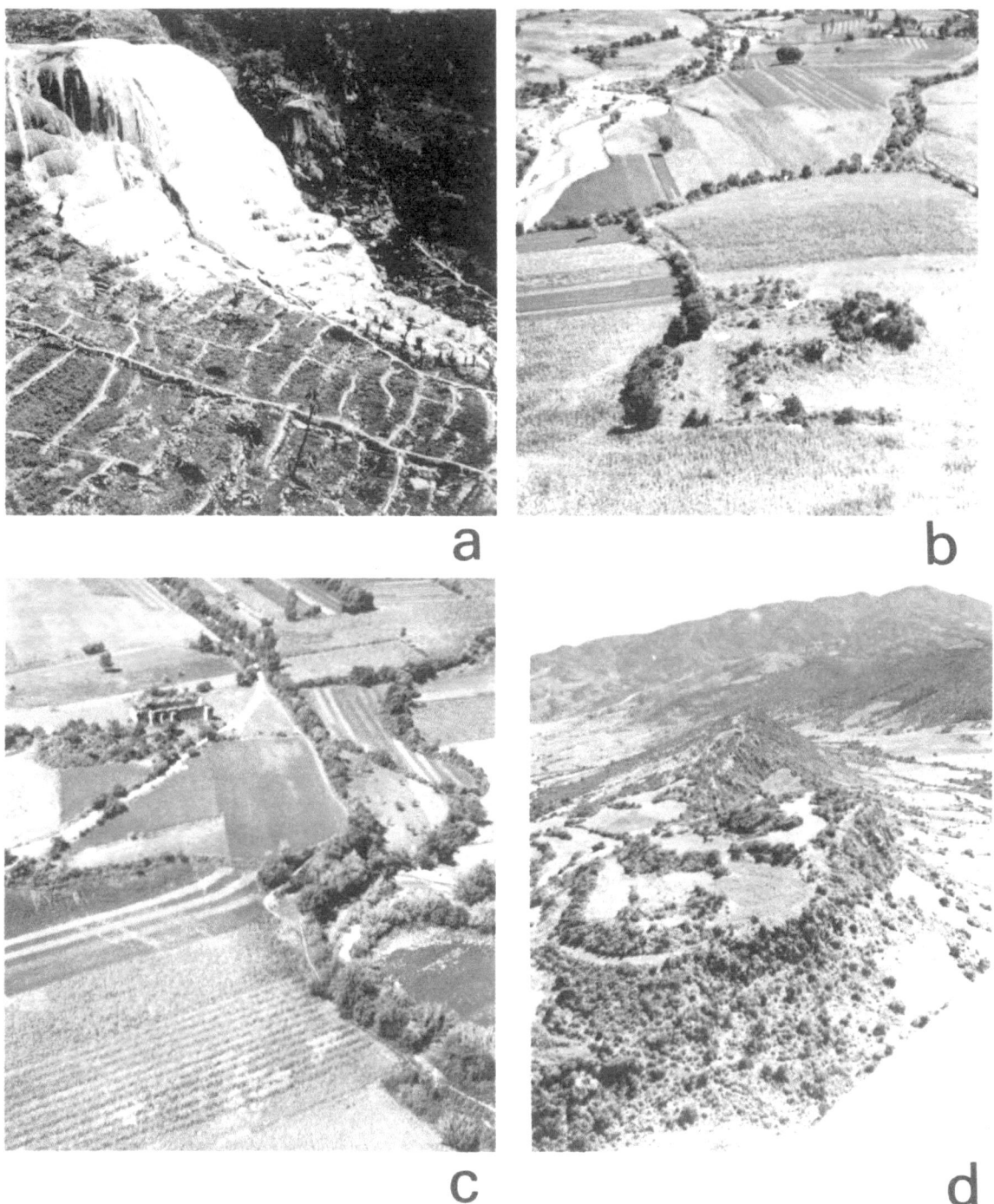

Plate 8. Archaeological sites in canal-irrigation settings: *a* Hierve el Agua in the mountains east of Mitla, showing pre-Columbian canals "fossilized" in travertine; *b* site B-39 (foreground), a Late Formative river-terrace village probably engaged in canal irrigation with the waters of the lower Magdalena Apasco River (background); *c* site B-37, a probable Late Formative canal-takeoff point in a loop of the Magdalena Apasco tributary near the old church of Santa Marta Etla; *d* site B-34, a probable Late Formative hilltop administrative center overlooking the Magdalena Apasco tributary. Numbering of sites shown in *b-d* (see Map 10) follows the surveys of Ignacio Bernal in the 1950s.